HUMAN RIGHTS AND
THE WORLD'S RELIGIONS

BOSTON UNIVERSITY STUDIES IN
PHILOSOPHY AND RELIGION

General Editor: Leroy S. Rouner

Volume Nine

Human Rights and the World's Religions

Edited by

Leroy S. Rouner

UNIVERSITY OF NOTRE DAME PRESS

Notre Dame, Indiana

Library of Congress Cataloging-in-Publication Data

Human rights and the world's religions / edited by Leroy S. Rouner.
    p.   cm. — (Boston University studies in philosophy and
religion ; 9)
    Includes indexes.
    ISBN 0-268-01086-2 :
    1. Civil rights—Religious aspects.   2. Civil rights and
socialism.   I. Rouner, Leroy S.   II. Series: Boston University
studies in philosophy and religion ; v. 9.
BL65.C58H84   1988
291.1'77—dc19   88-17303
                                                              CIP

Manufactured in the United States of America

Contents

PART IV: CONFUCIANISM

Preface

Boston University Studies in Philosophy and Religion is a joint project of the Boston University Institute for Philosophy and Religion and the University of Notre Dame Press. The essays in each annual volume are edited from the previous year's lecture program of the Institute. The Director of the Institute, who also serves as editor of these Studies, chooses a theme and invites participants to lecture at Boston University in the course of the academic year. The papers are then revised by their authors, and the editor selects and edits the essays to be included in these Studies. In preparation is Volume Ten, *On Freedom.*

    The Boston University Institute for Philosophy and Religion is a Center of the Graduate School, and is sponsored jointly by the Department of Philosophy, the Department of Religion, and the School of Theology. The Institute is made possible by regular financial support from the Graduate School. This year our budget has been supplemented by a generous grant from the Humanities Foundation of Boston University. The Institute is an interdisciplinary and ecumenical forum. Within the academic community it is committed to open interchange on fundamental issues in philosophy and religious study which transcend the narrow specializations of academic curricula. Outside the University it seeks to recover the public tradition of philosophical discourse which was a lively part of American intellectual life in the early years of this century before the professionalization of both philosophy and religious reflection. At a time when too much academic writing is incomprehensible, or irrelevant, or both, we try to present readable essays by acknowledged authorities on critical human issues.

    This book summarizes a two-year lecture series on human

rights. The first year's lectures were on civil rights, the second year on social and cultural rights. The program was part of our commitment to a public philosophy. It is a theme on which most of us have strong feelings and dogmatic views, but relatively little sense for the complexity of the issues, and almost no knowledge of values and practices in other religious and cultural traditions. We hope the book will widen horizons, temper dogmatisms a bit, and contribute to the current conversation on human rights.

For Elie Wiesel,

eloquent advocate for the human rights of all human beings. His Institute lectures have instructed and inspired us, lending courage to our memory of atrocities past, and hope to our work for a better world yet to come.

Acknowledgments

Special thanks are due this year to our authors, who have been patient with a year's delay in publication, and gracious in response to my extensive editing of their essays. Our former Dean, Geoffrey Bannister, and our present Provost, Dennis Berkey, made it possible for us to computerize our editing process. The resulting savings in time and energy and the new flexibility in manuscript preparation are difficult to exaggerate. Our gratitude to both of them grows daily. Here in the office Ted Gaiser has helped Barbara and me overcome our initial fear of our imposing new equipment and has done much of the leg work on our authors' biographical data. Barbara Darling-Smith, my peerless Administrative Assistant, having mastered a personal computer, is now more peerless than ever. Her superb copy editing and her legendary good cheer make her an ideal co-worker.

Greg Rockwell oversees the production process for the University of Notre Dame Press, and he continues to streamline the actual making of the books. Editor Ann Rice has been patient and helpful as always. Her quiet professionalism and relaxed good humor are only two of the many reasons we look forward to our annual contact with her. Jim Langford, Director of the University of Notre Dame Press, not only oversees the series for the Press, but also participates in discussion of possible themes for future programs and suggests names of participants. During this past year he has been one of our lecturers, and his essay will appear in next year's volume *On Freedom*. It is not often that one's publisher is also a philosophical colleague, and we continue to be grateful to him for making this series possible.

On rare occasions we include essays which have been revised

after earlier publication elsewhere. Much of the material in W. Theodore de Bary's essay appeared in *Confucianism: The Dynamics of Tradition*, edited by Irene Eber, under the title "Human Rites: An Essay on Confucianism and Human Rights."

Contributors

ROGER T. AMES received his B.A. and M.A. at the University of British Columbia and his Ph.D. at the University of London. He also did graduate work at the National Taiwan University and at the Tokyo University of Education as a Research Fellow. He has written *The Art of Rulership: A Study in Ancient Chinese Political Thought* (1983) and (with David Hall) *Thinking through Confucius* (1987). Most recently he has co-edited *Environmental Philosophy: The Asian Tradition* (1988). He is editor of *Philosophy East and West* and Associate Professor of Philosophy at the University of Hawaii at Manoa, where his specialties are Confucianism, Oriental philosophy, comparative philosophy, and process philosophy.

JOHN B. CARMAN is Professor of Comparative Religion at the Harvard University Divinity School and Director of the Center for the Study of World Religions. Born in India of Christian missionary parents, he studied at Haverford College, Yale University, and the University of Leiden. He has also been a Research Fellow of the Christian Institute for the Study of Religion and Society in Bangalore, India. In addition to many articles, his publications include the translation of W. Brede Kristensen's lectures in phenomenology of religion, *The Meaning of Religion* (1960). He is the author of *The Theology of Rāmānuja* (1974) and (with P. Y. Luke) of *Village Christians and Hindu Culture* (1968).

W. THEODORE DE BARY holds the John Mitchell Mason Professorship of the University at Columbia University, where he has also served in numerous other capacities, including Executive Vice President for Academic Affairs and Provost, and Carpentier Professor of Oriental Studies. His latest books are *Neo-Confucian Orthodoxy and the Learning of the Mind and Heart* (1981), *Yüan Thought: Essays on Chinese Thought and Religion under the Mongols* (1982), and *The Liberal Tradition in China* (1983). Among other honors he has been named a Guggenheim Fellow (1981–82) and the Ch'ien Mu Lecturer at the Chinese University of Hong Kong (1982) and has been a member of the council of the American Academy of Arts and Sciences.

MANSOUR FARHANG is Professor of Politics at Bennington College and has written extensively on Iran, international relations, and United States foreign policy. He served as revolutionary Iran's first ambassador to the United Nations, resigning in protest when the Ayatollah Khomeini broke his promise to accept the United Nations Commission of Inquiry's recommendation to release the American hostages in Tehran. In the early period of the Iran-Iraq war, he also served as then-President Bani-Sadr's envoy in negotiations with international peace missions attempting to settle the conflict. He has written (with William A. Dorman) *The United States Press and Iran: Foreign Policy and the Journalism of Deference* (1987).

MICHAEL FISHBANE is the author of *Text and Texture: Studies in Biblical Literature* (1979) and *Biblical Interpretation in Ancient Israel* (1984). He edited (with Paul Flohr) *Texts and Responses: Studies Presented to Nahum N. Glatzer on the Occasion of His Seventieth Birthday by His Students* (1975). He has taught at the Hebrew University and at Stanford University, and is now Samuel Lane Professor of Jewish Religious History and Social Ethics at Brandeis University. In 1984 he was awarded a Guggenheim Fellowship. He has served as Executive Secretary of the Association of Jewish Studies, as a Member of the International Committee on Interreligious

Consultations of the World Council of Churches, and as President of the New England Region of the Society of Biblical Literature.

NIKKI R. KEDDIE studied History and Literature at Radcliffe College before taking her M.A. in History at Stanford and her Ph.D. at the University of California, Berkeley, in 1955. Her research travels have taken her to Europe, Iran, Senegal, Nigeria, Morocco, Tunisia, Egypt, Yemen, Syria, Pakistan, Indonesia, and Malaysia. She is Professor of History at the University of California at Los Angeles and has written and edited many books and articles. Among her most recent books are *Iran: Religion, Politics, Society* (1980); *Roots of Revolution* (1981); *Religion and Politics in Iran* (1983), which she edited; *The Iranian Revolution and the Islamic Republic* (1982; updated and revised, 1986) and *Shi'ism and Social Protest* (1986), both of which she coedited.

MIHAILO MARKOVIĆ has written many books, including the following in English: *The Contemporary Marx* (1974) and *From Affluence to Praxis* (1974). He received his B.A. in the philosophy of science and his Ph.D. in logic at the University of Belgrade, and another Ph.D. in the philosophy of logic at the University of London. He has taught at the Serbian Academy of Sciences and Arts and on the Faculty of Philosophy at the University of Belgrade. He has also been Visiting Professor at the University of Michigan. Currently he is a member of the Yugoslav Academy of Sciences and Professor of Philosophy at the University of Pennsylvania.

ANN ELIZABETH MAYER appeared in 1987 in an Amnesty International feature on human rights in Iran since the Islamic revolution. She is Associate Professor of Legal Studies at the Wharton School of Business of the University of Pennsylvania and has been Visiting Associate Professor (part-time) at Princeton University. Her B.A., M.A., and Ph.D. (in Middle East-

ern history) are from the University of Michigan and her J.D.
is from the University of Pennsylvania Law School. She received a Certificate in Islamic and Comparative Law from
the University of London's School of Oriental and African
Studies. The author of many articles and recipient of many
fellowships and grants, she has edited *Property, Social Structure and Law in the Modern Middle East* (1985).

TRUTZ RENDTORFF is on the Protestant faculty of the Institute
for Systematic Theology at the University of Munich. He is
the author of many books, including *Protestantismus und
Revolution* (1969), *Gott, ein Wort unserer Sprache?: ein theo-
logischer Essay* (1972), *Kirchenleitung und wissenschaftliche
Theologie* (1974), *Politische Ethik und Christentum* (1978),
and *Charisma und Institution* (1985). *Church and Theology:
The Systematic Function of the Church Concept in Modern
Theology* (1971) and *Ethics* (1986) have been translated into
English. He is widely known as an ethicist and human rights
specialist. His interests include developments in contemporary
American theology, and he has traveled and lectured through-
out the United States.

HENRY ROSEMONT, JR., took his Ph.D. at the University of
Washington and later did postdoctoral work at the Massachu-
setts Institute of Technology and the University of London.
He has held visting appointments at various universities, including Fudan University in Shanghai and the University of
Hawaii. He is now Professor of Philosophy at St. Mary's College of Maryland. From 1976 to 1978 he was President of the
Society for Asian and Comparative Philosophy, and since
1972 he has been Book Review Editor of *Philosophy East and
West*. He also serves as Editorial Associate of the *Journal of
the American Academy of Religion*, and is a member of the
Columbia University Seminar on Oriental Thought and Religion. He is the author of numerous articles and reviews. He
has translated and edited Leibniz's *Discourse on the Natural
Theology of the Chinese*, and is coeditor (with Benjamin I.

Schwartz) of *Studies in Classical Chinese Thought*. His current work in progress is a book on *Confucianism and Contemporary Ethics*.

LEROY S. ROUNER is Professor of Philosophy, Religion, and Philosophical Theology at Boston University, Director of the Institute for Philosophy and Religion, and General Editor of this Series. He did his Ph.D. with John Herman Randall, Jr., at Columbia University on the philosophy of William Ernest Hocking, and is the author of *Within Human Experience: The Philosophy of William Ernest Hocking*, editor and co-author of the Hocking *Festschrift, Philosophy, Religion and the Coming World Civilization*, and, with John Howie, of *The Wisdom of William Ernest Hocking*. He taught for five years in Bangalore, India, and drove his family overland by Land Rover from India to England in 1966–67. He has been Visiting Professor at the University of Hawaii. His work in progress includes a book on Christian contributions to a world culture, and a memoir, *The Long Way Home*.

ROBERT A. F. THURMAN is Professor of Religion at Amherst College. He has been visiting professor at a number of universities: Harvard University, Smith College, Wesleyan University, Williams College, and Doshisha University in Kyoto. He has received grants from the American Institute of Indian Studies, the Institute of Advanced Studies of World Religions, and the National Endowment for the Humanities, and he is a member of the American Oriental Society, the Association for Asian Studies, the American Academy of Religion and the American Philosophical Association. He has written the *Holy Teaching of Vimalakīrti* (1977), *The Life and Teachings of Tsong Khapa* (1982), and *Tsong Khapa's Speech of Gold in the Essence of True Eloquence: Reason and Enlightenment in the Central Philosophy of Tibet* (1984).

TAITETSU UNNO is Professor of World Religions and Director of the Ada Howe Kent Program at Smith College. He did his

B.A. at the University of California, Berkeley, and his M.A. and Ph.D. at the University of Tokyo. He has taught at the University of California at Los Angeles, Ryukoku University in Kyoto, the University of Hawaii, and the University of Illinois. He is the translator of numerous works, including *Buddhism, Shinran in the Contemporary World,* and *Passages on the Pure Land Way.* He has also published numerous articles and reviews including a group of articles in the *Kodansha Encyclopedia of Japan,* the *Encyclopedia of Religion,* and the *Oxford Encyclopedia of Religions of the World.* In April of 1984 he was Codirector of the Symposium in Honor of Keiji Nishitani at Smith and Amherst Colleges, and later that spring was Codirector of the Symposium on Shin Buddhism and Christianity at Harvard University.

Introduction

LEROY S. ROUNER

FREE INDIVIDUALS, standing for their rights, are "the best fruit of modernity." So wrote William Ernest Hocking in *The Coming World Civilization* (1956). That judgment has general acceptance today. If it is not entirely clear what these rights are, or which of them is fundamental, it is nevertheless widely believed that we do indeed have them, and that they are somehow inalienable. We are also persuaded that our rights remain fundamental to our relations with others, so they are not only primary in our self-understanding, they are inviolable in our interactions. Human rights have become functioning absolutes for increasing numbers of people everywhere. The widespread violation of human rights in the twentieth century only strengthens our conviction about them. Confronted by holocaust after holocaust, and war on war, where the burning of children is commonplace, and the suffering of all unspeakable, we know beyond any possible doubt that these things are wrong. We have a right to be free of such suffering.

Two separate affirmations are involved in this conviction, however. One is the belief that the individual human being has inherent dignity and worth. The other is that *human rights* is the most significant symbol of that worth. The first conviction remains strong in moral philosophy, East and West. The second is now being reexamined in the West, either directly or indirectly. Alasdair MacIntyre's book *After Virtue* is an example. And among Eastern philosophers, *rights* has never been a primary category. The Buddhist scholar Hajime Nakamura spoke for most Asian philosophers when he commented, "We don't usually speak of rights in our tradition."

Hocking represented a Western liberalism which integrated individuals into society through idealistic concepts such as Josiah

1

Royce's "Beloved Community." Philosophical absolutes are more difficult to defend since the rise of analytic philosophy, however; and the moral optimism of liberal idealism has been virtually destroyed by world wars, holocausts, and the threat of nuclear annihilation. In such a climate, how is it possible to celebrate individual human rights as well as a human community for which individuals are responsible, and from which they derive much of their value as human beings? For surely there is no value in life, liberty, or the pursuit of happiness, alone. The notion of individual rights is therefore somewhat misleading. The rights of the individual person are always the rights of individuals in a community, whether they guarantee freedom for creativity, or freedom from encroachment on that creativity by others. But the assertion of individual rights sooner or later runs counter to the needs of the larger community. Can the free individual have dignity and worth without fundamental rights? But, if individual rights are fundamental, how is a viable community possible?

The essays which follow explore the role of religion as ground for belief in rights. Our authors represent many of the major religious traditions, and are agreed on the inherent worth and dignity of the individual human being. They are not agreed, however, that a theory of rights is the best symbol for that value. Our Buddhist and Confucian scholars raise this question most directly, but our Marxist colleague is also critical of much rights theory. This disagreement does not reject individual human rights; it argues for an enlargement of individual rights to include all social and economic groups within the community. It also argues that different groups are concerned with different rights. Mansour Farhang, for example, notes that the most precious rights for the urban poor in Iran today are not the personal civil rights so cherished in the West but the rights to public dissent. A further complication is the relation of different communities to each other. How do religious communities regard the human rights of individuals in other religious communities?

Not all of our authors answer each of these questions, and our book offers no final resolution to these various issues. Once again we present a small volume with a large title, but we do not pretend to be definitive. We do, however, include some of the most knowledgeable and perceptive current thinking on these issues as our contribution toward better understanding. I confess that I originally planned this volume as a celebration of Ernest Hocking's view that individual human rights are "the best fruit of modernity." I now find my own liberal individualism both enlarged and chastened by the colleagues and friends who have instructed me in this book. My hope is that, whatever your initial persuasions in these matters, you too will find them challenged and changed by these essays.

We begin with two sections on Western religions, one with single essays on Judaism, Christianity, and Marxism, and one with three essays on Islam. The emphasis on Islam reflects current American interest in the Muslim world, especially in Iran and the human rights situation there. We conclude with two sections on the religions of Asia: the first on Hinduism and Buddhism, the second on Confucianism. The special attention to Confucianism is not for current political reasons this time, but for the thoroughgoing intellectual challenge it presents to that liberal individualism which many of us presuppose.

Muslim and Christian views of human rights are both rooted in the religion of Israel, so we begin with Michael Fishbane's essay on "The Image of the Human and the Rights of the Individual in Jewish Tradition." He emphasizes the absolute worth of human life and the unique value of the individual human being in the Jewish legal tradition. He contrasts this view sharply with the legal traditions of other ancient Near Eastern cultures where both property and human life had an economically calculable value. For Judaism, human life was of incalculable worth.

Fishbane then turns to the rights of non-Jews within the Jewish community. In ancient Israel non-Israelite male slaves could participate in the Passover ceremony, after undergoing the rite of circumcision. Further, Israel regarded all persons as bearers of inalienable human rights, if they accepted and performed the minimal moral duties of the Noachide laws. These criteria — prohibitions against idolatry, blasphemy, bloodshed, sexual sins, theft, and eating living animals, as well as the positive obligation to establish a legal system — later helped provide common theological and legal ground among Jews, Muslims, and Christians in the Middle Ages. Since it constituted a universal revelation, it gave the Jewish community a means of participating in the common moral enterprises of the larger human community. Maimonides, for example, argued that there is a basic human duty to establish a structure of human rights within society.

Within Judaism, however, there have been groups whose rights have been marginalized by Jewish law, and Fishbane turns in conclusion to the difficult task of evaluating traditional law in the light of contemporary sensibilities, especially regarding the rights of women. He concludes that the Jewish tradition exhibits an ongoing concern to generate a self-correcting and self-reflective legal system based on a strong sense of the person.

Trutz Rendtorff is concerned with the historical contribution which Christianity has made to human rights in the West, and the relation of religious freedom to human rights. His essay on "Christian Concepts of the Responsible Self" explores the possibility that the Christian view of the person is a major influence on the modern concept of human rights. He concludes that it has been, but notes a distinction between the liberal North American emphasis on presocial individual rights, and the Eastern European socialist concepts of social responsibility. The Lutheran mid-European position which he advocates proposes to balance the rights of the individual with social responsibility. Since this is a goal many are seeking, Rendtorff's route to it is of special interest.

He argues that individuals are not inherently free. Freedom is the gift of God's prevenient grace, prior to any human action. Christian freedom is thus utterly independent of the world, so moral life can never be a means for achieving freedom. We know that things are now right with us in relation to God. We are therefore free to care for the worldly needs of the neighbor and the community. Is this thoroughly Christian rationale for rights exclusive? Rendtorff acknowledges that rights need to be specific and concrete, not sectarian or abstract. But he is unwilling to run the risk of an ultimate and exclusive definition which would inevitably lead to totalitarianism. For him, the continuing distinction between church and state, religion and society, is an important way of keeping the world open for the individuality of the self.

Fishbane finds common ground for various religious views on human rights by appealing to the Noachide law. Rendtorff makes no appeal to specific common ground, but implies the possibility of a cooperative pluralism for religious communities within the life of the state. Mihailo Marković argues that human rights is central to the existence of the state. His secular Marxist appraisal is that human rights developed through political and social revolutions during the past three centuries. With the rise of the bourgeoisie as a dominant economic class, however, *human rights* was narrowed to civil rights, since socioeconomic rights were of interest only to the working class. Marković's thesis is the need to enlarge the conception of rights beyond the necessary but not sufficient condition of individual civil rights to the economic and social welfare of the larger community. Rendtorff hopes this may happen through Christian influence on a pluralistic society. Marković is specific in pointing to transformation through sociopolitical movements like the New Deal in America.

Marx's criticism of previous revolutionary movements was that they created a society divided into two sharply different spheres, civil and political. In the economic life of civil society the fundamental freedom is that of buying and selling commodities, and inevitably involves domination and exploitation. Marković endorses Marx's view that until there is socioeconomic emancipation civil rights remain abstract and formal.

Marković is critical of the Soviet solution to the problem of rights, where duties prevail over rights while sanctions and prohibitions stifle individual liberties. He is also critical of capitalist cultures for the failure to guarantee social and economic rights, thus making civil rights more formal than substantive. The formal negative constraint supporting the civil right of free speech, for example, is only one of several necessary conditions of speaking freely. Positive requirements include alternative choices, the freedom to act on those choices, and sufficient control over external obstacles so that they cannot prevent the fulfillment of one's project. He notes that there has been progress in human rights until the recent rise of conservatism and militarization in the politics of the Northern Hemisphere, and he concludes with a plea for fighting against those reversals.

The conservatism which concerns Mansour Farhang is not the economic policy of Thatcher and Reagan but the religious policy of the Ayatollah Khomeini. His essay on "Fundamentalism and Civil Rights in Contemporary Middle Eastern Politics" focuses on the alliance between state coercion and Muslim fundamentalism. As Western ideas like civil rights penetrate Islamic cultures, and as Middle Eastern economies become increasingly integrated into world markets, the pressure increases toward the transformation of traditional Islam. Emulation and fascination vie with resentment and resistance in this struggle between modernity and tradition.

Farhang notes that Islamic doctrine on the rights of the person is theoretically in tune with the United Nations Universal Declaration on Human Rights, but that Islamic governments have generally ruled with arbitrary power. Traditionally, individual rights have constituted obligations toward the divine, with the state enforcing the *shari'a*, the laws derived from the Qur'an. He notes, however, that a separation between religion and the state has existed in the Muslim world for at least eleven of Islam's fourteen centuries. Fundamentalism is not a historical norm but results from the failure of modernists and secularists to create a viable synthesis between Islam and modernization. This failure became critical in the lives of the urban poor, whom Farhang takes to be the determinative social force in the disintegration of the Pahlavi state and the establishment of the Islamic Republic. Traditional resistance to cultural change, combined with economic and social deprivation under the Pahlavis, made modernization so disrupting for the urban poor that classical anomie stimulated anxiety, hostility and fantasy. Fundamentalist preachers then readily drew the disaffected to the dream of a sacred utopia which had existed in the past, and would now become the Islamic Republic of the future.

Farhang rejects the view that Islam is an overriding motivational force in the Middle East and regards the upheaval in Iran as an indigenous rejection of modernity. The indigenous culture is, however, Islam. The secularization of education and the acceptance of cultural pluralism threaten both "the old ways" and the power of the clerics to enforce them. He points out that the critical civil rights issue in Iran today is not personal privacy and lifestyle, as it is in the West, but the need for peaceful political dissent. For the fourth straight year Iran has executed more of its citizens than the rest of the world combined, and he expresses no optimism about the immediate future for civil rights in Iran.

Nikki Keddie's topic is "The Rights of Women in Contemporary Islam." She has recently traveled widely in the Muslim world, and her essay is a contemporary report in historical perspective. There are many Western stereotypes about Islamic women and Keddie notes that their history is obscure, controversial, and complex. Women were subordinate to men in premodern Islam, but no more so than in other great traditions. Resistance to male-female equality in contemporary Islamic countries is strong, however, since the equality of women is often seen as part of a Western cultural offensive against Islam. Attachment to the Qur'an and Islamic law is strong for most Muslims, not only because of the sacred nature of these texts, but because of their definition of what it means to be a true Muslim in the face of Western cultural onslaughts.

Keddie notes many positive steps toward women's equality in the twentieth century, including the expansion of women's education, the opening of public jobs, and legal reforms, especially in the 1920s in Turkey, where women got the vote well before they did in France or Italy. Tunisia and South Yemen were also leaders in women's rights. In Turkey, women's progress was very much the result of Westernization. Elsewhere, indigenous Muslim reformism effectively advocated women's rights. These progressive reforms followed World War I. After World War II there were three changes which helped create an "Islamist" constituency, or what Farhang calls a "nativist" group: the cultural alienation of the newly Westernized elite from the majority; Western cultural influence and the power of Israel; and the socioeconomic dislocations resulting from rapid urbanization, oil-backed modernization, and the increasing gap between the rich and the poor.

Islamism is populist in its appeal, but its social egalitarianism has not extended to women, partly because matters affecting women make up one of the few legislative areas in the Qur'an, and a return to the traditional injunctions on polygamy, adultery, and so forth, is a good way to show that one is a good Muslim. Keddie notes hopeful signs in Pakistan and elsewhere, however, where women are studying the Qur'an and Islamic law to find a basis for an egalitarian position. Perhaps most importantly, there has been little repeal of legislation favoring women in the Muslim world.

Ann Mayer's essay on "The Dilemmas of Islamic Identity" summarizes many of Farhang and Keddie's specific interests. Islamic tradition has not had a developed doctrine of human rights, but a broad range of rights flourished earlier in a rich and open rural folk culture, despite the official strictures of high urban orthodoxy. Mayer argues that this was the real Islam for most Muslims. The rise of the centralized state meant that culture became assimilated into propaganda and ideology. As cultural energy was depleted human rights violations increased, and Islamist restraints on human rights became normative. In the 1979 Constitution of the Islamic Republic of Iran, for example, human rights are guaranteed "according to Islamic standards." But these standards limit press freedom, the right of association, freedom to demonstrate, the right to choose a profession, and more.

Mayer is particularly concerned with social and cultural rights. She agrees with Farhang that Islamism is driven by the alliance of religious fundamentalism and the coercive power of the state. She asks, "How does one find or impose a cultural identity via a religion?" The answer is given by those Muslims for whom Islam is a religious culture, and who speak of Muslim architecture, cities, and science in such a way that religious orthodoxy becomes the criterion for cultural value, and censorship becomes the political order of the day. Mayer finds the cultural climate in most Muslim countries discouraging to intellectuals facing the critical task of reformulating Islamic thought in response to the challenges of modern life. She is hopeful, however, that voices now stilled may yet be heard advocating cultural freedom within the context of a modified and modernized Islam.

To turn from Western religions to the religions of the East changes the climate of the discussion and finds us groping for a new vocabulary. For all their differences on human rights, Jews, Christians, and Muslims share a common understanding of what it means to have a right. John Carman's "Duties and Rights in Hindu Society" shows that individual rights is not an independent notion in Hindu philosophy and culture. It exists in a context of duty which structures daily social interchanges as well as Hindu ritual practice. He uses an illustration from Louis Malle's film portrayal of India to show how Westerners regularly misinterpret Hindu cultural life because they regard rights as distinct from duties. A vast throng at night near the Mylapore temple in Madras City gathers around hundreds of devotees pulling on ropes which move a giant temple car. Malle saw in this the dark, incomprehensible chaos of the exotic East. Carman points out that it is actually a complicated but orderly example of particular outcaste groups exercising caste rights in the performance of a religious and cultural duty. This fulfills the law of *dharma*, the cosmic order of things into which each person is born with a particular duty to fulfill. *Dharma* is an order of perfect cosmic justice, determined by the actions of one's past life. Duty is therefore an expression of one's true persona, more one's participation in maintaining the cosmic order than an alien constraint.

British justice in India gradually dismembered this integrated law of *dharma*, substituting a disparate collection of individual rights. Carman points out that the Indian constitution now uses the language of rights to replace the language of duties, and many of these new rights challenge not only the traditional Hindu system of caste duties, but the notion of *dharma* which structured them. What, then, is the prospect in India for a modern doctrine of universal human rights, apart from the traditional doctrine of *dharma*? Carman analyzes legal records dealing with the *dharma* notion of honor traditionally granted to certain groups and finds them "filled with human foibles but also with . . . the blotting out of a magnificent cosmic vision of the divine-human community. . . ." Can *dharma* be conjoined with the Western idea of universal human rights? Carman clearly hopes so. His is an important Western Christian voice reconsidering the primacy of individual rights in our thinking about the value of human being.

Ty Unno argues the Buddhist case for a conception of duty, felt with sincerity, as the appropriate way of being in a consensual society. He notes that Buddhism emphasized a sense of gratitude, rather than rights, as essential for a truly human life. Of critical importance for him is the distinction between the classical Buddhist notion of the not-self and the contemporary Western notion of the person. This differs from the distinction which John Carman was making in the case of Hinduism, since a major school of Hindu thought argues for a strong sense of inner self (*ātman*) which is identical with the Holy World Power (*Brahman*). Buddhism teaches the virtue of self-emptying so that the individual person becomes egoless. Unno makes it clear that this does not mean the loss of personality or individuality, but rather a lack of possessiveness in one who can now make the ritual announcement, "This is not mine, I am not this, this is not myself." Buddhism recognized the difficulty of eliminating the deep roots of self-centeredness, however, and the awareness of this difficulty led to the development of the Pure Land Tradition. Here the Primal Vow of Buddha Amida comes to the aid of those lost in ignorance of the not-self. Religious fulfillment is thus made possible by the Other Power of Buddha.

Unno proposes a way of understanding individuality taken from the contemporary Japanese philosopher Keiji Nishitani who argues that reality is neither subject nor object but rather an "in-itself." When we lift something from its elemental mode of being our consciousness transforms it into an object, but its original condition "in-itself" is prior to subjectivity or objectivity. Unno argues that this is a valid way of understanding all reality, and that the question of rights must therefore be broadened to include nature as well as human society. Especially in light of the current ecological crisis he urges the relevance of Buddhist thinking for contemporary Western culture.

Unno's primary focus is on personal rights and rethinking the nature of the individual. Robert Thurman turns to the question of "Social and Cultural Rights in Buddhism." He begins by examining the Buddhist view of the universe and then turns to aspects of Buddhist culture before finally summarizing some of the Buddha's teachings on human society. Thurman admits that Buddhism never had much success in affecting the political, legal and economic life of premodern Asian societies. He suggests, however, that Tibetan Buddhism has developed a form of modernization which is interior rather than exterior. The monasteries became the dominant institution in Tibetan life between the fifteenth and seventeenth centuries. Rather than become secularized and "external" in the modernizing process of shaping nature through technology, "the monasteries became the seats of the national industry, the inner perfection of minds and souls through education and contemplation."

The view of Buddhist metaphysics which he sketches at the outset is one of numerous universes in which the Buddhas simultaneously perceive both the ultimate reality of pure bliss and the historical reality of human beings caught in delusion and suffering. The Buddha force is omnipresent in our historical world providing an ideal opportunity for us to develop and become free. Against this background Thurman sketches the Buddhist view of society and culture, beginning with the Buddhist notion of *social individualism*. He argues that Buddhist "selflessness" enabled many in role-ridden, hierarchical ancient societies to break out of social, cultural, and religious stereotypes. This social individualism was also the cornerstone for Buddhist monasticism which enhanced ancient cultures by providing a free space beyond role requirements and social obligations where individuals could pursue self-realization. Thurman also points out that the human individual is the result of a long process of innumerable reincarnations. Since actions of one's past life influence one's present, we are in part self-created and therefore responsible for our own destiny. By the same token we have earned our rights and no one can rightfully deprive us of them. Thurman concludes with a call for further reflection on the Tibetan experience of "interior modernization" as one way of meeting the Western need to balance individual rights with social responsibilities.

Our concluding section on Confucianism begins with Henry Rosemont's question, "Why Take Rights Seriously?" He uses Confucian philosophy as a critique of contemporary Western philosophical thinking on human rights, thereby providing a context for the essays by Theodore de Bary and Roger Ames which focus directly on the Confucian tradition. Rosemont is persuaded that the Western notion of the autonomous individual is not the most appropriate way to characterize human beings. He is particularly critical of abstraction in the Western doctrine of universal rights, arguing instead for "concept clusters" through which various cultures may learn from and adapt to one another. His essay uses Confucian concept clusters to clarify the difficulties and dangers of Western views of rights based on the autonomy of the free-standing individual. His project is to analyze the concept cluster of rights in a given culture, then partially decontextualize those concepts without, however, deconstructing them. He would also simultaneously recontextualize them by contrasting them with a second culture, in this case Confucianism. His project assumes that there are universal elements in any doctrine of human rights, but that universality is always concretely embodied in a particular cultural context.

Rosemont argues that early Confucianism is not a moral philosophy in the Western sense, and that Chinese is only one of a number of languages in which there is no word for *moral*. He goes on to show that relativism can be avoided by noting that particular actions are regularly deemed appropriate in particular social contexts. In the Chinese context, for example, an action is not abstractly moral; it is concretely fitting. He argues that Confucian ethical alternatives can alter our perspective on the question of rights and make an important contribution toward reconstituting the entire discipline of philosophy.

Theodore de Bary begins his essay on "Neo-Confucianism and Human Rights" observing that *human rights* is a relatively recent Western invention. This does not mean, however, that Eastern philosophical traditions have nothing to contribute to the discussion. He is persuaded that fundamental ideas in the Neo-Confucian tradition contribute to a better understanding of what it means to have a right and how rights function in a cultural context. The Confucian contribution is centered in its focus on "humaneness" and the reverential attitude which Confucius had toward the meaning of being truly human. De Bary regards Confucianism as a religious humanism and stresses the importance of reverence for life and the sources of life. But the functional notion of rights in Confucian culture is based on equity in social relations, not equality. The relations between parent and child, for example, are equitable but not equal. He also stresses that relationships change in the course of time, thus altering the specific rights of those involved in the relationship. *Reciprocity* and *propriety* are central conceptions in the Confucian cultural context.

The Neo-Confucian view of the inherent goodness of our moral nature provides a premise somewhat akin to the Western idea of the inherent dignity of humankind, on which our doctrine of rights is based. This view also emphasized the reciprocal nature of responsibility in the classical paradigmatic relationships of parent and child, ruler and minister, husband and wife, elder and junior, friend and friend. Chu Hsi, the chief architect of Neo-Confucian philosophy, emphasized ritual order as the embodiment of principles inherent in the universe. These principles were static and structural and, at the same time, vital processes of change. Chu sought to avoid moral relativism and pragmatism on the one hand, and the autocratic state on the other. De Bary argues that the Confucian tradition worked continually to conceive a better human state in which the rights of all would be protected by an adequate system of laws.

Roger Ames begins his study of "Rites as Rights: The Confucian Alternative" with an examination of the basic concept *li*. The term is very broad and is translated as "rites," "ritual practices," and "propriety." He argues that ritual practice is "a pliant body of practices for registering one's own importance." Ritual practice is also a necessary condition for Confucius' vision of social harmony because it not only permits but requires personalization. Because humanity itself is regarded as a progressive cultural achievement in the Chinese tradition, ritual practice is a fundamental form of social and cultural structuring.

Ames argues that the Western conception of individual human rights is a cultural response to the rupture between the small familial community where custom and tradition guaranteed fundamental dignities and the modern nation state in which mobile and atomized populations claim their humanity from an impersonal government. He reverses this argument to show that China has not been under the same compulsion to develop a doctrine of individual rights because of continuity in familial communities. Ritual practice, he points out, has been a major instrument enabling that continuity.

A major strength of the Chinese understanding of human dignity is the extent to which ritual practice wove humanistic values into the cultural fabric, maintaining them by social pressure rather than punishment or legal action. From the Chinese point of view, reliance on the application of law, and the interpretation of human rights as a legal doctrine, dehumanizes and impoverishes the natural sources of that dignity. Those sources are the processes of mutual accommodation and the compromise of a particular responsibility in order to discover conduct appropriate to a particular occasion in a specific context.

Ames concludes with a proposal for rethinking rights in the West in the light of these considerations from the Chinese tradition. He notes especially the Marxist criticism that the dominant bourgeois culture limits human rights to civil rights. Ames argues that this criticism could be blunted in the West by recognizing the immediate and inseparable relationship between cultural conditions and the variable content of abstractly defined human rights.

Common to virtually all of our authors is the conviction that Ernest Hocking's "free-standing individual" suffers as much from autonomy as he or she gains. While all will not agree on the structure of cross-cultural adaptation sketched by Henry Rosemont, it is evident that most of our authors are involved in some sort of intercultural conversation. Ernest Hocking was persuaded that *The Coming World Civilization* was inevitable, short of nuclear holocaust, because of the demands of world politics and a world economy. He had his own scheme for connecting the autonomous individual to a familial community. Our authors have been quick to criticize the Western notion of universal rights as abstract. Hocking argued that it was an invaluable resource. Vague and abstract though it is, there can be no cross-cultural understanding without a significant common basis for conversation. Without some common ground among cultural concept clusters, for example, Henry Rosemont's proposed interchange between Western and Confucian approaches to rights would not be possible. So liberal individualism may have its own contribution to make to the ongoing conversation. In the light of current human rights violations it is clear that the conversation needs help from all sides.

PART I

Judaism, Christianity, and Marxism

1

The Image of the Human
and the Rights of the Individual
in Jewish Tradition

MICHAEL FISHBANE

I. THE IDEA OF THE PERSON AND HUMAN RIGHTS

THE FUNDAMENTAL PRESUPPOSITION of the rights of the person in Judaism is a belief in the absolute and uncompromisable worth of human life. This belief is grounded in the unique value of the individual in the divine scheme of creation and is variously articulated in both biblical literature and rabbinic tradition. The biblical view, itself formative and foundational for historical Judaism, contrasts sharply with ancient Near Eastern law. In this latter — be it Babylonian, Assyrian, or Hittite law — a clear correlation emerges: life has an economic evaluation, on the one hand, while property is correspondingly calculable in terms of life. Thus, in Hittite law, punishment of a murderer may take the form of the surrender of other persons of equivalent social value "instead of blood," or, in an Assyrian phrase, to "make good the dead person." A hierarchy of payments is listed for the intentional murder of a free man or woman, less for unintentional homicide, and still less for the intentional or unintentional murder of a slave. A most valuable item, a Hittite merchant, is worth one hundred minas of silver. The concern of the law in such cases is thus to make up a social-economic deficit.[1] By the same token, property crimes may be compensated or made good by the life of persons of a worth estimated as compensatory for the material loss sustained. Thus

17

Babylonian law requires the life of a person for breaking and entering with intent to steal, or for actual theft.[2] Safeguarding property is thus a preeminent legal consideration and allows for the exaction of a death penalty—just as property is worth a person's life. In a word, life and property are commensurable values, used interchangeably in this legal system, there being presupposed an exchange rate between persons and things.

In biblical law there is no correlation between persons and property, no commensurable exchange between human worth and economic value—a fact which also leads to some stark results. Thus, in ancient Israel intentional murder is punishable by death, there being no substitution. "You shall not take a ransom for the life of a murderer who is guilty of death," states the law, "but he shall surely be put to death" (Num. 35:31). The only exception provided for this harsh rule involves the case of homicide not committed personally or with intent to produce harm, as, for example, in the case of the negligent owner of a vicious ox which kills a person. In this case, the ox must be killed as the direct agent of death, though the law allows the owner to make a ransom payment of a sum fixed by the slain person's family (Exod. 21:28–30). The juridical postulate underpinning this biblical view is clearly formulated in Gen. 9:5: "For your lifeblood I shall require a reckoning; of every beast I shall require it. . . . Whoever sheds the blood of a man, by man shall his blood be shed, *for in the image of God was man created.*"[3]

This value principle may, in turn, elucidate what appears to be a more brutal system of punishments—one which does not permit any economic exchange in the case of murder—in biblical as against comparable Near Eastern law. For at the core of the biblical system is the perception that the person is of absolute and inviolable worth: created in the divine image. Hence, while a human may kill creatures of lesser value, like animals, with impunity —since they are not in the divine likeness—an animal which kills a person or a person who kills another person must bear the maximal punishment, death, "for in the image of God was man created." A human system of exchange cannot, then, replace the divine worth of the person. Significantly, Genesis 9 is a free adaptation of Genesis 1, where this value was first proclaimed.[4] From this overall perspective the corresponding biblical situation, which does not envisage any property offense that can be compensated by a human life, is fully understandable. The absolute and inestimable value of the person is thus the fundamental presupposition and preamble for our investigation of human rights in Judaism.

These various considerations become even clearer in rabbinic law and tradition. The invaluableness of life led to a virtual abolition of the death penalty—not by reintroducing any form of exchange principle but by making the requirements for conviction of a capital offense so extreme that it was quite unlikely that such an adjudication could ever come down. The provisions included the necessity that witnesses be present *in flagrante delicto* and warn the murderer that he or she was about to commit a capital offense, so that the potential murderer was forced to take cognizance of the act and his or her clear intent to act with premeditation. To best appreciate the animating spirit of these rabbinic attitudes toward human life, a text found in the legal code of the Mishnah from the second-third century C.E. is most instructive. In this source we learn that witnesses in capital cases were admonished by the judges as follows:

> It was for this reason Adam was created alone: to teach you that anyone who destroys a single life, it is to be accounted to him by Scripture as if he had destroyed the whole world, and whoever preserves a single life, it is accounted to him by Scripture as if he had preserved a whole world . . . and also to teach you the greatness of God: for a person stamps many coins with one die, and they are all similar; but God has stamped every person with the die of Adam, yet no one is similar to his fellow. Therefore, everyone must say: "For my sake was the world created." (*M. Sanhedrin* 4.5)

The human being is of inestimable worth, an incomparable divine creation: each one unique, like Adam at the beginning; each one a whole world, a cosmos in miniature. All humanity is bound up in the life of each person. The burden of this mighty presupposition weighed heavily upon the culture, and some Mishnah manuscripts even revised the admonition to refer to "a single life *in Israel*"—a safer and homier prescription. But the original reading is confirmed by the orientation of the text itself and by ancient manuscripts and medieval citations[5]—together with a full citation in the Qur'an.[6] And it is this original sense which lies at the heart of Judaism and explains its more passionate dialectics and demands with regard to human rights in complex situations.

The exhortation to witnesses in the Mishnah just cited stresses the uniqueness and value of each person, who, as a descendant of Adam and a bearer of his image, may legitimately say, "For my sake was the world created." But this may lead, in certain circumstances, to a clash between rights and duties — between one's own right to life and one's duty to die and not be the agent of death.

> In every other law of the Torah, if a man is commanded, "Transgress and do not suffer death," he may transgress and not suffer death, excepting idolatry, incest, and shedding blood. . . . Murder may not be practiced to save one's life. . . . Even as one who came before Raba and said to him: "The governor of my town has ordered me, 'Go and kill so and so; if not, I will slay you.'" Raba answered him: "Let him rather slay you than that you should commit murder; *who knows that your blood is redder? Perhaps his blood is redder!*" (b. Sanhedrin 74a)

No commensurability between persons is envisaged here. Each person is an absolute creature, so that one may not substitute one life for another. This is certainly an extreme — though consistent — rabbinic admonition. It underscores the value of the human being created in the divine image, so that no exchange between persons is allowable.

Now the problems of compliance or resistance to a tyrannical order, as well as the formulation of a minimal list of behaviors which exemplify ultimate obedience to God and the Torah, derive from the historical situation of terror experienced by the Jews during the Hadrianic persecutions of 132–35 C.E., when Rome was the occupying force in ancient Palestine. These concrete cases undoubtedly provoked contemporary debate and, in their wake, a whole series of subsequent rabbinic discussions which are largely preserved from the general era before Raba and shortly thereafter (the third through the fifth centuries C.E.). Clearly, in the text just cited, Raba reflects an absolute and uncompromising position: there is no exchange of value between one person and another. But under what conditions is the right to life of the one subordinate to the right to life of the many, so that a person may become the accessory to another's death?

To illustrate a rabbinic approach, here is a Tannaitic text, from the Roman period in question, which has been preserved in the *Tosefta*. The advice is directed to

> a company of men to whom Gentiles said: "Give us one of you that we may kill him and if not we shall kill all." [The answer was given], "Let all be killed but let no soul [life, person] of Israel be handed over; but if they specifically mention one, as for example they single out Sheba ben Bichri, they (the Jews) may give him to them, that not all of them be killed." R. Judah (ben Ilai) asked: "To what (case) does this apply?" "When he (the identified one) is within (the city) and they (the others) are without [then compliance is forbidden]; but if both are within, insofar as he would be killed and they would be killed, they may give him up to them that all not be killed; as Scripture says: 'And the woman came to all the people in her wisdom' (2 Sam. 20:22), (which means) she said to them: 'Since he would be killed and they would not be killed, give him to them that you not all be killed.'" R. Simeon rejoined: "It means that she said thus to them: 'Anyone rebelling against the kingship of the house of David is deserving of death.'" (*Tos. Terumot* 7.20)

This text is enormously complicated and has been subject to much traditional and modern discussion.[7] The legists are concerned to emphasize that no one can make a judgment of individual worth, even *in extremis*, even if collective death would result, if faced with an unspecified demand that one person be sacrificed for the many. In such cases, mass death is enjoined rather than compliance with such a tyrannical request. On the other hand, the sages do agree that compliance is permitted when the mob explicitly designates the person by name, and the person and the rest of the community are together in a besieged place. Conceivably, R. Judah adds his rider in order to soften this severe ruling, or, as I think just as likely, in order also to soften or qualify the conditions of compliance involving indirect complicity in another's death. He says: one may comply only if the *entire* group is in mortal danger; that is, if there is any chance of escape, compliance is not allowed, but otherwise the safety or preservation of the majority is an overriding consideration. R. Simeon's view, on the other hand, appears to suggest that one may never comply with such a dictatorial demand — but perhaps he hints that one may hand over a named person who has already been condemned to death. This is not directly stated by R. Simeon, but it was an ancient opinion and is a contextually possible inference here. If so, R. Simeon's strict view would both refuse compliance and allow it, at once preserving the community from complicity in murder and preserving national rights to determine capital punishment.

In the foregoing episode the community is struggling with its extreme value of the noncommensurability of life and the practical demands for survival in a reign of terror. Obviously the guidelines of the Sanhedrin were not the end of the matter, and debates ensued with regard to the proper action *even if* a person were specified. Finding a proper and just balance between the religious-legal ideal and the constraints of practical moral choice and its impinging considerations was no easy matter. An insight into the complexity of deliberations is offered by a midrashic tradition in *Genesis Rabba* (94), which preserves a version of our episode and adds two other cases to it.

In the first case, R. Joshua ben Levi (third century) received and gave sanctuary to a criminal. Realizing the danger, he persuaded the man that it was better that he give himself up for death than that the community as a whole be punished. Though such complicity was legally correct, we learn that such behavior was not deemed to be of the highest standards — not the way of *hasidim* ("pious ones") — and was rejected in heaven. One wonders whether the editor of the Midrash, appropriating the case from the Jerusalem Talmud (*jer. Terumot* 46b), adds it here in order to comment on the view of R. Judah, cited earlier — who *did* make a trade of lives: one for many. In any case, the Midrash follows this episode with a related legal *topos*: an instance concerning Nebuchadnezzar. According to this rendition, this Babylonian king, upon besieging Jerusalem, announced that if King Jehoiakim, who had rebelled against him, was given over to him, he would lift the siege. Jehoiakim, who fights for his life with casuistic vigor, is presented in legal debate with the rabbinic authorities.

"Is such done?" he asked. "Does one push away a soul for a soul? Is it not written: 'You shall not surrender a (fugitive) slave to his master' (Deut. 23:16)?" They (the Sanhedrin) answered: "Did your old one (the wise woman) not do thus to Sheba ben Bichri? [for Scripture reports that she said]: 'Behold his head is thrown over to you' (2 Sam. 20:21)." As he (Jehoiakim) refused to comply (and give himself over) they overpowered him and dismembered him (passing him over the wall, like Sheba).

This legal discussion shows the difficulty of formulating a hierarchy of rights to life within the society. The following ancient mishnaic ruling deals with the same problem:

(With respect to) the woman who has difficulty giving birth — one cuts up the fetus in her womb, and takes it out limb by limb, because her life takes precedence over his. If the fetus has largely emerged, one does not injure it, for one does not push aside one soul for another. (*M. Oholot* 7.6)

According to this law, when a woman has difficulty in childbirth her life must be saved and an embryotomy performed on the fetus in her womb. Indeed, saving the life of the mother and destroying her fetus is not only permitted but required. But if the fetus has largely emerged one has no right to intervene, since the fetus is now viable and no human can choose which life is the more important. Feticide is not regarded in the preceding Mishnah as a capital offense. A conservative construction of the rule also has serious implications for cases where a fetus may become genetically damaged — due, for example, to exposure to such diseases or drugs as rubella or thalidomide. Indeed, conservative rabbinic jurists in the modern period are quite strictly opposed to natal infanticide even for genetic reasons and are also opposed to medical procedures like amniocentesis in principle; for genetic screening — in Jewish circles Tay-Sachs is the flare point — is often linked with arguments for genetic abortion, and feticide is not permitted *except where the mother's life is imperiled*. Rabbi I. J. Unterman, a former chief rabbi of Israel, has argued in this vein, and also against neonatal infanticide (for example, by starvation), *even* where the child is born deformed or severely genetically damaged. He states:

> This very thought appears to me as opposing the outlook of the Torah on human life, whereby even in the hardest moments it is forbidden to sacrifice life for any reason whatever other than the sanctification of the Divine Name (martyrdom) or the saving of the mother's life.[8]

The position of the eighteenth-century Talmudist Rabbi Jacob Emden[9] has been expanded in our day to produce a decidedly lenient approach to the abortion of a fetus with Tay-Sachs disease, for example. Rabbi Eliezer Waldman, former head of the Court of Jewish Law in Jerusalem, thus ruled in 1976 that such a fetus — deemed not viable — could be aborted until the seventh month! He also extended the notion of *great need* to cases of a deformed Down's Syndrome fetus where the family would be under great stress.[10] In other lenient rulings, great need can mean psychological stress to the mother, as in cases of impregnation by rape.

In brief, we see in the foregoing deliberations conflicting resolutions of the ideal of human life in Jewish legal sources, as the deciders struggle with inherited legal cases and give different exegetical emphasis to the mother and her rights and needs, or to the fetus and its rights. In Jewish law there is great hesitation to permit ungovernable medical acts which regard the doctor as a source of healing. Yet Jewish teaching overall regards the doctor as the proximate agent of divine activity (cf. *b. Berakhot* 6a). Therefore it has built into itself the capacity to temper its strong aversion to so-called tampering with nature with clear permission for therapeutic interventions which may, *inter alia*, correct congenital abnormalities, affect gene design *in utero*, result in sterilization, or more generally allow for risky procedures that offer the promise of a cure.

Significantly, in so-called right-to-die cases — as against those involving the right to life or the duty to die — if the individual is in the natural death process no nonnatural interventions are permitted. However, until that moment, every effort must be made to save the life of the ill person and prevent his or her exposure to mortal risk or suicide. Despite a strong commitment to the absolute value of life, and an equally strong aversion to life-for-life equivalencies, hierarchies of value are unavoidable and Jewish law inevitably legislates priorities. Withal, the historical diversity of opinion in halakic literature on all these points is the strongest argument against legal dogmatism and for the open-endedness of this juridical system.

II. THE RELATIONSHIP BETWEEN LEGAL-RITUAL DUTIES AND HUMAN RIGHTS

As with other ancient religious-legal systems, Judaism, since antiquity, has excluded nonmembers from participation in ritual practices and has even developed a whole hierarchy of marginal status. Thus, for example, a non-Israelite male slave in the biblical period could participate in the Passover ceremony after undergoing the rite of circumcision; and there was also an inner-biblical development which imposed certain civil and cultic laws on the non-Israelite "stranger"— just as on the "native-born"— even though the "stranger" was not religiously naturalized. With the development of proselytism and various preproselyte stages within ancient Judaism, new duties were imposed upon or permitted to the novitiate in proportion to the degree of his or her entry into the normative ritual community. Thus, not-fully-converted non-Jewish "God-fearers," who nevertheless observed the Sabbath and celebrated festivals in Jerusalem, constituted a distinct category; males of the same group who also undertook the covenant of circumcision changed status. At each point along the path from alien to Jew, and as a matter of principle, our sources evince a clear relationship between rights and duties: the more duties, the more rights; contrariwise, the diminution of duties implies and effects a lower standing with respect to the larger notion of rights. The above issues have nothing whatever to do with the larger Jewish recognition that all persons are bearers of basic and inalienable human rights, *insofar as a set minimum of humane duties are performed.*

The duties involved are the so-called Noachide laws — seven minimal moral duties enjoined upon all persons (*b. Sanhedrin* 56–60). These are listed variously as prohibitions of idolatry, blasphemy, bloodshed, sexual sins, theft, and eating living animals, as well as the positive obligation to establish a legal system. In Jewish law, then, persons performing these minimal duties were accorded fundamental regard as persons in the full human sense. This category, it may be added, also proved salutary in providing a certain common theological-legal ground for Jews, Christians, and Muslims in the Middle Ages. Similarly, the category of Noachidism provided the mechanism for determining the *non plus ultra*: cases where persons might be deemed as having gone beyond the pale of human behavior and no longer deserving of the rights and protections offered by civil society.

Maimonides, for example, shows the role of the Noachide laws in his thinking. For him, Holy War — the only justifiable war — is permitted in order to extend Noachide law and its basic principles. Moses, he states, "was commanded by God to compel all people to accept the commandments enjoined upon Noachides. Anyone who does not accept them is to be put to death" (*Hilkhot Melakhim* 8.10).[11] While Maimonides is clearly concerned with the divine duty to purify the Holy Land and rid it of idolatrous seductions, a more overriding issue is involved: the impositions of the minimal human duties of social-political morality — the minimal repair of the state of nature, we might say. In effect, the religious-legal duty to destroy non-Noachides points beyond the issue of idolatry *per se* and to the basic human duty to establish a structure of human rights within society — a minimal moral order.

The Noachide category provides an ancient minimal statement on human rights. It protects humans from certain nonsocial behaviors and even guarantees protection under law. This category is not a species of natural law but a feature of the divine law in the broadest sense. The list of Noachide laws are *exegetically* derived from Gen. 2:16 (cf. *b. Sanhedrin* 59b; *Genesis Rabba* 34). Thus the Noachide laws are a type of universal revelation, though technically derivative of the moral law. The Sinaitic law, on the other hand, with its more elaborated structure of rabbinic rights and duties, is a particular revelation to Israel and its descendants.[12]

There is a class of Jews given marginal status in Talmudic and post-Talmudic law, however. What are their rights? The class frequently comprises idiots, minors, androgynes, and women. Such persons are not allowed, for example, to bear witness or to give legal testimony — presumably, for idiots and minors, because of their defective or immature powers of judgment.

The disempowerment of women here, as elsewhere, is more complicated and probably not simply reducible to stereotypes in the traditional sources — where women are often portrayed as gadabouts, superstitious, or simply uninformed. The inferior position of women in classical rabbinic law probably comes down to something much more fundamental, namely, that the legal category of *person* in Jewish law is a male construct, so that women (like minors and so forth) are, in effect, conceived of as incomplete males. The category *woman* is a mirror category, a negative requiring a positive for self-definition. The woman is defined by male categories and found wanting. To be sure, already in ancient sources *woman* is a positive category with respect to familial duties. But this extralegal social classification only supports the point at issue, for these latter activities are not religious-legal duties but their shadow side. Indeed, they are primarily invoked by the rabbis to "explain" why women's positive, required duties are so few. Being responsible for family affairs, a woman is not free — and hence not obligated — to perform religious duties which, from the legal point of view, are regulated by fixed times. From the positive legal viewpoint, in fact, women have but three fundamental obligations: to light Sabbath candles; to perform a paracultic ritual connected with the baking of bread; and to heed the rules of menstrual purity. To these three behaviors women have inalienable rights. But apart from them, a more complicated gradation of duties is imposed — moving from permissible to forbidden behaviors. No such gradation affects the corresponding "normal male," who has maximal duties (and hence maximal rights) within the halakic system. Thus, for example, a woman may, time and family obligations permitting, pray the time-bound morning prayers and even wear phylacteries; but, traditionally, she may not be counted as a person in determining a prayer quorum, and she is not permitted either to lead prayers in a male quorum or to read from the Torah scroll during public worship. To be sure, women may have their own quorum where they may lead prayers and read from the scroll of the Law; yet even here some restrictions are imposed which leave these "rights" defective compared with the normative male obligations. As we have had occasion to observe earlier, the fundamental correlation between rights and duties — so prevalent in Jewish law — occurs here as well.

In another range of instances, a woman's rights are severely compromised — and one cannot but conclude that this is directly due to the fact that she is not an independent legal person. The issue at hand involves a set of legal problems dealing with a particular aspect of female victimization. I shall simply indicate the problem; the various ancient and modern solutions — at pains to rectify the situation, while constrained to work within the framework of traditional legal reasoning and certain dogmatic presuppositions — cannot be treated here. The legal *topos* is known as *agunah* and concerns the situation where a woman has been left by her husband without a divorce. Abandoned, not permitted to remarry, she is in limbo, an *agunah*. Now the law does not make distinctions between intentional, punitive desertion by the male and the latter's accidental or forced separation from his wife. Both intentional and unintentional abandonment invoke the *agunah* status of suspended rights upon the woman, though constraints are brought on the intentional deserter to force him to return home or give his wife a divorce, and lenient rules of attestation of death are permitted in cases of death under tragic or combatant circumstances. Nevertheless, the woman cannot herself directly rectify her liminal situation. Legally, she cannot initiate divorce or simply demand an annulment of her marriage. In the case of negligent desertion, the inability of the woman to receive alimony or child support only makes her *agunah* status all the more poignant. Legal fictions in this case can neither alleviate nor hide the woman's fundamental lack of rights of redress or self-help in a situation produced against her will, or at least against her best legal interests. Rights are a social-legal category, such that even the broad principle of the person as one created in the divine image is a functional norm within a specific system — which latter can enhance, moderate, or actually eclipse the principle in certain cases.

In the preceding discussion we observed the inner-cultural suspension or limitation of rights. We now briefly focus on the suspension or qualification of duties in the face of higher duties — all of which bear on the notion of the person and his or her rights in the overall halakic system. I choose three examples from classical rabbinic sources. The first involves the principle of *piquah nefesh,* or the concern for health and life, as an overriding duty. Already in ancient sources one's right to life and one's duty not to put oneself in mortal danger often requires the suspension of certain halakic duties — the commandment of Sabbath rest, for example. As important and overriding as this commandment is under normal circumstances, modern authorities have seen fit to rule that one may desecrate the Sabbath rest in order to protect or save a person's life. Some include under this category the duty to help someone threatening suicide, even if that threat is merely a hint or one does not even know for sure whether the person really intends to carry out the threat. The absolute value of human life takes precedence over other divine commandments and even qualifies them in certain instances.

A second example is the principle of *yosher* ("justice" or "equity"), especially where it indicates that one owes allegiance to a higher authority (*dinei shamayim*, "the laws of Heaven" [God]). It shows that there are metalegal concerns in the Halakah to sustain certain personal rights which fall through legal loopholes. A case noted in the Mishnah (*Baba Qama* 6.4) and the Talmud (*b. Baba Qama* 55b), and treated by later commentators as well, involves a case of torts where the tortfeasor is legally exempt from payment of compensation according to human law but is liable according to the laws of Heaven. Given this latter, one commentator (Yam shel Shelomo, *ad M. Baba Qama* 6.6) states that the courts "should bring pressure to bear on [the tortfeasor] verbally, without compulsion; others object to such constraint, but require that the individual be informed that 'we do not compel you, *but you shall have to fulfill your duty to Heaven.*'" In this way, the rights of the person to be compensated for damages is endorsed in conjunction with an appeal to a higher authority and duty.

Finally, I return to the problem found in *Genesis Rabba* 94, where R. Joshua ben Levi gave sanctuary to a person wanted by the government. Although he did not literally hand the man over to the authorities, R. Joshua did persuade the refugee to hand himself over, in order that the community be spared. While this appears to be a favorable moral solution, the text goes on to report that while legal, and acceptable by normal human standards, R. Joshua's behavior was nevertheless *rejected* by Heaven! For, though he had acted correctly, he had abandoned *mishnat hasidim* ("the law of the pious") — a higher obligation than the dictates of mere legality. The rights of persons being absolute, R. Joshua could not even be an indirect accomplice in another's death. In effect, he had acceded to a tyrannical request in handing over Ullah bar Qosheb to the government. This act of collaboration cost him divine favor. He was deprived of visitation from the prophet Elijah, an ancient sign of grace and inspiration. Realizing that he had sinned, R. Joshua fasted for thirty days. When Elijah subsequently reappeared, the rabbi asked him why he had been absent. In response, the poor sage was roundly rebuked. "Am I an associate of betrayal?" queried Elijah. R. Joshua, still perplexed, asked: "Is there not a ruling (which deals with permissible extradition in cases where a person is specifically mentioned?" (cf. *Tos. Terumot* 7.20, cited above). Elijah responded: "Is this *mishnat hasidim?*" And then came the prophet's sequel, which somewhat qualifies the judgment: "It was necessary for this matter to be done, but not by you!"

In effect, the sequel owns that the valid law condones or concedes extradition in this case; but it adds the caveat that the truly pious person should not be an accomplice to such an act. Let the law stand, the prophetic voice admonishes, but let a higher standard be exemplified as well: the principle of the incommensurable value of the person should be retained as a guiding norm, even if such an absolute standard be compromised in tyrannical times for the sake of the right to life of the community. That this *quid pro quo* for the sake of collective redemption could itself be a fiction, a lie of non-Noachides, was never so clear as in our own brutal era. The demonic choices imposed upon Jews and their leadership in the ghettos of eastern Europe—the promise of life for the many in exchange for the extradition to death of the few— are still within living memory. As for the decisions of R. Joshua ben Levi in antiquity, or of Adam Czerniakow, the first head of the Warsaw Judenrat in World War II, who would judge them; who could dare? Our rabbinic sources certainly do not. They are, rather, powerful testimonies to the anxieties and cautions, even the conflicts and compromises, of moral choice: at once mindful of the absolute ideal of the human right to life, and anxious to perform a noble duty before God in ambiguous, degrading, or all-too-human circumstances.

This is the Jewish position. At times, to be sure, the burdens of precedent, the weakness of will, and the pressure of presuppositions have produced morally problematic decisions — at least by certain modern standards. But as a body of thoughtful decisions overall, even as a legal-religious system which places the rights of the person as its *Grundnorm*, there can be little doubt that the Jewish tradition provides monumental testimony to an ongoing concern to generate a self-correcting and self-reflective legal system — based on the highest moral principles. By the same token, the Jewish legal tradition may, overall, also provide a powerful resource for contemporary reflections on human rights and duties in our time. From this perspective, the issue is neither to praise nor to criticize the system for its historical achievements; it is rather to reflect on the presuppositions and solutions of the Jewish legal and moral tradition as we, in turn, try to dignify human action and provide principled standards of moral choice based on a clear notion of the person. All concerns for human rights will founder, as so much ideality and cheap legality, if they are not grounded in a strong and shared sense of personhood.

NOTES

1. See J. B. Pritchard, *Ancient Near Eastern Texts Relating to the Old Testament*, 2d ed. (Princeton: Princeton University Press, 1955), "The Hittite Laws," pars. 1–4; and G. R. Driver and John C. Miles, *The Assyrian Laws* (Oxford: Clarendon Press, 1935), p. 35.

2. Pritchard, *Ancient Near Eastern Texts*, "The Code of Hammurabi," pars. 6–10, 21, 25; "The Laws of Eshnuna," par. 13; "The Middle Assyrian Laws," par. 3.

3. Moshe Greenberg was the first to articulate this fundamental difference between biblical and ancient Near Eastern legal collections. See his "Some Postulates of Biblical Criminal Law," in *Yehezkel Kaufman Jubilee Volume*, ed. Menahem Haran (Jerusalem: Magnes Press, 1960), pp. 5–28. Recent attempts to qualify this insight in details, or by methodological considerations, do not, to my mind, undermine his seminal insight.

4. Michael Fishbane, *Biblical Interpretation in Ancient Israel* (Oxford: Clarendon Press, 1985), pp. 318–21.

5. See the note of Chanoch Albeck in his edition of the Mishnah, *ad loc.*, and, particularly, the exhaustive review of E. E. Urbach, "*Kol hammiqayyem nephesh ahat*," *Tarbiz* 40 (1970–71): 268–84 (in Hebrew).

6. "Therefore we decreed for the Israelites: anyone who kills a human being (who did) not (commit) murder or corruption on the earth is as though he destroyed all mankind, and anyone who keeps him alive is as though he kept alive all mankind" (Qur'an 5:32).

7. For diverse solutions, see Saul Lieberman, *Tosefta ki-Feshutah* (1955) 1:420ff.; and also David Daube, *Collaboration with Tyranny in Rabbinic Law* (London: Oxford University Press, 1965), chap. 2, on this topic and related considerations.

8. Quoted by Immanuel Jakobovits, "Review of Recent Halakhic Periodical Literature: Deformed Babies," *Tradition* 5 (1963): 268.

9. For this conclusion he produced an ingenious reading of *b. 'Arakhin* 7a. The matter has been discussed in English by D. Sinclair, "The Legal Basis for the Prohibition of Abortion in Jewish Law," *Israel Law Review* 15 (1980): 124.

10. Sinclair, "Legal Basis for Prohibition of Abortion," pp. 126ff.

11. Translated by M. Herschmann, *The Code of Maimonides: The Book of Judges* (New Haven, Conn.: Yale University Press, 1949): p. 230.

12. On these matters see S. Schwarzchild, *Jewish Quarterly Review* 52 (1962): 302; Jose Faur, *Tarbiz* 38 (1968): 43–53. Maimonides notes that Noachides should not accept the seven commandments on their merits but as revealed legislation. Cf. *Yad, Melakhim,* 7.11.

2

Christian Concepts of the Responsible Self

TRUTZ RENDTORFF

I. THE AMBIVALENT STATUS OF HUMAN RIGHTS AND THE PROBLEM OF THEIR FOUNDATION

THE STATUS OF HUMAN RIGHTS today is marked by an ambivalence which is hard to understand. On the one hand, the idea of human rights enjoys broad, even universal, recognition. One could hardly name a second moral and political idea which receives an equally high degree of recognition in most parts of the world. The idea of human rights embodies something like a universal ethical norm of almost ecumenical range. On the other hand, the permanent and repeated disregard of human rights by so many striking and obvious violations shows how fragile the moral obligation is which follows from the idea of human rights. In the foreground of public debate, questions of the realization and the accomplishment of human rights are asked. But these questions have to be raised and these demands have to be brought forward because the idea of human rights lacks its own irresistibly convincing power. Here one might debate the different ideological and political systems and their historical and structural linkage to the idea of human rights. One could develop the empirical conditions under which human rights are being recognized or disregarded. No doubt there exist great and relevant differences. They show up when we look at the ways and means in which human rights take concrete shape as civil rights. Here, at this level of concrete political reality, the differences seem to be whether human rights belong, in the first place,

33

to the individual person as part of his or her self-determination, or whether human rights are looked at as a function of the human species or class. In the first case, the self-determination or self-definition of the individual person forms the norm and shapes the kind of civil rights by which human rights are to be recognized. The individual person comes first and the rights and obligations of citizenship come second. In the other case, the definition or evolution of class or human society forms the norm and determines the type of civil rights which are bestowed on the individual person as part of the overall societal structure. Are rights originally given with the individual person? Or are rights derived from the person's existence within society?

II. RELIGIOUS ELEMENTS IN THE DEVELOPMENT OF HUMAN RIGHTS

This problem of the development of human rights in the modern age raises the role of the Christian tradition. Is the Christian tradition of the human person as created by God, redeemed through Christ and expecting the kingdom of God, the root of the modern concept of human rights? And does this tradition furnish the criteria for the transformation of human rights into civil rights? Which tradition should be named here in the first place among the controversial strands of historical Christianity? Further, if we claim historically a Christian foundation for the modern idea of human rights, does that also mean that a recognition of human rights today necessarily includes a recognition of the Christian tradition? Does the Christian tradition form not only a historical condition for the emergence of human rights but also a permanent norm on which the inner obligation to recognize human rights depends? When we ask this kind of question it is quite obvious that we are moving in the realm of far-reaching problems: continuity or discontinuity in the relation of modern political history to historical Christianity. Wherever a "loss of legitimation" is discussed today, the discontinuity of our secular political world with its religious origins is under discussion. And wherever one seeks a moral and political obligation which grounds human rights, one is asking for something like a religious foundation or something which is apt to replace it.

A. *The Discovery of Religious Roots of Secular Rights: Religious Freedom (Georg Jellinek)*

The search for Christian elements in the rise of modern human rights is a task of historical research. But it is also a search for today's motivating power in the concept of human rights. Both questions were present in the much-debated work of Georg Jellinek. In 1895 he published his famous essay on "The Declaration of Human and Civil Rights." A fervent scholarly debate ensued. The time then was ripe for the question: Are there continuities between the Christian tradition and the modern age? Jellinek put forward the thesis that the American Bill of Rights in 1776 was based on the right of freedom of conscience, that the idea of the inalienable rights of the individual had a *religious* rather than a political origin. He argued further that in contrast with the French Declaration of 1789, the Americans drew a firm line to protect those areas into which the state should not intrude. For Americans, asserted Jellinek, rights of freedom are not positive but negative, demanding not that the state take a particular action but that it *abstain* from action. Liberty in America is not to be achieved by the political organization of society. Freedom is not the goal of political action; it is the presupposition. It is founded in the religious conscience, in the religious self-awareness of people who are free in faith and therefore not dependent on the state for that condition which constitutes them as free persons. Jellinek contrasts this American view with the French concept of freedom as a secular or political "ought" in which freedom is to be established by political institutions. The original idea of human rights in America is already a consequence of the freedom which is constituted in the radical independence of religious belief. In his discussion Jellinek was in favor of a normative function of religious freedom in constitutional law.

There are two points which need to be followed up more closely. One is the tension between the freedom of the self and the freedom granted by civil rights. The freedom of the self is constituted in its own inner realm as a religious believer receives personal identity from God. To that same person freedom is granted by the civil rights of citizenship. How is this tension to be understood? The other point is the present meaning of the historical connection. Are the religious roots of human rights necessary today for the moral obligation to respect human rights? Both points are closely related.

B. Continuity or Discontinuity in the Development of Human Rights (Max Weber, Ernst Troeltsch)

I take up the second point first, the relevance of historical development. It is worthwhile to remember that Max Weber felt very much inspired by Jellinek's thesis in developing his own thesis: the spirit of capitalism as a fruit of Protestant ethics. Weber regarded Jellinek's essay as what today, after Thomas Kuhn, we would call a change of paradigm. Jellinek had argued that what had previously been thought to be caused by secular political revolution was instead caused by the Reformation. Weber used this insight in his reformulation of the genesis of modern capitalistic society. He transformed the material of Jellinek's constitutional history into a model for the development of modern society. He wanted to show that not only materialistic economic forces could change the world but religious forces could do so as well—and had done so in the case of the rise of Western society. His thesis has been debated even more than Jellinek's essay, but in Weber's case the outcome was specifically different from Jellinek's. Weber's research led him to the conclusion that modern industrial society no longer needed the religious foundation out of which modernity had developed. Although post-Reformation Protestantism formed at least one of the major strands which made possible the modern world—the independent, unworldly self-consciousness of the ascetic believer—present society seemed to Weber to be self-containing, no longer in need of its historical religious roots. Ernst Troeltsch, who worked in close relation with Weber, came to similar results. At the core of the Christian religion he identified the concept of the individual person as independent from the world and linked to worldly affairs only by compromise. But he saw modern society as a "hard rock" from which this religious idea was excluded. This metaphor expresses the same idea as Weber's "steel-hard house of capitalism." Lest reference to Weber and Troeltsch seem tangential to our topic, let me make the connection clear. What happens to the foundation of human rights in religious self-consciousness when religion no longer has influence in the contemporary world? What becomes of the constitutionally guaranteed rights if, under changed conditions, there is no religiously based concept of individuals who are free in themselves but who now expect the fulfillment of their basic wants from state and society? The correlation of Jellinek's thesis with Weber's rather pessimistic outlook throws new light on the question of the foundation of human rights. The inner foundation of human rights cannot be achieved by law or by civil rights. The law is not productive but only protective. That was Jellinek's understanding. The protection of the individual, which is independent on religious grounds, served as the historical legitimation for constitutional law. Does it not lose this legitimation if, according to Weber, Troeltsch, and many others, the history of society has gone beyond its religious foundation?

It would be tempting to go further into the issue of religion in modern society. In my opinion, those sociologists and historians who claim the "end of religion" in modern society are quite wrong. This assertion is one of those almost mythological prejudices under whose guidance much analysis has pointed in the wrong direction. As Paul Johnson has shown in *Modern Times: The World of the Twenties to the Eighties*, the predicted disappearance of religion was the major *nonevent* of our day. This observation is doubtless true and eventually will gain credence in the dominant concepts of sociological and political theory. But it is also true that a revision of those theories which have been built along the "decline of religion" line will not, in itself, clarify the relation between human rights and religious beliefs. The issue of civil rights is a good example. States set up civil rights protections to give human rights a specific political form. The notion of human rights calls for a concept of the person as citizen, unconditioned by any religious claims or religious authorities. In this sense the pure secularity of civil rights is a must. But human rights in the form of civil rights cannot bring the ultimate fulfillment which the religious believer finds in relation to God. The French Revolution in

its early stages promised society the fulfillment of life in an ultimate sense through worshiping the goddess of reason. This was
also the promise of Marxist philosophy of history. But fulfillment of
these promises is also among the significant nonevents of our day.

C. Basic Rights as Social Rights of Participation (Rudolf Smend)

The debate around the Jellinek thesis refers to a Christian
concept of human rights which has its roots in Calvinism. But
Rudolf Smend, a German Lutheran scholar of the history of constitutional law, notes a different approach to the issue. On the
Continent, basic rights (*Grundrechte*) were meant for citizens as
responsible agents within the political community. Such civil
rights differ from *human* rights insofar as they are not founded
on the independence of the single individual. They were a function of responsible individual citizenship within the political community. The historical genesis of this concept of civil rights is
found in the Christian teaching of "status" in society (*Standelehre*):
each person has a certain status, *status politicus, status ecclesias-
ticus, status oeconomicus vel familiaris*. This status defines a concrete state of responsibility. The starting point of this concept is
not the self-realization of the individual but the responsible participation of individuals in the common good. In modern constitutions these states of responsibility are transformed into basic
rights (*Grundrechte*). They define and guarantee the autonomous
responsibility of citizens within the political community. The concept of basic rights implies that every person is called to social responsibility, to responsible participation in the communal life. This
calling now includes a religious and ethical dimension. It is a calling by God in the sense in which Martin Luther has reformulated
the spiritual vocation (*Beruf*) into the worldly vocation (*welt-
licher Beruf*). The worldly vocation is the situation in which a person is addressed by God and is asked to fulfill neighbor love in
free, spontaneous responsibility. This is a different emphasis from
the Puritan tradition of Calvinism. The basic rights, as Rudolf
Smend pointed out, are not founded in a realm before the social
and political community, but they protect and ensure the self-
responsible position of the citizen within the community. In this

understanding basic rights are, at the same time, rights of liberty *and* social rights.

In the first part of this century a debate occurred between Anglo-Saxon and North American ideas and the Continental concept of basic human rights. In this discussion it was argued that the German tradition balanced rights and duties; moral and social duties legitimated the individual's rights. The Western tradition, on the other hand, seemed to put all the weight on the inherent, presocial rights of the individual as such. This, of course, is too rough a comparison, but for our purpose it can serve as a convenient mirror to reflect some of the basic questions. The present debate focuses on the tension between the classical liberal concept of the individual rights of freedom on the one hand and social human rights on the other. In this tension between liberal Western concepts and socialist Eastern concepts, the Lutheran, mid-European tradition which Rudolf Smend has evaluated takes a position in the middle.

III. THE CHRISTIAN CONCEPT OF FREEDOM AND RESPONSIBILITY: JUSTIFICATION AND CIVIL DUTIES

How does Christianity understand this free individual who is the responsible bearer of rights? The Christian is not inherently free. The Christian is freed basically in relation to God through justification. Christian freedom is freedom from sin and the accusations of the law. It is freedom in the state of grace. Christian selfhood is not self-determined but determined in relation to God through Christ. Christian freedom is received freedom, not natural freedom. It is granted by God and received in faith. The Christian self finds itself constituted in the social relation to God. This relation is totally dependent on confidence in God's prevenient grace, the grace which comes before any human action. In relation to God the Christian self is resting in confident passivity, not in any activity to achieve freedom. The justice of the believer is not his or her own justice; it is "alien justice," *justitia aliena*. This alien justice contains freedom from sin and guilt. By virtue of this origin Christian freedom makes the person utterly independent of the world. It is ultimate freedom in the sense that it cannot be destroyed by the world since it cannot be reached through worldly activities.

The consequence of this radical freedom of the self is that moral and social life are not means to achieve freedom. Freedom is already contained in faith. Individual freedom finds its continuation in social duties, but Christian freedom belongs totally to the individual person. Religious freedom is grounded in the order of personal life, not in the order of society. This distinction lies at the root of Luther's often misunderstood distinction between the two realms, the realm of Christ and the realm of the world. But how do we get from here to the responsible self?

A. Civil Responsibility in the Worldly Realm

The moral and social activities of the individual are set free from the burden of achieving freedom because they have radical freedom as their foundation. This freedom works to serve others and contributes to the common good. The basic needs of the self are taken care of in faith, and in faith alone. That is the core of Luther's teaching on justification. The person's needs for God, for the fulfillment of life, and for righteousness, are not the subject of moral and social activities. These activities must be guided by the worldly needs of the neighbor and of the community. The traditional natural law represents God's will in asking human beings to do what is good. In free Christian self-consciousness the will of God is done spontaneously, not because of the demands of the law. Luther can go so far as to say that Christians may set up new decalogues, out of freedom. Looking at the law from the other side, from the world under the rule of sin and evil, the moral law has to be enforced and obeyed even by those who do not accept its spiritual meaning. But this, the enforced law, is only the secondary order, necessary in a world not yet redeemed. The primary order, the original meaning of God's will, is recognized by the responsible self without outer force, spontaneously.

This distinction between moral spontaneity and enforced law follows from the quality of the person. Here is a certain ambiguity. The moral and civil law as representative of God's will is a secondary substitute for the freedom of such persons who fulfill the will of God without compulsion. The law is necessary because of the weakness of such persons who have to be moved by coercion to follow the law. To put the same distinction differently, it is the original *right* of freedom to do God's will in the world, but it becomes a necessary *duty* to follow the moral and civil law for those who are not living out of this freedom.

In the first case, the moral law or public authorities cannot ask from the free person what he or she does not recognize autonomously. In the second case, the right of freedom is replaced by the duty of obedience.

B. Tensions among Theological Concepts of Christian Responsibility

Among Christian theologians today there is much debate over what is actually at stake when Christians take a stand on moral and political struggles for civil rights. The question is not one of general morality, of informed rationality, or of engaged partisanship. The question is a theological controversy over the specific Christian responsibility within the secular, political world. But there exists no real consensus among Christians about Christian responsibility. Does it constitute a specific prophetic office over against the world, on a high level of sovereignty? How is this responsibility mediated by the concrete situation in which we find ourselves?

The issue centers in Christology. One version of Protestant Christology argues that Christ has achieved everything for us, but until the consummation of the world Christ exercises his power through believers as his representatives in the fight against sin and evil in the world. Until Christ comes again it is up to his believers to continue his work and exercise his kingdom. Christ is not idle; he is working in the motives and in the decisions of his believers. This concept imposes an enormous significance on the responsibility of the individual Christian. He or she is the representative of Christ in the world during his absence. He or she must put the kingdom into effect and realize Christ's government. In confessing Christ the Christian is claiming to enact Christ's own government. Each "case of confession" then is at the same time a case for political action and proclamation. What may look like just another type of political commitment when seen from the outside is, seen from the inside, a commitment to carry on the kingdom

of Christ. The moral and political responsibility of the Christian
is this specific privilege, furnished with an extraordinary authority, which is indivisible and has to be carried out without compromise. The foundation of this responsibility is open only to the
believer; it cannot be shared with others on common grounds.

A second version of Protestant Christology has the same starting point but has developed in quite a different direction. Christ
has achieved for us everything we need for eternal life. The confession of the kingdom of Christ then goes on to affirm that the
future course of the world is also ruled by the government of Christ.
But his government is hidden before the eyes of the world. Our
part in his government is to trust confidently in the sufficiency
of Christ's own activity. To confess Christ means to confess that
we can only receive what he has to give. The individual Christian
as human being is not called into any world government, nor is
the Christian a representative of the kingdom of Christ. As a Christian, he or she is called to concrete tasks and to specific offices
within the world. His or her motives and decisions, in which he
or she tries to fulfill a vocation according to conscience and ability, are human motives and human decisions without any privileged authority or quality. Christ does his work alone. In this
Christology the Christian recognizes that his or her responsibility
is within the world and is not different from the responsibility of
any other person or citizen.

The first of these Christologies is essentially Calvinist; the second is essentially Lutheran. Historically these two positions are
complex and sometimes overlapping, but the controversy between
them as to the nature and task of the responsible self remains unresolved.

IV. CHRISTIAN RESPONSIBILITY
BEYOND THE BOUNDARIES OF DOGMATICS

A. *Toward the Political Form for Individual Freedom*

The modern concept of civil rights follows basically from
the freedom of the individual person as the foundation of all human rights. Basic individual freedom had to be qualified in a con-

cept of the responsible person who accepts in free decision the duties of sociality. Responsibility because of freedom was the ethical ideal of the Enlightenment. The religious and moral tradition was transformed into the ideal of a constitution of free persons. The model was that of an unconstrained ethical revolution. The stronger the inner, free self-responsibility becomes, the less is there a need for the coercive function of moral and civil law. On this line religious responsibility was imagined as the evolution of human freedom. Kant employed the image of a universal kingdom of God to be realized by rational ethical persons. The Christian implication in his thought was the argument that human beings are not free, rational, and good by nature; they have to educate themselves to become so through the efforts of ethical reason. To form an ethical kingdom means to work on moral self-education and to construe political structures which support morality. Not nature but the ethical form of Right constitutes the consciousness of universal humanity. Hegel teaches that Right makes all individuals of identical worth simply because they are human. This estimation is not based on the natural history of the human race. It is the explicit and conscious work of rational penetration and transformation of reality by ethical consciousness built into the concept of Right. We may take these as examples for what later has been called secularization. The step beyond dogmatic foundations has also been taken by liberal theological thinkers like Schleiermacher.

Secularization as rationalization means to express the Christian concept of freedom and responsibility in nontheological language, thus giving human freedom a universal form. This process intends to bestow upon the individual a structural form which recognizes in the individual more than its fragile empirical disposition. That is the continuous Christian content in modern concepts of human rights.

Within the abstractness of such contemporary philosophical concepts as the order of law, or of Right, one can still identify the same motive which we find in the originating theological doctrines. The individual person does not possess freedom and human dignity inherently. Freedom and dignity are given to the individual. The concepts of freedom and dignity appeal to a responsible self, which responds to this idea. In the case of Christian faith this response finds its expression in religious doctrine and practice. They form a specific world-independent realm for the expression of freedom and dignity. State and society are called upon to respect this religious realm of ultimate independence. But they are also challenged in their own specific realms to grant to the individual a firm and inviolable basis for human rights. Religious freedom is real only for believers. Human rights in the secular realm are meant for every person, including those who are not religious believers as well as those who do not have the economic or political, psychological and social means to achieve freedom and dignity by themselves. Thus the "weak" Christian concept of love for the poor and the needy had to be transformed into the "strong" concept of rights and legal claims. The modern secular concept of human rights recognizes these rights independently from the empirical disposition and social fragility of the individual. This concept corresponds to the religious idea of freedom as independence from the empirical world. But the secular concept itself proclaims that it is unconditioned by religion, race, sex, and so forth — that it is universal by intention.

Further, religious freedom is built up by religious teaching, preaching, liturgy, and the whole complex of religious institutions. The individual person does not "have" religion as a natural possession. Individuals need meaningful forms of expression to realize ultimate freedom consciously. By the same token, universal human rights had to be developed into political and constitutional forms of concrete civil rights which are supported and guaranteed by the state. Human rights need specific practical means which help the individual to enjoy those rights. Otherwise human rights would remain as abstract and irrelevant as religious freedom would be without the reality of concrete religious forms of expression. There would be no real religious freedom without churches, and there would be no real civil rights without states.

The theological and philosophical debate on the final foundation of human rights, complex as it is historically and systematically, may remain undecided. No church and no state can serve as an ultimate and exclusive definition of humanity. Wherever people have tried to put into effect such final and concluding definitions, politically or otherwise, the end result was inhuman totalitarianism. The distinction between church and state, between society and religion, is one fundamentally important way to keep the world open for the individuality of the self. The organization of state and law and the development of economic conditions are other ways. The foundation of human rights leads to the pluralism of institutions which help make responsibility in freedom possible.

B. The Role of Religious Freedom

I have spoken of the correspondence between the Christian concept of the individual self and its freedom, and the relevance of human rights as civil rights. This correspondence does not lead to identity. It would be poor theological teaching to proclaim such an identity and to view the political realm as the field for the final fulfillment of religious promises. The liberal ideals of the Enlightenment are not to be renounced. And Christian religion has, no doubt, contributed to a sharpened consciousness of ethical responsibility in many fields. Still, there do exist conflicts which cannot be solved by political or social action, and the integrity of individual persons may be endangered by expectations which cannot be fulfilled by economic or psychological means. It is an essential part of the dignity of the person to have the freedom to acknowledge "shortcomings" which withstand successful secular management, and it is also part of our dignity to stick to hopes which will not be fulfilled by state and society. Specifically religious insights may represent a dimension of inner freedom which gives to public freedom its proper measure and contour. Religion is not called upon to rule the world or to overrule it. But religious consciousness continues to contribute to finite human freedom and dignity in politics and society.

3

Political Rights Versus Social Rights

MIHAILO MARKOVIĆ

I

HUMAN RIGHTS IN GENERAL and political or civil rights in particular are great achievements of political and social revolutions during the last three centuries. They express some basic needs of all human individuals; and although they are incomplete and not always effective, the very fact that certain needs of all human beings have been equally recognized and given legal form constitutes a major breakthrough in the history of humankind and one of the demarcation lines between traditional and modern society. Traditional society rests on a principle of authority and cultivates the virtue of serving that authority. Modern society, although so far in a limited way, emphasizes the principle of individual freedom and equality before the law. Human rights are necessary — although not sufficient — conditions of a free human life in any society. That each individual should live and develop under those conditions is a modern idea. To be sure, there is almost nothing in modernity that was not anticipated in ancient Greek and Roman democracies. Male adult citizens enjoyed political liberties, participated in running the state, and were entitled to some economic and cultural goods and services, such as food and entertainment. Stoic philosophers were the first to assert that all human beings are equal by virtue of their reason.

René Descartes expressed a similar idea a millennium later. Hobbes, however, was the first philosopher to express the idea of equality in the form of a *right*. Since all humans equally need to continue their motions and all are equally liable to destruction, they all equally have a right to life and a right to the means of preservation of life. Hobbes was quite modern insofar as he did not derive the idea of human rights from either divine authority or natural law. Locke was less consistent. He obtained his rights from a natural law, and some of them (rights to the preservation of one's life and to inheritance) he claimed were derived from God-given desires. However, Locke's conception of rights was more developed, more articulated, and more adapted to the needs of a liberal bourgeois society. From the natural right of everyone to do anything Hobbes derived a need for absolute monarchy in order to guarantee safety. Locke's government was limited since the law of nature limits human freedom. No one ought to harm another in life, health, liberty, or possessions. An important constituent of Locke's social contract theory is the right of citizens to overthrow a government that pursues its own selfish interests, violates the social contract, and brings society back into the state of nature.

It is characteristic of Locke and other early philosophers of human rights that they did not reduce human rights to civil rights. Locke followed Hobbes in asserting the right to life and subsistence. Furthermore, and especially in his later work, he insisted on an unlimited right to property and accumulation of wealth. Macpherson was, of course, right when he qualified Locke's "natural man" as a typical "bourgeois man." It is interesting, however, to note that at this relatively early stage of modern society, when the new bourgeois class felt an ideological need to legitimate its rapidly acquired economic power, it did not separate civil and economic rights. Rights are derived not only from the status of an individual as the citizen of a political organization (the state), but also from general human capacities and desires, such as the capacity to make agreements and give consent and the desire to have more property than one needs.

II

The concept of human rights was narrowed down and reduced to civil rights once the bourgeoisie emerged as a dominant economic class which entered into open conflict with state absolutism. Any elaboration of socioeconomic rights would be of help only to the working class that appeared now as a critical historical force. What at this point constituted the historical need of the entire third estate was the demand for guarantees of human freedom against the arbitrariness of state power. The Declaration of Rights delivered by the British Parliament to the Prince of Orange in 1688 listed as illegal the following: suspension of laws or execution of laws by the regal authority; prosecution of citizens for exercising their right to petition the king; keeping a standing army in a time of peace. Election of the members of Parliament, and speech and proceedings in the Parliament, were declared free. The 1793 French constitution, which protected personal freedoms, stated explicitly that the need to proclaim rights of free expression of thought, free gathering, or free religious festivities resulted from the memory of autocratic excesses. Freedom was recognized as a natural and inalienable right. Laws were supposed to put an end to usurpation and tyranny and to protect the citizen from the abuses of the rulers. The state as a public power had to cease being used for the private goals of its functionaries. An idea of justice emerged which was stated explicitly for the first time in the American Declaration of Independence, and which made an essential distinction between justice and positive laws. The idea of justice is constituted by the inalienable rights of citizens.

The interests of the state; the imperatives of "state reason," have to be subordinated to the principles of justice. Laws and state acts which violate those principles lack legitimacy. The focus of legality has now been shifted from force and sanction to civil liberty. In such a way the great revolutionary democratic process, which started with the Enlightenment and with the formulation of the first theories of a rational natural law, was completed.

III

It was socialist theory that raised again the issue of socioeconomic rights. While praising the bourgeoisie for achievement of civil liberties, while expressing the view that political emancipation was a necessary phase of any human emancipation, Marx pointed out the limited significance of those revolutionary achievements. He saw human society as divided into two sharply differentiated spheres: civil society in which individuals pursue their economic and other particular interests, and political society in which individuals observe law and order and respect the rights of other individuals. In such a way a human being is split into an immoral economic egoist and a moral abstract citizen. Freedom in civil society turns out to be merely a freedom of buying and selling commodities, including human productive capacity which is turned into a commodity. This narrow conception of economic freedom involves a tremendous amount of domination and exploitation. Equality reduced to a mere equality before the law permits a huge and growing inequality in social and economic conditions for individual survival and growth. That is why for Marx political emancipation had to be conceived as only the initial phase of an ongoing radical and universal human emancipation that would end up with a state of affairs in which the freedom of each would become a condition of the freedom of all and in which freedom would be conceived as a process of the self-realization of each individual. Such bringing to life of the full creative potential of each person would be possible only if all alienated dominating forces and institutions (such as capital and bureaucratic state power) could be abolished and if political liberties could be supplemented by socioeconomic freedom and equality. That would be possible, as Marx explained his idea of freedom in volume 3 of *Capital*, only when associated individuals take into their own hands the responsibility for the entire process of production and regulation of public life without capitalists and without state bureaucracy. In the absence of such a socioeconomic emancipation all civil rights remain abstract and all liberties remain formal.

The Constitution of the Russian Federal Socialist Republic of 1918 in its Declaration of Rights of Exploited Working People laid down as its basic task abolishing the exploitation of human beings by other human beings and stated as its general principles true freedom of conscience, thought, choice, association, and education for working people. There was an obvious intention in the first Soviet constitution (no matter how utopian under the conditions of a primitive rural society) to remove the contradiction between the form and the content of democracy. On the other hand, by proclaiming the dictatorship of the urban and rural proletariat and the poorest peasants the first Soviet constitution deprived earlier ruling classes of many rights. The Soviet legal theory of that time defined the dictatorship of the proletariat as the power of coercion over the bourgeoisie, unconstrained by any law. Such a view was interpreted at that time as a legal revolution. Soviet legal theory justified the complete subordination of law to politics in the transition period by claiming revolutionary expediency. The danger of bureaucratization was completely overlooked. Yet the dictatorship of the working class was reduced to that of the Party, which in its turn degenerated into a dictatorship of one single Party leader.

In the new system there was no place for the associations of citizens and producers that Marx spoke about. There was indeed no place for any organization that rested on self-determination and self-initiative of liberal individuals. Duties prevailed over rights, prohibitions and sanctions over liberties. The legitimacy of an utterly voluntaristic state practice was based on an assumption of suprahuman "objective laws" which were supposed to act independently of the consciousness and will of actual, living people. "The masses" were construed as purely mechanical, passive material modeled according to the twists and turns of this nonhuman necessity. What started as a critique of bourgeois law ended up as a conservative justification of political caesarism.

What remained of proclaimed real liberties of conscience, thought, education, and organization were caricatured forms only. Citizens were "free" to think, but if they took that liberty they were suspect until they proved that their thinking was loyal and "constructive." They were free to elect as their own representatives only those who were previously chosen by "big brother." They were also free to join all those organizations which underwent strict and permanent Party control. Education was subordinated to the pragmatism of daily politics and the imperatives of a thoroughgoing pseudorevolutionary indoctrination. The citizen was turned into an *Untertan*, a subject of the state who did not even dare to ask what the state did in his or her name and how it spent the surplus product of his or her labor.

Even the most naive Soviet citizens hardly believe today that all those articles of the constitution which guarantee their freedom of thought, conscience, speech, publication, and organization were really written for them. They know that they could be held responsible for a crime against the people and the state, or end up in a mental hospital, if they take the constitution of the country seriously and behave according to it. One of the most oppressed strata of this pseudosocialist society is precisely its alleged "ruling class." The workers do not even have the traditional rights which they exercised in capitalist society before they were "liberated": the right to organize into trade unions, to bargain for their wages and working conditions, to strike. Compulsory work based on the full subordination of citizens to the state cannot be a historical alternative to the politically free labor on which capitalism rests.

IV

On the other hand, however, political freedom and civil rights when divorced from socioeconomic rights are indeed very limited.

First, in what civil rights do assert they remain formal and ineffective since some social preconditions for their implementation do not obtain, or obtain in such a limited and distorted way that activity in accordance with them appears meaningless.

Second, civil rights in a capitalist society do not and cannot assert certain political rights which follow from the idea of political freedom and which have temporarily been implemented in the past. Thus they are essentially incomplete.

The formality of civil rights consists in the fact that they only deny legal constraints for various political freedoms. The law asserts my freedom to speak up, to publish, to organize, manifest, demonstrate. However, absence of legal obstacles is only one of several necessary conditions of being free. Being free involves at least the following necessary conditions:

1. There must be objective alternatives among which to choose.
2. I must be aware of those alternatives.
3. My choice must be autonomous, that is, made on the basis of criteria that I have laid down myself.
4. I must be able to act according to my choice.

5. I must be in sufficient control over the field of reality in which I act so that no external obstacles prevent bringing to life my chosen project.

In a society in which social and economic power is unjustly distributed and in which no socioeconomic rights are guaranteed, many individuals have no objective alternatives among which to choose. There will be one school — the cheapest; one job that is available — if any; one environment into which one is thrown by birth; and the choices among political candidates will often be between one who is hostile and one who does not care. There could also be some hidden possibilities but one must have enough education to be aware of them. It is very difficult to build up an autonomous will when one is pressed by life necessities, by the traditional culture of limited surroundings. Autonomy of the will requires not only a rebellious, critical self-consciousness that challenges all that has been learned in the earlier stages of life; it also presupposes enough knowledge about cultural alternatives.

When one is socially and economically underprivileged it can be extremely difficult to act according to one's desires and choices. I could be very creative and could desire to publish a book or start a journal. I have a legal right to do so; but this right is abstract and formal, since I have no financial means to invest in that project, and those who have them may be interested not in creativity but in profits. I could be a political genius, but unless I sell myself to those who would be willing to support my political career materially I cannot even begin to promote myself as a political leader. On the contrary, money can turn almost any mediocrity into apparent stardom. Hired speech writers provide spirit and eloquence, hired mass media make one seem an able communicator, and a hired efficient political machine makes one look strong and powerful. The greater the monopoly of economic power in a society, the less effective its civil rights, and the more expensive not only beauty, health, and knowledge, but also justice. Under the conditions of an unequal distribution of wealth, therefore, civil rights are not only formal but also incomplete. There is a considerable gap between existing civil rights and those political rights which a citizen could have in a fully developed democracy.

To be sure, democracy cannot be reduced to the political

sphere only. Thus the very idea of economic and cultural democracy involves the recognition of socioeconomic rights. But if we concentrate for the moment only on political democracy, then the very meaning of the term implies the citizen's right of *cratei*, "ruling." In modern society the right to *cratei* would have to be understood, on the one hand, as the right of direct participation in decision making in living and working communities to which an individual belongs. On the other hand, it involves the right to control the exercise of the power delegated to elected representatives for various purposes of higher-level coordination and direction of social activities.

The presupposition of democracy is the recognition that *demos*, "the people," are able to make basic policy decisions — directly at the microstructure level of society and indirectly at the social macrolevel. More specifically, that means the right of self-government in a sufficiently decentralized society. To the extent to which in a modern political society local and regional autonomy have to be coordinated within the society as a whole, citizens will elect their representatives and delegate to them their decision-making power. But the election must be free, without any mediators, and the representatives must be directly responsible to the electorate and recallable by it. With the nineteenth-century political parties, powerful mediators between citizens and their representatives appeared on the historical stage. It was not *demos* that ruled but political parties in its name. Parties in their turn were controlled by small oligarchies.

In the twentieth century another even more powerful mediator emerged: the state bureaucracy. The state greatly expanded and centralized its governing functions. Those civil rights that Jefferson had in mind were not only not implemented; they fell into oblivion. Few people know that according to Jefferson citizens have the right to reexamine and change all laws every twenty years, since "the dead should not rule over the living." In Jefferson's view citizens should also have the right to debate and vote on all major issues of national politics in their local communities, which Jefferson called "wards." With our present electronic technology such an institution of direct democracy is quite feasible but, except in Switzerland, is never even considered as a practical possibility. The right to *cratei* has been turned into a right to give consensus to one or another similar policy, to one or another similar party. The right to vote has emerged as a basic civil right. But how much it means can be seen from the fact that often nearly one-half of the population decides to give it up. Consequently the governments come to power with the support of less than one-third of the electorate.

The language still preserves the initial idea of civil rights. Functionaries of the state are still called "civil servants." Servants, however, tend to turn into masters, and nowhere is that so visible as with those governmental institutions that in the name of national security spy upon their own citizens. An alarming growth in intelligence services and the modernized technology of data collection not only defy popular control but effectively deny the individual right to privacy. Once human emancipation is reduced to political liberty, once human rights are reduced to civil rights, these liberties and rights will actually exist in very limited and slowly eroding forms.

The contradictory nature of civil rights stems from the fact that liberal representative democracy serves the capitalist system better than any other form of political organization. Economic domination by corporate power goes together with a limited political freedom of citizens. The market economy requires freedom of movement, freedom of labor contracts, and legal responsibilities of each citizen. The freedoms of speech, organization, and manifestation are harmless since economic power can always be easily translated into political power. Once civil rights are used to organize powerful movements for social change, civil rights will be violated. Liberalism will, at least temporarily, turn into authoritarianism and, in extreme cases, into fascism.

Contemporary bourgeois society can neither abandon its basic values nor live in harmony with them. This ambivalence is most obvious in international relations. The rights proclaimed in the developed West are not granted to developing countries of the Third World. A weak, parasitic, and hedonistic local bourgeoisie in those countries is unable to deliver a minimum of economic goods to its people and also unable to prevent the use of civil rights for the emergence of powerful and radical emancipatory movements. Hence the tendency of Western superpowers to tolerate and support repressive dictatorships in Latin America, Africa, and Asia.

Narrowly conceived national interests, growing out of confrontation with other superpowers, give rise to a paradoxical practice: suppression of freedom in the name of the "free world," glorification of tyrants as "defenders of democracy."

V

In spite of all this the recognition and practical implementation of civil rights and political liberties, no matter how formal and incomplete, is the necessary condition for any further social emancipation. In the absence of civil rights, socioeconomic rights either are impossible to achieve or remain crippled and deformed.

We now have more than six decades of experience with social revolutions which sought the abolition of economic exploitation, the elimination of material misery, greater social justice. The goals of those revolutions were not formulated in terms of human rights. Some of their leaders labeled the very concept of rights "bourgeois," partly because they do constitute elements of bourgeois ideology, and partly because those leaders, including Marx, tried to legitimate their revolutionary projects as scientific, that is, devoid of any normative elements. But if we abstract from those terminological idiosyncracies it is quite clear that the basic objective of those revolutions was the implementation of some essential socioeconomic rights.

It was believed that those rights could be realized quite independently from civil rights. Before the revolution such rights were not granted to citizens by prerevolutionary authoritarian regimes: the czar's absolutism in Russia, the Kuomintang in China, a repressive monarchist regime in Yugoslavia, and the dictatorship of Batista in Cuba. As a consequence revolutionary movements took the form of clandestine, authoritarian, rigidly disciplined vanguard organizations. After seizing power those vanguard parties consciously and deliberately introduced regimes in which the very concept of *civil rights* did not make much sense. Some of the economic improvements were remarkable. Industrialization, urbanization, abolition of abject poverty, elimination of epidemic diseases, and mass education were among them. And yet whatever resembled the achievement of socioeconomic rights bore the mark of a basic authoritarian relationship between the citizen and the state. For example, the new regime offered a chance to each citizen to get a job. But it turned out to be more a duty than a right. The Soviet poet Joseph Brodsky was prosecuted for not being employed, for merely writing poetry. And the jobs were assigned. Employees were distributed all over the country depending on the needs of the plan rather than on individual preferences.

Nationalization of the means of production did not go together with the implementation of the workers' right to self-government. And where self-government was partially implemented, as in Yugoslavia after 1950, it was given in small doses to the people by the leadership, not claimed by workers and citizens themselves as their inalienable right.

Mass education greatly developed and became free in the sense of being financed by the state, but not free in the sense that every citizen had free access to any school. Rather than being a right, access to higher education became a government's reward to a family for loyalty and past merits. Heavily subsidized culture and art flourished, with the exception of Mao's cultural revolution. However, the fast growth and material well-being of cultural institutions stood in glaring contrast to an extraordinary drabness of content. The right to culture turned into the right of a bureaucracy to decide which books, plays, movies, or musical works were good for the people. Hence, a type of society that promised true social justice produced enormous inequalities in incomes, in the standard of living, housing, medical treatment, and old-age benefits. These differences are the result not of unequal work contributions but of unequal social status. One right affirmed in all social spheres was the right to material privileges for loyalty to the state.

A general lesson that can be drawn from all those experiences is that substantial progress in the realization of socioeconomic rights cannot be made without full recognition of civil rights. It is true that imperfect solutions are sometimes better than no solutions; mixed and contradictory new social forms are sometimes preferable to stagnant old forms. However, comparisons should be made not only between the old and the new but also between the actually existing and the potential. The optimal historical possibility in modern societies is the struggle for human rights without the rigid separation between civil rights and socioeconomic rights.

More specifically that means that the struggle for human rights, wherever historically possible, should have the form of broad democratic, pluralistic movements, such as the Polish Solidarity movement or the German Greens. Only those movements that fully incorporate civil rights as the principles of their own organization are able to bring them to life in the society at large, once they emerge victorious. And only under those conditions could socioeconomic rights be realized with dignity and self-respect.

VI

When we embrace both civil and socioeconomic rights within the concept of human rights our language indicates the only possible way in which we could legitimate those rights. We have those rights not because God implanted certain desires in us, nor because of a law of nature, nor because some enlightened benevolent rulers happened to grant them, nor even because some liberal political representatives agreed to pass them in the form of a law. What human rights formulate in a normative form are the necessary and objective conditions of the very possibility of growing as a human being and staying human. The basic assumption here is the idea of reciprocity between society and the individual. Human society can exist and develop only because individuals belong to it and invest a tremendous amount of work and care, in order to maintain its structure and functioning and in order to further develop and improve its overall performance. Since the contributions of individuals are unequal total social rewards will be unequal. However, there is a minimum of needs of its members that society must equally meet just in order to be a genuinely human society and not a mere collection of individual egoistic achievers. Since both the character of society and individual needs change, the concept of human rights must change too. When society is loose, poorly organized, limited in its functions, and when individual needs are primitive and few, the idea of human rights exists only in a vague form. Modern society produced a wealth of human needs but also an extraordinary web of social institutions that survive and quickly develop owing to an increasing input of energy and creativity from its members. Rights are simply social returns for this growing individual investment. In the late twentieth century they embrace much more than the traditional rights to life, liberty, and property, and especially much more than civil rights.

Before one can function as a human being each individual must survive as a living organism. It is therefore entitled to a certain amount of food, clothing, shelter, and communication, and to belong to an elementary human community. These are elementary vital rights or survival rights. All other rights are some kind of superstructure on this basic foundation. They formulate the necessary conditions of human development through work, political life, and cultural activity. As a productive being each individual also has the right to a job, to participation in the decision making in one's immediate working community, to a share of the collective's revenue corresponding to his or her contribution. It is clear that a superior idea of social justice at which humankind arrived, after two centuries of experience in the capitalist jungle, requires a revision of Locke's idea of the right to property. Appropriation of unlimited wealth produced by hired people cannot be a right because it deprives others of the results of their own work and violates the principle of equality. The very meaning of the concepts of domination and exploitation exclude equality. They are possible only, to use Orwell's phrase, if some are more equal than others. Thus the right to property must be interpreted to mean the right to appropriate the results of one's own work.

As a political being each individual has, in the first place, traditional civil rights to freedom of speech, publication, organization, movement, public gathering, manifestation, and so forth. Such a limited conception of civil rights, corresponding to an anthropology of rugged individualism and to a political philosophy of bourgeois liberalism, could be expanded and generalized once we recognize that an individual is also a social being and that each citizen has the necessary capacities to participate actively in political life. Consequently, the right to political liberty must be interpreted as the right to equal self-determination or briefly as the right to self-government.

As a cultural being each individual has both the capacity and the need to learn, to create symbolic forms, to communicate, to play. Consequently, each person has the right to an education which corresponds to one's interests and gifts; and each person has the right to enjoy the culture which we inherited from earlier generations. Furthermore, as a functional being each person has the right to cultural creativity, within the constraints of the level of material development society has achieved at a given historical moment. To be sure, contemporary societies, especially the most developed ones, could offer almost unlimited facilities for cultural creativity once they reduced the tremendous waste of human and material resources involved in military expenditures and expenses of huge and costly bureaucracies.

Until recently there were good reasons to believe that considerable progress had been made in both the conception and the universal implementation of human rights. Since the beginning of the New Deal and especially after the Second World War, traditional civil rights have been supplemented with many socioeconomic rights. Roosevelt declared that every American had the right to a job and a home. The welfare state everywhere in the West introduced various forms of social security: protection of the unemployed, retirement benefits, free health service, stipends for higher education, and so forth. On the other hand, in "socialist" countries Stalinist cliches about purely abstract and formal bourgeois democracy gradually gave way to greater respect for citizens' rights, greater freedom of cultural expression, and increasing tolerance of dissent.

Universal acceptance of basic human rights is a fact of enormous historical importance. In spite of all differences in social orders, political cultures, and basic values, it was possible for the governments of East and West to agree, first, on the United Nations Declaration on Human Rights, and then on the 1975 Helsinki Convention which spelled out both civil and socioeconomic rights in considerable detail. Whatever differences remained, whatever the gap between declaration and implementation of those rights, the fact remains that, in the conditions of relative peace, détente, and increasing collaboration between different social systems, an impressive progress in the area of human rights was possible everywhere.

Unfortunately we are witnessing a reversal of this trend during the last decade and especially during the last few years. The present wave of neoconservatism and militarization tends to destroy all that was created during the last fifty years and especially after the Second World War. Unfortunately we see the same trend everywhere in the West: in this country with Reaganism, in England with Thatcherism, in Germany with Kohl and the Christian Democrats, and now in France with Chirac's government. Increasing military expenditures lead to slashing welfare programs, to a large-scale violation of human socioeconomic rights in the West. The new armaments race and the poisoned international atmosphere strengthen to some extent Stalinist forces and reduce the level of respect for civil rights in the East.

If we are serious about human rights we have to fight against those reversals and fight for peace. This present madness of wasting trillions of dollars on weapons which will never be used — or if used would amount to the collective suicide of humankind — must be stopped or else all our high-brow deliberations about human rights will mean nothing.

PART II

Islam

4

Fundamentalism and Civil Rights in Contemporary Middle Eastern Politics

MANSOUR FARHANG

FACED WITH THE CHALLENGE of the modern world and subjected to the pressures of historical forces, the Muslim societies are currently undergoing profound transformations. The personal and political crises caused by this situation exhibit two contradictory tendencies: (1) a progression in the consciousness of freedom as manifested in the rise of popular demand for participation in the political life of the community; and (2) an unprecedented expansion in the coercive apparatus of the state along with the emergence of religious fundamentalism as a major ideological current. These developments are related to the integration of the Middle Eastern economies into the world market system as well as to the Western cultural penetration of the Islamic societies. Indeed, all the major political upheavals and ideological conflicts in the Middle East since the turn of the century have been variously influenced by the Western challenge to the native culture patterns in the region. Emulation and fascination as well as resentment and resistance characterize the attitudes of Middle Easterners toward this historic encounter.

Like nationalism, liberalism, socialism, and Marxism, the contemporary idea of civil rights is essentially a Western import into the Middle Eastern countries. It is a preconception of the Universal Declaration of Human Rights that in spite of the diversity in cultures and differences in existential conditions in the world, a common standard of rights can be established for all peoples and nations. Thus the Declaration claims that "all human beings are

born free and equal in dignity and rights", that some basic rights
are inherently human. Among the civil and political rights included
in the Universal Declaration are rights to freedom from discrimi-
nation, to life, liberty, and security of the person, to freedom from
slavery, to freedom of assembly and association, to freedom from
torture and cruel punishment, to equality before the law, to freedom from arbitrary arrest, to fair trial, to protection of privacy,
and to freedom of movement.

From a theoretical perspective, one could interpret Islamic
doctrines in a manner largely consistent with the letter and spirit
of the Universal Declaration. But historically — that is to say, in
Islam as a cultural system — governments have generally ruled with
arbitrary power and the individual has lived at the mercy of the
state. Thus, before analyzing the fundamentalist view and treatment of civil rights, it is necessary to outline the general Islamic
concepts regarding such rights. In Islam, the rights of individuals
constitute obligations connected with the Divine. The state must
enforce the *shari'a* (the laws derived from the Qur'an), the *sunnah*
(normative practices associated with the Prophet), *ijma* (the consensus of the community) and *ijtihad* (the counsel of judges on
a particular case). In the Islamic state, sovereignty belongs to God
alone and legislation is restricted within the limits prescribed by
the *shari'a*. The Islamic state is charged with maintaining a balance between the rights of individuals and the duties of government; it must prevent individual freedom from threatening the
interest of the community. The liberal notion of freedom from
external restraint is incompatible with Islamic theology because
freedom in Islam is not an inherent right. Individual freedom is
perceived as personal surrender to God. It is only in relation to
obligations that human rights are recognized in Islam.

Yet Muslims do not have a unified and monolithic perception
of their faith, any more than do the followers of other religions.
For example, the contemporary interpretations of the Qur'an by
various Muslim thinkers range from extreme left to extreme right,
or any combination of themes from the two polar positions. Discourse on such controversies often revolves around the meaning
of revelation or the intentions of the Prophet, but it is in fact a
manifestation of deep-rooted conflicts and contradictions in the
socioeconomic structure of the society. For contrary to the recent

media/academic assertion that ascribes to Islamic societies a special proclivity to link religion and state power, separation between state and religion has been the norm in the Muslim world for much of its history. Muslims, for the greater part of their history, have lived under regimes which had only the most tenuous link with the *shari'a* or the religious law.

Despite the *shari'a*'s grasp of nearly all aspects of individual and social life, there is no unified Islamic legal system, enshrined in integrated codes and accepted by all Muslims. Besides the sectarian divergences in interpreting the *shari'a*, the willingness of the state in the application of the law, which is often a function of its ideological and political underpinnings, is also a determining factor. For example, Saudi Arabia, Libya, Pakistan, and Iran all consider themselves as Islamic states but none of them is recognized by the others as authentic. To the extent that Islamic doctrines have been instrumental in the formulation of criminal or private codes in the four nations, it has stemmed only from what their leaders perceive to be true Islam — a perception shaped by a host of political, psychological, social, economic, and historical factors.

In the century-old cultural encounter between the West and the Islamic Middle East, four response patterns have tried to meet the challenge:

- *The secularists* — they perceive their societies as backward, both economically and socioculturally, and maintain that only scientific education, economic development, industrialization, and modernization can remedy the ills of the society.
- *The traditionalists* — they reject modern ideas and wish to retain the political authority structure as well as the sociocultural values of the past.
- *The religious modernists* — they favor a liberal and scientifically based interpretation of Islam and call for radical reform in both the socioeconomic and political order of the society. They maintain that the progressive aspects of Western thought already existed in original Islam.
- *The fundamentalists* — they portray Islam as a civilization superior to the Western tradition, including both Marxism

and capitalism. They are convinced that Islam will defeat
the West in the ongoing confrontation between them. They
present Islam as the only moral order and regard themselves as the exclusive representatives of the Divine on earth.

The emergence of Islamic fundamentalism as a popular movement has to be comprehended in the context of the failure of the
secularists and religious modernists to reach a functioning synthesis between Islam and modernization. In Iran, for example, Islamic fundamentalism could not thrive until the Pahlavis' blind
Westernization drive produced massive sociocultural alienation and
the secular alternatives to the Shah's dictatorship were fatally sup-
pressed. As the economic gap between the privileged few and the
wretched many increased, so did the cultural gap. The enclaves
of wealth and power in Tehran, Shiraz, and Isfahan also became
enclaves of imported cultures and lifestyles. One could make a
reasonable case that the rapidity of political disintegration in Iran
in 1978 was primarily due to the lack of minimal capacity on the
part of the regime to contain or accommodate a peaceful popular
challenge. Indeed, the Pahlavi state proved to be much weaker
than expected, not only in its relations with the society at large
but, more importantly, within itself. The arbitrary rule of one family could no longer be maintained in the face of new socioeconomic
realities which, besides causing cross-class disaffection, entailed
a massive increase in the urban poor population.

To understand the Islamic fundamentalist view of political
life in general and civil rights in particular, it is essential to acknowledge the desperate existential conditions of its principal
constituency—the urban poor. As a society moves away from its
traditional setting, people often find themselves in unexpected
situations. Individuals and groups respond to this challenge in diverse ways. The mediating or intervening mechanism is the inter-
nalized cultural orientation. As Barrington Moore has explained
in his classic study of modernization, "The residue of truth in the
cultural explanation is that what looks like an opportunity or a
temptation to one group of people will not necessarily seem so to
another group in a different form of society."[1]

It is due to the intervening variable of native culture that
modernization as a concept and as a policy can be seen to be either

a hope or a curse. For example, whatever else it might be and regardless of its equity or inequity, modernization historically has involved a change from conservative toward liberal values in the realm of culture. Almost everywhere, this process seems to produce disturbances because it dramatically threatens the habits, customs, living conditions, and values of individuals and social classes. The nature of such disturbances cannot be generalized simply because there are variations in premodern conditions. Diversity in experience, past and present, leads to different results. Thus each society produces its own distinct response to the challenge or demand of modernization. When the inevitable traditional resistance to cultural change is combined with feudal politics and the deepening of relative deprivation, as was the case in Iran under the Pahlavis, then the social disruptions caused by the process of modernization could create anomie in the classical sense, which often results in the growth of anxiety, hostility, and fantasy.

Under these circumstances, the fundamentalist preachers and organizers can be quite effective in appealing to the disaffected sectors of the population. Since the problem of cultural identity is an instance of the crisis of national disillusionment, the fundamentalists can easily transform the disorientation of the individual into a collective hatred toward the *other*. Hatred toward the enemy, both internal and external, real or imagined, is an indispensable characteristic of the fundamentalist political consciousness. Indeed, it is hard to see how a fundamentalist regime or movement can function without an intense and hateful confrontation with the *other*.

The great revolutions of the past sought, at least theoretically, to create a new society. The fundamentalist revolutionary movements, in contrast, seek to reestablish a sacred utopia presumed to have existed in the distant past. For the fundamentalists maintain that their project is to restore the Islamic institutions and beliefs to their original pristine purity. They reject any attempt to interpret Islamic doctrines in modernist terms. Thus, in pursuing their political objectives, they inevitably run into violent conflict not only with the secularists but also with Islamic modernists and traditionalists. They believe that they alone are able to resolve the problems facing the world today.

The fundamentalist view of society and history is derived from a supposedly timeless struggle between good and evil. The attitude of the fundamentalists toward the world revolves around the question of how things have deviated from the sacred principles. They contend that the Islamic laws and doctrines as revealed in the Qur'an were enacted by Prophet Muhammad 1400 years ago in the first divinely inspired state in history. This conception of the past, it should be noted, is an invention of the fundamentalist imagination, not an accurate portrayal of history. To be sure, the Islamic state under the leadership of Muhammad was a progressive experience in the life of the Arabian peninsula, but the subsequent mythology about this state was a by-product of the fantastic territorial expansion and military successes of Islamic forces during the century following Muhammad's death in 632 A.D.

History or theology aside, the ongoing fundamentalist current in the Middle East is primarily a nativist response to the crisis environment at home and the cultural challenge from abroad. The word *native* is used here without normative connotation because, as we have learned from the revolutionary experience in Iran, native values do not necessarily serve the interests or aspirations of the community. Furthermore, even though the fundamentalist currents in the Islamic societies have certain important characteristics in common, each movement has to be understood in the context of its national environment. Needless to say, the establishment of the Islamic Republic of Iran has provided impetus for militant action by both Shiah and Sunni fundamentalists throughout the Islamic world, but such a source of inspirational influence does not change the significant differences in the nature of the crises which fuel the fundamentalist current within each nation. In this regard, it is also worth mentioning that contrary to Khomeini's claim that he leads a transnational movement beyond national boundaries or identification, the Ayatollah is an *Iranian* Shiah fundamentalist par excellence. He preaches Islamic universalism but pursues a messianic form of nationalism with the purpose of extending Iran's influence in the region. In a more general sense, the emphasis on Islam, or any particular interpretation of it, as the overriding motivational force behind the current upheavals in the Middle East is analytically misleading.

Islamic fundamentalist thinkers in various Middle Eastern countries have written extensively on the issues and problems facing their respective societies. Their primary effectiveness is in providing emotionally satisfying answers to the existential and sociocultural concerns of certain strata of population caught up in the disruptive processes of disorganic development. For example, the urban poor and the newly rich petty bourgeoisie are attracted to fundamentalism because it promises to end all deprivation and alienation in the framework of a moral language and psychocultural symbolism rooted in their deepest sensibilities, fears, and hopes.

It is now clear that in all his anti-Pahlavi postures Ayatollah Khomeini was expressing not so much an opposition to political or economic inequities as a reaction against the observable consequences of Westernization in the cultural sphere. Indeed, it is only on cultural matters such as education, art, entertainment, courtship, and sociosexual mores that Khomeini has a coherent idea of what he wants — a quick return to an imagined puritanical past. In each of these spheres of activity he prescribes behavior down to the last details. Khomeini maintains that the corruption of the Islamic Iranian culture began with the success of the constitutional revolution at the turn of the century. It was the constitutional movement that paved the way for secular reform in the judicial and educational institutions of Iran. Thus the fundamentalist clerics regard the reestablishment of Islamic cultural and judicial standards and practices as the principal goal of the 1979 revolution.

The sociocultural policies of the Islamic Republic are astonishingly consistent with the specific concerns and priorities expressed in Ayatollah Khomeini's first political treatise, *Kashf al-Asrar* (Key to the secrets), published forty-five years ago. In this book Khomeini repeatedly refers to the unveiling of women, mixed swimming pools, coeducation, dancing parties, and the drinking of alcohol as the most undesirable and destructive reforms of Reza Shah's period. He vehemently condemns the permissive government policies with respect to such vices and asks the authorities to suppress the violators as well as the critics of the Islamic moral codes. He wrote:

We expect the Islamic government to support the religious ordinances, prevent the publication of antireligious material, and publicly execute the responsible persons. These seditious

characters who corrupt the earth must be done away with
so that others like them will not indulge themselves in treach-
erous agitation and discussions against the sacred religion.[2]

The dominant issues in *Kashf al-Asrar* are the general impact
of Western values on the society, unveiling, the emergence of woman
as a public person, the practice of liberal manners in courtship,
and male-female contacts. There is hardly a page in the book without an execrating remark about these issues. The following is quite
typical:

> The mixing of the newly pubertized men with the young li-
> bidinous ladies, atrociously exposing their hair, legs, jewelled
> chests, and listening to joyous and lustful music played on
> the radio. . . . [The] poisonous education given to them by
> the lecherous instructors. . . . What corruptions they cause
> in the country.[3]

Kashf al-Asrar illustrates the nature of the fundamentalist
response to the value transformations in Iran under the Pahlavis.
It is important to note, however, that the book was virtually unknown to the general public before the rise of Khomeini as the
leader of the 1979 revolution. Even most of Khomeini's clerical
followers did not begin to take the book seriously until the
mid-1960s. For during the 1940s and the 1950s there was no up-
rooted or dramatized social class whose alienated members could
be attracted to the lure of religious fundamentalism.

Thus, given the fundamentalist view that secularization of
education and acceptance of cultural pluralism threaten the moral
authority of the clerics, it is understandable why the present rulers
of Iran regard the re-Islamization of the country's sociocultural
institutions as the first priority of their domestic agenda. They reject all secular studies of humankind and society as unnecessary
at best and blasphemous at worst. Thus even in the universities
most of the social science, humanities, arts, and music departments
have been abolished. Books considered contradictory to Islamic
doctrines or values have been destroyed or removed from libraries
and bookstores. The fundamentalists simply believe that their version of Islam contains perfect and eternal knowledge about all aspects of individual and social existence. They reject the very no-

tion of objective investigation of human conduct. Even students applying for admission to engineering and medical colleges must pass a comprehensive examination on *feqh* or religious law.

The Islamization of the elementary and secondary schools is complete. Textbooks have been rewritten to reflect the Shiah fundamentalist view of society, science, and history. Just as was the case under the Pahlavis, the new interpretations of Iranian history in the official texts suffer from much distortion and inaccuracy. Faith and belief are supposed to compensate for evidence and proof. Virtually all secularly oriented teachers have been dismissed; even the mathematics and geography instructors have to pass examinations on *feqh* to keep their jobs. Schoolchildren are subjected to daily indoctrination. Some are interrogated to provide information about their parents' private lives; others are persuaded to spy on their neighbors.

Ayatollah Khomeini has repeatedly emphasized the crucial importance of complete Islamization of the country's educational institutions. Once he said to a group of students visiting him at his house:

> My dear ones, we are not afraid of economic sanctions; we are not afraid of military invasion; what frightens us is cultural dependency. We are afraid of the imperialistic universities which train our youth to become servants of the West or communism.[4]

Parallel with the transformation of the schools and universities, the fundamentalist rulers of Iran have acted decisively in re-Islamicizing the country's judiciary, particularly in the area of criminal law. The Islamic Code compels judges to base their sentences on the edicts of the Qur'an and the supposed sayings and practices of the Prophet. Thus prostitutes have been stoned to death, and fingers of petty thieves have been cut off. With thousands of minor officials claiming to speak in Khomeini's name, each with an individual interpretation of Islamic norms, it is difficult to escape the puritanical wrath of the regime. The very arbitrariness of law enforcement is a source of terror and uncertainty. Thousands of Iranians have been arrested and publicly whipped for drinking or playing cards. The Ayatollah has gone so far as to issue a *fatva* (religious judgment) holding that chess, which some believe originated in Iran, is a sinful game; players can be punished by the Islamic justice system for pushing a pawn.

The detailed examination of such developments in the Islamic Republic of Iran is essential for an adequate comprehension of the intentions and the potential of the fundamentalist currents in the Islamic world. For Iran is the first country where the fundamentalists have established their hegemonic control over the state and society. Before this historic achievement, the only other fundamentalist organization which exerted great influence on society was the Egyptian Brotherhood, which was founded in 1928. Between the two world wars, Egypt was plagued with socioeconomic crises and conflicting ideological currents. This situation created a favorable environment for the appeal of the Brotherhood. Hasan al-Banna, the leader of the Brotherhood, was a charismatic leader with a message of spiritual and sociopolitical salvation. By the mid-1940s, the Brotherhood had a million followers and was perceived as the most formidable contender for power against the monarchy.

Members of the Brotherhood were totally devoted to their cause and the organization controlled all aspects of their lives, including family affairs, athletics, and finances. By the late 1940s, the Brotherhood had virtually established a state within the Egyptian state. The relationship between the Brotherhood and civil society was explained by Hasan al-Banna in a famous statement addressed to his followers:

> My brothers, you are not a benevolent society, nor a political party, nor a local organization having limited purposes. Rather, you are a new soul in the heart of this nation to give it life by means of the Qur'an; you are a new light which shines to destroy the darkness of materialism through knowing God; and you are the strong voice which rises to recall the message of the Prophet.[5]

The Brotherhood's violent activities brought a reign of terror to Egypt, leading to Hasan al-Banna's assassination in 1949. His successor, Sayyid Qutb, the most influential fundamentalist theoretician in the Arab world, was accused of plotting to assassinate President Nasser in 1965. He was tried and hanged in the same year. The Brotherhood continues to be the most significant source of influence on the current fundamentalist movement in Egypt.

Before coming to power, the fundamentalists, like other anti-status quo political formations, criticize their governments for civil rights abuses and present a rather humane conception of Islamic laws and values. This tactic can be used in a credible fashion because the sources of *shari'a* are open to diverse interpretations. Ambiguity is in the nature of all religious texts and traditions. Muslim theologians and judges are perfectly capable of interpreting their laws and doctrines in such a way that the absolute domination of the society by the state is seen as legitimate. Iran is a vivid example.

Unlike the West, where civil rights are largely focused on lifestyles and matters of privacy, concern for civil rights in the Middle East centers around the need for peaceful political dissent. Only a tiny segment of the urban population think about civil rights in terms of choices in the private sphere. In the countryside and in the urban slums, where the vast majority of the people live, consciousness of individual or collective rights revolves around basic human needs and resentment of privilege. The distinct absence of respect for civil rights on the part of the state has to be seen more as a problem of political culture and socioeconomic inequalities than as a manifestation of religious dogma. Secular Syria is at least as repressive a state as traditionalist/religious Saudi Arabia. Radical nationalist Iraq is more tolerant of dissent than fundamentalist/theocratic Iran.

Nearly all Middle Eastern countries are ruled by armed minorities who do not recognize any rights for their opponents. There is a tragic scarcity of political civility in the societies of the region. Amnesty International Reports of the 1970s and 1980s portray the Middle Eastern states as the worst violators of human rights in the world. These reports document the sorry fact that throughout much of the region freedom of expression is nonexistent and torture of political prisoners is routine. Since the 1979 revolution Iran has executed more people than the rest of the world combined. In both Iran and Iraq to question the wisdom of continued conflict in their seven-year-old war is regarded by both regimes as a crime against the state. The war magnifies the unresolved sociopolitical contradictions which underlie the uncivil politics of the region. The absurd and tragic theater of the war, which is characterized by the use of human wave tactics and poison gas, has become a place where the psychopathology of politics and the pathology of the cult of personality, in both their secular and religious varieties, can be watched and studied.

Even though in the position of power fundamentalists do not seem much different from their secular rivals, the impact of fundamentalism on the civil rights situation in the Middle East has a unique significance of its own. The essence of this uniqueness lies in the fact that the fundamentalist rulers truly believe in their justifications when they abuse the rights of others. Khomeini is an *authentic* man. But authenticity is not necessarily a virtue, a realization that can be existentially painful in certain circumstances. The agents of the Shah's secret police were ashamed of what they were doing. Khomeini's executioners feel proud. Since the fundamentalists deny the very humanity of their critics, they naturally perceive them as opponents without rights. Under these circumstances, the ends always justify the means.

The fundamentalist project does not differentiate between politics and daily life. In the past when Iran was under traditional despotism like that of the Pahlavis, politics was merely one component of life; it did not interfere with the thought and being of the passive or uninterested citizen. But under the totalitarian regime of the fundamentalists, politics provides the method of constructing a supposedly organic society in which every aspect of life is to be integrated with the basic purpose of the state. As the fundamentalists define this basic purpose, no citizen is allowed to stand apart. Constant propaganda, pervasive terror, character assassination, the presence of organized gangs in the streets, and the perpetuation of big lies — all tools of modern totalitarianism — are used to maintain order and exalt the cult of personality. This is a great leap backward because in the Middle East restraining the cult of personality is a precondition for the development of civil society.

Yet Muslim fundamentalists must be seen in their sociohistorical environments. Simply to label them as fanatics, as if that would be an adequate characterization of their being, is an emotional condemnation of a mode of behavior without any effort to understand the causal relations that produced it. The fanatic is always the *other*. This is why in the mass media Muslim fundamentalists are presumed to be frenzied, irrational, thoughtless and brutal. Paraphrasing John Stuart Mill, this picture is at best a falsehood that contains an element of truth. Fanaticism is an enduring ingredient of history and thus those who wish to comprehend their motives and actions ought to refrain from substituting labels for analysis. For fanatics of destruction or rebirth have played a decisive role in inventing our religions, our countries, and our revolutions.

NOTES

1. Barrington Moore, Jr., *Social Origins of Dictatorship and Democracy* (Boston, Mass.: Beacon Press, 1966), p. 485.

2. Imam Khomeini, *Kashf al-Asrar* [Key to the secrets] (Tehran: Ministry of Islamic Guidance, 1980), p. 105. This book was originally published in 1942 and is currently available only in Persian.

3. Ibid., p. 249.

4. Imam Khomeini, *Imam va Enghelab-e Farhangi* [Imam and the cultural revolution] (Tehran: Teachers Training College, 1983), p. 21. This book consists of a collection of statements by Ayatollah Ruhollah Khomeini on cultural issues; it is currently available only in Persian.

5. R. Hrair Dekmejian, *Islam in Revolution: Fundamentalism in the Arab World* (Syracuse, N.Y.: Syracuse University Press, 1985), pp. 81–82.

5

The Rights of Women
in Contemporary Islam

NIKKI R. KEDDIE

THE HISTORY OF WOMEN'S POSITION in the Muslim world, and of
Muslim attitudes toward women, is full of obscurity and controversy, and it is far less simple than may appear on the surface.
One may say that the subordination of women to men in premodern times was not strikingly different in the Muslim world from
that in other great civilizations but that many Muslims have been
far more resistant to modern trends toward male-female equality
than have been their counterparts elsewhere. The reason usually
given for this difference is that certain points about the status of
women and their relations to men are embedded in the Qur'an,
believed to be the unalterable word of God, and in the holy law,
or *shari'a*, which also has a high religious status. Without denying
these points I would like to suggest that there are also other reasons for resistance to change — and particularly Western-authorized
change — among many Muslims. These reasons relate primarily to
a centuries-long hostility between the West and the Muslim world,
and a consequent reluctance by many Muslims to borrow ways
from the modern West, which many Muslims see as bowing to
neocolonialism. The rise of Islamic politics in recent years involves
not only conservatives and reactionaries but, more often, young
people with technical and scientific educations whose views on
women — whether they themselves are men or women — are generally more nuanced than Westerners realize. These Islamists,
as we are beginning to call them, see Western attitudes toward
women and Western clothing and behavior as part of a Western

cultural and political offensive directed especially against Muslims.

In order to understand better than most Westerners do the position of women in the Muslim world, we must take an excursion into history, and even into prehistoric times, where information is often scanty. Regarding prehistory, many scholars are beginning to posit a more equal status and relationship between men and women than they formerly presented. Some tools that had been seen as men's hunting tools are now considered to be women's agricultural tools, while other women's tools and implements are believed to have been more perishable than men's, though not therefore less important. While the earliest division of labor was that between the sexes — male hunters and female food gatherers in hunter-gatherer societies are one widespread example — this division did not necessarily imply inequality. Among contemporary hunter-gatherers in Africa it has been found that women contribute the great majority of the food. Some argue that despite this men's work is more highly valued among hunter-gatherers, but clearly there is not the gap in status, sexual behavior, and permitted activities among hunter-gatherers that developed in later, class-divided societies. And the same greater equality is found among most preliterate, preclass societies.

The regular cultivation of crops, the domestication of animals, and the foundation of the first cities, which could feed different classes of specialized workers owing to the new agricultural surplus, brought new possibilities for the appropriation of private property in land, animals, movable goods, and later money. Along with private or group property went a new concern over its inheritance. Women, whose role in childbearing and rearing had already limited their participation in warfare and politics, were now to be subject to new controls. These were largely aimed, whether consciously or not, at assuring that a man's own children inherited his property. To assure this nearly all civilized peoples adopted measures to reduce the possibility of a wife's marital infidelity, often by keeping her under the eyes of her mother-in-law (which also served to acculturate her, sometimes brutally, into the new family). Social intercourse between women and men also tended to become more limited, and value was put on bridal virginity. Many peoples, including Jews, Christians, ancient Greeks, and some Muslims, developed myths about women as the source

of evil and/or sexual temptation, and the idea grew that women
were dangerous and had to be controlled. This idea was based,
among other things, on the notion that the same actions that were
normal and accepted in men were evil and dangerous in women.
Men were generally assumed to be polygamous by nature and to
be doing nothing wrong if they indulged in a varied sex life or,
where it was legal, in polygamy. Although various popular traditions, including many in both the Christian and the Muslim worlds,
consider women lustful, the nonmonogamous satisfaction of wom-
en's sexuality was seen as evil. Often this male-female distinction
is recognized and its basis made explicit among Muslims: polygamy is all right for a man, they say, because it will always be known
who the mother is, but polygamy for a woman would lead to an
impossible confusion about paternity.

Measures to control women seem to have been especially
strong in various Near Eastern and Mediterranean civilizations
from ancient times until very recently. As many of the customs
normally considered Islamic—notably the veiling and seclusion
of women—really go back to pre-Islamic Near Eastern civilizations, something must be said about these customs as a prelude
to a direct discussion of Islam.

The earliest textual reference we have regarding veiling comes
in an Assyrian text of about 1200 B.C., and its point is prohibiting
prostitutes to veil. This indicates that then, as later, veiling was
a sign of status and respectability. Respectable Athenian women
were generally secluded, and veiling was known in the Roman
world. Strabo says that it came to Greece from Persia, with Medea,
whom he sees as a Mede, and this may reflect an actual Oriental
origin. It is known that the veiling and seclusion of women existed
in pre-Islamic Persia and also in the Byzantine Empire, the two
areas conquered by the early Muslims.

Veiling and seclusion clearly form part of the protection of
daughters and wives from any male contact, which helps assure
the husband's paternity and also makes the wife easier to control.
In addition, in precontemporary times veiling has been a sign of
status; a husband who can veil and seclude his wife demonstrates
that she is better protected than others from sexual harm, and that
she is not so poor as to need to go out to work or even to shop.
Women who did work, including almost all of the great majority

of women who were rural, have, to our knowledge, almost never veiled, with some very recent exceptions.

Veiling, seclusion, and noncontact with marriageable males are thus not exclusively Muslim phenomena, and indeed the evidence is overwhelming that the early Muslims adopted them from the peoples they conquered, who made up the majority of the population in the Islamic empire. The customs of other Mediterranean peoples, such as the Spanish, the South Italians, and the Greeks, had much in common with those of Muslims when it came to guarding girls and married women from male contact, as well as other aspects of male-female relations.

This similarity of male-female attitudes around the Mediterranean has been noted and partly explained by a French anthropologist, Germaine Tillion, in a book translated into English as *The Republic of Cousins.* According to Tillion, Mediterranean peoples are especially prone to endogamy—marriage to relatives—and endogamy increases the desire to control the women in a tightly interrelated lineage. She notes that the ancient Egyptians and Persians favored unions that we would call incestuous, while most Mediterranean peoples have favored cousin marriage. Building on what was written by Tillion, and on a paper by Leila Abu Lughod, I would suggest that nomadic tribal groups, who were very numerous among the Arabs, and also among the other chief Middle Eastern Muslim peoples—the Iranians and the Turks—have a special incentive to control their women and to favor cousin marriage. This incentive extends to tribes who are not pastoral nomads, like the agricultural tribal peoples in Yemen.

First I should be clear about what I mean by *tribe*, a term that has been so loosely used and misused that in some circles, notably among Africanist scholars, it is now avoided altogether. While Africans and Africanists may justly react against a word that is often misued to characterize a nation of millions of people just because they are Africans, there is a useful role for the word *tribe* in Middle Eastern studies. It corresponds to terms in Arabic, Persian, and Turkish that refer to contiguous population groups who claim descent from a common ancestor, and hence a blood interrelationship. A tribe is a political unit, and often an economic one; and tribal leaders, nearly always chosen from one family, are accorded more respect and loyalty than is a central government.

Tribes flourish when central governments are weak, and central governments usually try to weaken tribes, which are most often armed.

Tribes as we have known them in history are not primitive. Pastoral nomadic tribes, which are the most common ones in the Middle East and Central Asia, can only come into existence after the domestication of animals and the creation of a settled agricultural and urban population with whom nomads can trade animal products for agricultural and other ones. The cohesion of tribes and subtribes is necessary to their economy, which requires frequent group decisions about migration or other matters. Such decisions are not imposed from the top, and to make them amicably groups and subgroups closely connected by kinship ties are a desideratum. The practical benefits of close kinship in maintaining tribal politics and economics are surely one reason why cousin marriage has long been preferred among the Arabs, and also among other Middle Eastern peoples. Cousin marriage encourages the most thorough family integration by the bride and permits control over the wife by both sides of the family, which are closely related.

Tribal structures also place special emphasis on premarital virginity and marital fidelity by the woman, since tribes and subtribes are held together by kinship in the male line, and any doubt thrown on the purity of this kinship would be even more disastrous in the tribal than in the nontribal environment. Hence it appears likely that strict controls on women have a connection with the pervasiveness of tribal structures in the Middle East even though most nomadic women are not veiled and secluded.

It was in a situation of marked sexual inequality among both Arab tribes and non-Arab empires that the Qur'an was written. The question of whether it, and later Islamic law, improved the position of women, and if so, to what degree, is a subject of controversy. The predominant Muslim view is that before Islam Arabs lived in a state of ignorance and barbarism, so that as regards women, as on other questions, the divinely revealed Qur'an provided a tremendous, and indeed perfect, step forward. Some Western scholars, however, notably Robertson Smith and Montgomery Watt, found conditions of matriliny and high female status in pre-Islamic Arabia, which would imply a less reforming role for Islam; and this view has been adopted by some recent feminist scholars.

The predominant Western view is that the Qur'an marked an improvement on previous practices, though not as dramatic a one as is held by believing Muslims. In my view, some scholars in the last group view what do indeed appear to be matrilineal and matrilocal customs among some pre-Islamic tribes — including free divorce for women — as signs of disorder, as do Muslim believers, and hence regard the suppression of such customs as progress. On the other hand, the matriarchy-feminist position seems to take reports of matrilineal and matrilocal customs from a minority of tribes and generalize them to all tribes or all Arabs.

The Qur'an may be seen as prescribing an improvement in the conditions of most women, but not necessarily those from matrilineal tribes. This improvement seems not to have been revolutionary, nor do we know enough about the practices of all tribes to evaluate it precisely. A clear Qur'anic reform was the outlawing of female infanticide. Also an apparent improvement were regulations decreeing that females should inherit half of what males did and allowing women to control their property — which was known, however, among pre-Islamic Arabs, as seen in Muhammad's first, merchant wife.

Much less favorable were free divorce for men — while for women it remained very difficult — and polygamy for men. The latter is presented by the Qur'an as helping the condition of unprotected widows and orphans, who were numerous in those warlike times. Men are first admonished not to take additional wives unless they can treat them all equally, and then told that no matter how hard they try they will not be able to treat all equally. This contradiction is taken by modernist Muslims to show that the Qur'an meant to discourage or forbid polygamy. Veiling and seclusion are nowhere enjoined in the Qur'an, although later Muslim interpretation says that they are. One version of the Qur'an tells women to veil their bosoms and hide their ornaments. "Ornaments" was later taken to mean everything except the hands, feet, and perhaps the face, though this interpretation makes no logical or linguistic sense. In addition, if everything was to be veiled, there would be no point in ordering bosoms veiled separately. Another verse tells women to draw their cloaks tightly around them so that they may be recognized and not annoyed. And these are the only words taken to refer to veiling.

The above are the most important Qur'anic points on female behavior except for the punishment of adulterers—where there are *four* eyewitnesses to the act—by lashing. It is often said, with some truth, that Islamic practices regarding women are so resistant to change because they have the sanction of the Qur'an, which believing Muslims take to be the literal word of God. Although this has some truth, we should be aware of how much breaking and bending of Qur'anic admonitions there has been throughout Muslim history. To limit ourselves to women, it has been often noted by anthropologists and others that many, and possibly the majority, of Muslim women have never inherited as the Qur'an says they should. It should be realized that the inheritance rules of the Qur'an were very hard to follow in rural and nomadic societies, as daughters marry out of the family, if often to close relatives; and land or flocks given away reduce the property of the patrilineal line. Hence, especially in rural areas, means were found to ignore or evade women's inheritance rights. Nor could a woman, whose husband had powers of threat and coercion, always hold onto or manage her own property, as she was supposed to. Adultery or fornication has rarely been published Qur'anically; certainly four eyewitnesses are not demanded, and very often the girl or woman is killed by a member of her own family—frequently her brother. Stoning to death, a custom practiced by Jews and Christians, was sometimes adopted, and in some countries is now considered Islamic, even though the Qur'an says otherwise.

In other words, and the examples could be extended, the Qur'an was often followed on sexual and other matters when it was not too inconvenient or repugnant to men or the patriarchal family to do so, and not followed when it was. The not following was mostly in the direction of reviving patriarchal tribal practices, as in Sunni legal rules of inheritance, or adopting customs like veiling and seclusion from the Byzantines and Persians and reading them back into the Qur'an. In some cases practice was less severe than a mere reading of the Qur'an might suggest, however, notably regarding divorce. Since marriages were carefully arranged and the groom's parents paid a significant bride-price, the groom could run into a great deal of trouble with his family if he divorced quickly or lightly. Polygamy was often favored over divorce.

Urban middle- and upper-class women, traditionally the most veiled and secluded, also were much more likely to inherit as the Qur'an said they should. This is a paradox only to a Westerner who reads back our concepts of women's rights into the past and thinks that a woman who has more such rights in one sphere should have them in another. Significant differences existed in women's roles according to time, place, and social status, and there has never been a single category of Muslim women operating under one set of rules. Particularly when Islam spread beyond the Middle East to South and Southeast Asia and to Africa, the position of women, traditionally freer than in the pre-Islamic Middle East, remained so. And these latter areas have the great majority of the world's Muslims.

This is not to suggest that the prescriptions of the Qur'an and of Muslim law counted for little or nothing among most Muslims. The rules on polygamy, divorce, and child custody (to the father after a young age) were very generally followed. If polygamy and divorce were far less widespread than Westerners might imagine, they remained a threat to a wife, and still do in many areas. Divorce was clearly the worse threat and condition in most cases.

On the whole, however, the condition of women did not change radically from its general "Mediterranean" status after the rise of Islam. Veiling and seclusion were stricter in Islam than in the European Mediterranean, but the general style of dress and deportment, including the stress on male and family honor residing in the proper sexual behavior of the female (and brothers' killing erring sisters, and occasional stoning) were all present. Different were polygamy and divorce, but one may have some sympathy with Muslim apologists who note that Western husbands were hardly monogamous in practice. When we turn to other great civilizations, such as South Asia and the Far East, we find similarly patriarchal customs with special restrictions for women of status, like footbinding, widow burning, and forms of seclusion. Hence the traditional status of most Muslim women cannot be said to have been significantly worse than that of women in other civilizations. The dramatic difference between Muslims and non-Muslims comes with the nineteenth- and twentieth-century Muslim resistance to change, and especially the current Islamic revivalist desire to return to strict Islamic ways. Regarding gender relations this has no precise parallel in other civilizations, even though the recent exposure of widespread bride burning in India (as opposed to traditional ceremonial *suttee*) indicates that the Muslim world is not the area of the worst atrocities toward women.

The special resistance of Muslim societies to modern or Western-inspired changes in women's status is tied to the sacred position of the Qur'an and of holy law in Muslim societies. But this is not the whole story. For one thing, we have already seen how Qur'anic provisions are ignored or evaded when they do not fit needs or desires in many cases. Second, whole categories of Islamic law have been made inoperative in various countries at a stroke of the pen in the past two centuries, and this has aroused little or no resistance. The last area of law to be left to the Islamic courts, after criminal and civil law were Westernized, was personal status law, which included the position of women. This is an area that many religious traditions have held onto most tenaciously — witness the Catholic Church on divorce and abortion — and also one that many governments hesitate to get into. But, more than that, it is an area which naturally felt the greatest resistance to the wholesale invasion by the West of the Middle East in the past two centuries.

If the close-knit family group felt a need to keep its women from the stares of strangers, how much more was this need felt by many when the strangers were European Christians — for centuries the chief infidel enemies of the Muslims. Nada Tomiche has noted that, with the French presence in Egypt after Napoleon's invasion, veiling increased as a reaction to the presence of Europeans; and in later Algeria some of the same reaction was seen.

There is no doubt that many Muslims became Westernized and adopted Western or Western-influenced modes of thought. But we should realize that these people tended to come from those in the middle and upper classes who had profitable contacts with Westerners in trade, politics, and society. For larger but less visible and articulate groups, Westernization was less popular or unpopular. The petty bourgeoisie and bazaar traders in particular tended to support traditional Islamic ways. Juan Cole has traced this process in Egypt, where the modernizing reformers and liberals tended to come from and appeal to the higher social classes;

those who defended veiling and traditional customs came from and appealed to the traditional petty bourgeoisie. Just as the upper classes were in politicoeconomic as well as ideological alliance with Westerners, so the traditional petty-bourgeois classes were in competition with larger-scale Western trade and manufacture, and tended to reject Western ways partly out of a desire to defend their economic and social position. Women were partly a pawn in this political and ideological game, which was really more about colonial and semicolonial relations than it was or is about women as such. Nonetheless it is striking how tenaciously the petty bourgeoisie stuck to essentially traditional positions for women. The idea that women who appear publicly are semiprostitutes could only be reversed when access to Western ways was possible and directly helpful. Also, upper-class men probably had less impetus to dominate their wives than did petty-bourgeois ones, both because of servants who carried out domestic tasks, leaving time for wives and daughters to undertake educational and vocational activities, and even more because upper-class men had various people they could dominate, while petty-bourgeois and lower-class men did not.

Within the parameters of different class positions there were, in most Muslim countries, nineteenth- and twentieth-century ideological and political battles and activities concerning women's rights which, until very recently, resulted in progress toward broadening those rights. The names most associated with the early struggles for women's rights were those of male intellectuals and political figures, but it must be realized that from the beginning there were women who worked to broaden the scope of their rights and activities. Women's activities and organizations became public and organized, and fought for women's rights and education, generally in the twentieth century. However, as recent Islamist trends have underlined, we should not imagine that the majority of either men or women were consciously involved in a movement or trend toward the broadening of women's rights.

Reformers on the question of women's rights had, from the first, to try to meet questions raised by the Qur'an and the holy law. Although a few — including the radical reforming Turkish ruler, Ataturk — took a secular position, legislating women's equality on the basis of European, and not Islamic law, this was a rare public

position to take. Far more widespread have been modernist or reformist interpretations of the Qur'an, associated with the Egyptian modernists Muhammad 'Abduh and Qasim Amin and many
other male and female writers down to today. I should reiterate
that attachment to the Qur'an and Islamic law is strong for most
Muslims not only because of the sacred nature of these texts but
also as a point of identity in the face of Western cultural onslaughts,
which have been especially pervasive in the Middle East. Hence
there was and is a strong impetus to ground one's arguments in
Islam, even for many who were privately secularists.

Modernist arguments are variable but often display a number of common features from their origins to the present. One such
feature is to say that the Qur'an has more than one meaning (a
position held before modern times by many Muslims), and that
its literal prescriptions were designed to meet the reformist possibilities of its own times, with later reforms suggested by many
phrases as interpreted by the modernists. An allied argument is
to stress the spirit of the Qur'an — to use the book title of the South
Asian reformer Ameer Ali — and to say that the Qur'an is egalitarian (largely true) and favors human rights, and that these general principles were meant to be extended to women's rights. There
is also extensive reinterpretation of particular verses and passages.
The Qur'an in the same chapter says that men can marry up to
four wives if they can treat the wives equally, and later that no
matter how hard they try men will not be able to treat wives
equally. Putting the two together, it is logically held by the modernists that the Qur'an was against polygamy, as the conditions
it lays down as requirements for polygamy it then says are impossible to meet. More generally, various passages are interpreted to
refer to male-female equality.

The reformists also tend, both on the woman question and
on others, to refer to the earliest sources — the Qur'an and the holy
Traditions about Muhammad — and to reject much of later interpretation. This allows them, in some cases, to call for radical reforms in Islamic law, which is seen, with considerable justice, as
being less reformist on women's rights than is the Qur'an. Particularly if the Qur'an is reinterpreted in the ways suggested, law should
similarly be reshaped. A reinterpreted Qur'an could bring restrictions on, or an end to, polygamy, an improvement in women's prop-

erty rights, and the like. Even an easier form of divorce for women has been found to date back to the time of Muhammad, however little it has been utilized in later times.

These arguments were put forth by men and women against the background of a rapidly changing economy and society that had entered into new relations with the West. The rise of capitalism and of new paid job categories created new positions on the labor market for women, who had always worked in the nomadic, rural, and domestic economies. In the Middle East the early demand was especially for teachers and for nurses, midwives, and doctors for women. Demand spread to low-paid factory work and later to white-collar jobs. Putting some women in the paid labor force could mean changing rules and ideals about sexual segregation and seclusion. In addition wealthier families, in contact with Western men and women, saw the advantages of women's education and participation in the wider, non–sexually-segregated world. Women's education was advocated by reformists both to improve and modernize child raising and to prepare some women for jobs. The earliest arguments stressed the need to educate women so their *sons* would be raised well, but men and women soon advanced to arguing for women's rights. Although steps toward more women's education, jobs, and freedom all met some resistance, until recently they moved forward, almost entirely in the direction of greater equality for women.

Among the steps that deserve mention are the creation and expansion of women's schools and women's or mixed universities in almost every Muslim country, the opening of public-sphere jobs to women, and some reforms in laws regarding women almost everywhere. The most radical reforms were those of the 1920s in Turkey, where Ataturk took the still unique path of ignoring Muslim law and practice and adopting Western codes that outlawed polygamy and created substantial legal equality for women. Women got the vote in Turkey well before they did in France or Italy. Turkey was able to move so radically partly because of a long contact with the West and experience of gradual reform, and partly because of the huge popularity of Ataturk, chiefly as a ruler who had taken territory back from Western powers—something no other Middle Eastern leader has done. The next most radical situations are found in Tunisia and Marxist South Yemen. In Tunisia

Bourguiba's Personal Status Code of 1956 outlawed polygamy on the Muslim reformist grounds suggested above and created substantial equality for women, while still retaining certain Islamic features and special rights for men. In South Yemen polygamy is allowed in a very few circumstances, but the family law is otherwise egalitarian, and women's organizations are encouraged to carry out education and propaganda for it. Elsewhere legal reform has been more limited, but it is still very significant in most Muslim countries. It is important to realize that, despite all the Islamist agitation, there has been very little retreat in women's reformed legal rights except in Iran and, on a few matters, in Pakistan.

The normal form of legal change outside Turkey, Tunisia, and South Yemen is to place restrictions on divorce, polygamy, and/or the age of marriage, often by finding Islamic precedents, and often by making men petition courts for divorce or polygamy. All this follows a general modern trend of putting personal and family matters increasingly under state control.

This trend toward progressive reform, however, which occurred mainly after World War I, was simultaneous with other changes, especially since World War II, that helped create an Islamist constituency in our own time. Among these changes I will stress three: (1) the growing cultural gap between the Westernized elite and the majority of the population; (2) the continued growth of Western cultural, economic, and political influence and of the power of Israel; and (3) socioeconomic dislocations resulting from rapid urbanization, oil-backed modernization, and growing income distribution gaps.

The gap between the elite and the masses has led me to speak elsewhere of Two Cultures with regard to Iran, and the same phenomenon may be seen elsewhere. The elite cultures tend to be highly Western-oriented, with young people getting a Western or Western-style education, and having very little contact with the traditional bourgeoisie or the masses. Sometimes the two groups literally speak different languages, as in much of French-speaking North Africa, despite some success for Arabization policies. The popular classes often identify more with Islam than do the elite, and identification with Islamic revival is especially strong for students from rural or petty-bourgeois backgrounds who succeed in entering universities but see little future for themselves or their countries.

To speak of the growth of Western economic and political influence, and particularly of cultural influence, may seem a paradox in a period of decolonization, but there are many more Westerners in most Muslim countries today than there were in colonial times, and they enter more crucially into increasing areas of the economy. Western cultural influence is all-pervasive, whether in clothing styles, other consumption articles, television, films, and music, or the total elite culture. The backlash of rejection of Western cultural dominance in favor of indigenous tradition is not surprising. In addition, Israel is widely seen as a Western-supported bastion of neocolonialism, which brings further reactions against pro-Western leaders and Western ways.

Socioeconomic dislocations, reinforced by first the rise, and now the decline, in oil income, include the following: very rapid urbanization, opportunities for the rich to get richer while the poor improve their condition little or not at all, the problems of resettlement of migrants into the city or abroad, and the breakdown of family ties and accustomed rural ways. Here again, Islamism provides a social cement that appears familiar in the face of these new problems.

The Islamic revival also included disillusionment with postcolonial governments that generally had a nationalist, not Islamic, ideology. These included the governments of the Pahlavis, of Sadat in Egypt, and of Bourguiba. In this situation nationalist and Western-style ideologies were discredited among many, who were attracted instead by new visions of Islam that had major implications for the position of women.

Islamic revivalist movements have become frequent ever since the first important Western economic impact in the Muslim world in the eighteenth century. Contemporary ideological Islamic revivalism, however, traces its roots to the interwar period, especially with the Egyptian Muslim Brethren, founded in 1928, and the work of Maududi for Islamic government in Muslim India. Islamist groups grew after World War II, especially after the 1967 defeat by Israel and the 1973 oil price rise, with its resultant economic dislocations.

Contemporary Islamism, which has various manifestations, generally advocates Islamic states and Islamic law. In this it is more innovating than it seems, as after the first four caliphs Islam

has traditionally been separated from rule, and Islamic law has
not been applied in a thorough, much less codified and centralized, way. So what is really demanded is a modern, centralized
theocracy. Modern economic and technological means are accepted,
although often with Islamic names.

Islamism is almost everywhere populist in its appeal, stress-
ing the defence of the oppressed and the socially egalitarian nature of the Qur'an. It is far from egalitarian about women, however, and to a degree takes what it sees as the Islamization of
women's position as a touchstone of being Islamic. This is in part
because matters affecting women make up one of the few legislative areas of the Qur'an; and a return to what the Islamists see
as Qur'anic injunctions on polygamy, adultery, and so forth, is a
highly visible way to show that one is a good Muslim. Dress is a
particularly visible symbol of Islamist beliefs, and one might almost say that the dress adopted by Islamist women is as important
as a badge of ideology as it is as a means to modesty or seclusion.
This shows up in the fact that Islamist women are not at all secluded from the world, but are heavily concentrated among students, young working women, and the like, and are also engaged
in political activity. Also, the dress of many Islamist women is not
traditional; this is true of the smocks, jeans, and running shoes
of the Iranian leftist Islamic Mujahedin-e Khalq, of the long belted
dresses and scarves of Tunisia's Islamists, and of the fitted sarongs
and cowls (both often brightly colored) in Southeast Asia.

There is, however, separation of the sexes among Islamists
when they gather or demonstrate. This is part of a widespread
Islamist ideology that can be stated, in terms familiar to the American past, as a separate but equal position regarding women. For
the Islamists I have read and talked to around the world do not
speak of inferior capacities or positions for women. They insist that
men and women are equal but have been made with different,
though not unequal, capacities, according to their different roles.
They go on to stress the dignity of child rearing without, in general, denying women the possibility of working, provided it does
not interfere with child rearing. Rhetorical justifications are found
for practices in the Qur'an and Islamic law that are unequal, as
again being based in men's and women's different natures and
needs. Polygamy is upheld as better than the prostitution and hav-

ing mistresses that are taken to be typical of the West but not of the Islamic world, and early marriage is seen as preferable to Western-style teenage promiscuity. (There is no doubt that Western problems with such things as teenage pregnancies and drugs helped turn many Muslims back to a traditional morality, or that Western dress and habits are profoundly shocking to many strict Muslims.)

Leading Islamists have usually been men with Westernized, or partly Westernized, educations, and to an extent this is still true. But on this as on many matters a new phase began with the Iranian Revolution, which was led, for reasons tied to the independence of the clergy in Shiah Iran, by clericals with a traditional education. These men were less inclined to compromise on questions concerning women's position than, say, the secularly educated leaders of Tunisia's main Islamist movement seem to be. But Iran's reversal of reforms regarding women cannot be taken as typical of governments calling themselves Islamic: Saudi Arabia has liberalized its position, especially regarding women's education and work; Libya has been quite egalitarian; and Zia al-Haqq in Pakistan has been able to put through and enforce very few inegalitarian measures in the face of an active women's opposition.

Islamist movements have had considerable appeal for women, especially among students and the traditional classes. In Iran more women actively supported Khomeini than opposed him, and the leftist Islamist Mujahedin-e Khalq have always had many women members. Elsewhere Islamist women are also numerous and well organized. The Islamists tend to encourage female activism and do not oppose women's rights on matters not covered by the Qur'an, such as education, jobs, or the right to vote. Many women have chosen to wear Islamic dress and, on questioning, one of the main reasons they give is that it keeps men from bothering them in the streets or in social relations. Islamic dress is once again a badge — here saying that this is a serious, respectable woman who should not be touched or annoyed. Unfortunately male socialization in many parts of the world has not taught that women in general should not be touched or annoyed.

Beyond the question of dress, however, there are other aspects of Islamism that appeal to many women. For one thing, Islamists in many countries have women's circles, organizations, or discussion groups where women are encouraged to speak up and discuss important matters in all-woman surroundings where they need not be intimidated by men. They are also encouraged to undertake religiopolitical propaganda activities. Girls and women whose parents or husbands would not let them out for other reasons will allow them to attend Islamist meetings or go to the mosque, and some, I was informed in Tunisia, can even reject proposed marriage partners on the grounds that they are not good Muslims.

In Nigeria I attended a three-day founding meeting of a Muslim women's group, and it was clear from the stress on education, work, and coming out of seclusion that the new Muslims are for many women advocating more progressive positions than those women now have. Also, it must be realized that the legal reforms in Muslim countries often affected only, or chiefly, the elite, so that for most women Islamism does not mean a step back from reforms from which they have experienced benefits. Those who have experienced benefits suffer under Islamist rule, but where Islamists are out of power they are often ambiguous about their position on women, thus facilitating their appeal to women. Thus the leader of Tunisia's main Islamist movement told me that the Personal Status Code should be amended to increase men's rights, while a young woman in the same movement told me that it was patriarchal, and this needed changing. As the official group position is simply that the code needs amending, either position can now be accommodated, though it is clear that male leaders and members want the code made more "Islamic" and favorable to men.

One of the most hopeful developments I witnessed in my travels around the Muslim world was in Pakistan, where oppositional women and men are undertaking more profound study than before of the Qur'an and of Islamic laws and traditions so as to find better Islamic bases for an egalitarian position. Thus far they seem to have gone beyond the achievements of the early modernists, while building on them, in order to show that the spirit of Islam is egalitarian and reformist, and that they are more in tune with that spirit than is the government. Benazir Bhutto speaks of the egalitarian nature of Islam as regards the sexes, and though this raises doubts among some Westerners, it has a real basis as well as a real appeal. Such interpretations of Islam are no more forced than our Supreme Court's varying interpretations of the U. S. Constitution.

And these Pakistani women and men may have found a better way to appeal to the masses, brought up with a loyalty to Islam, than have the highly Westernized liberals or Marxists of prerevolutionary Iran and elsewhere.

It should be mentioned that there are still modernists who take more radical and novel positions regarding Islam than those mentioned thus far. Among them is a recent Egyptian scholar who maintained that the legal parts of the Qur'an were intended only for the lifetime of the Prophet and have no current status or validity. A somewhat similar view is propounded by a small group of Sudanese, who claim that only the Meccan suras of the Qur'an (which have religious and not legal content) and not the legalistic Medinan ones have validity after the Prophet. From an abstract viewpoint such views are tenable, as there is nothing in the Qur'an that says that its legal provisions are valid for later times. Unfortunately, there is also nothing that says that its other provisions are valid for all times, so that the grounds for distinguishing between legal and other provisions are unclear. More important, such views are bound to be rejected by the great majority of Muslims today, whereas views that base themselves more solidly in Islamic texts, like some I have read and heard in Pakistan, seem more likely to gain a following.

A word of caution is in order against seeing Islamist trends as continuing to be powerful into the indefinite future. An Islamist like Khomeini is able to unite various kinds of discontented people, but once in power he arouses increasing discontent against himself. The other so-called Islamic governments — Saudi Arabia, Pakistan, the late government of the Sudan — are not supported by Islamists abroad, but at home they have contributed to disillusionment with Islamic government. In the one country where Islamists were allowed a legal party and participated in 1986 elections (Malaysia), they did very badly, even though many expected them to do well. The Islamist phase of the 1970s and 1980s may certainly continue, but it is unlikely to outlive widespread experience with so-called Islamic governments. Another hopeful sign for women is that even now there is no general trend toward repealing legislation favorable to women. Also, Islamism to date has brought advances for many women, at the same time as problems for others.

6

The Dilemmas of Islamic Identity

ANN ELIZABETH MAYER

ISLAMIC DOCTRINE
AND SOCIAL AND CULTURAL RIGHTS

HUMAN RIGHTS CONCEPTS WERE developed in the West and have not until the last decades had any direct counterparts in Islamic thought, which has only recently begun to seek to accommodate certain modern human rights concepts within an Islamic framework. The writings that have been produced on this subject by Muslims indicate that they are currently deeply divided among themselves on the question of what kinds of human rights protections Islam provides.[1] Some prominent Muslims have even condemned human rights concepts as incompatible with their religion.[2] Examination of the newly emerging "Islamic human rights" literature in isolation does not give a full or representative picture of where Islam stands on human rights issues. Consultation of a wider range of materials is necessary. I will therefore refer to aspects of classical Islamic civilization and Islamic law as well as a variety of writings and experiences in contemporary Muslim countries that illuminate how Islam has been and is understood to apply to issues of human rights.

The fact that Islamic thought did not have a developed theory of human rights did not necessarily mean that there was a pattern of state suppression in traditional societies in the Muslim world. Historically there was a general pattern of governmental abstention from interference in social and cultural matters in such societies. In past centuries nongovernmental institutions like ingrained traditions, the extended family, and the community loomed larger

94

as factors affecting the freedoms of the individual than governments did. These were not circumstances of a sort to create regular conflicts between the state and individual freedoms — or to
prompt Islamic thinkers to concern themselves with the protection of such freedoms against governmental intrusions, a concern
that underlies the development of modern human rights norms.

When one scans the great medieval juristic treatises in which
the classical *shari'a* rules are set forth, one finds that Islamic legal
doctrines directly bearing on social and cultural freedoms are scarce,
and that there is a dearth of discussion on the subject of how far
a government can go in restricting social or cultural activity. One
could argue that the only question of social and cultural rights,
as these are defined here, that was expressly addressed in classical
Islamic law was whether Islamic law permitted depicting the
human form. There were precepts banning any human representation due to the concern to prevent idolatry, which Islam strongly
abhors, but not all Muslims were convinced that this ban was necessary to prevent a lapse into idolatry — as the superb human depictions in Persian and Mughal miniatures attest. However, there
are certainly many classical Islamic precepts on ancillary topics
that, depending on their interpretation, could impair the ability
of individuals to enjoy the rights that international law says they
are entitled to.

In the premodern era, Islamic law was not normally interpreted in ways that limited artistic expression or intellectual freedom; and, during the period when classical Islamic civilization
was flourishing, Islamic doctrines do not seem to have placed the
barriers in the way of scientific inquiry that religion imposed in
the Christian West. There were, nonetheless, tensions in this area,
and many would argue that the pervasive hostility on the part of
members of the Islamic religious establishment toward rationalist
currents in Islamic philosophy did discourage the development of
philosophy and science in the long run — that is, that Islamic orthodoxy did ultimately have a chilling effect on certain kinds of
intellectual inquiry. Dogmatism on the part of defenders of Islamic
orthodoxy was one of the factors leading to the eventual stagna-
tion and decline in cultural development in the Muslim world. In
addition, there were occasional incidents of repression aimed at
crushing dissident sects or banning the dissemination of ideas con-

sidered heretical, so that some intellectuals with radical ideas must have engaged in self-censorship rather than risk public denunciation by religious authorities.

In any event, the splendid, enormously rich classical Islamic civilization that was produced in the great urban centers testifies to the fact that Islam by itself did not stunt social and cultural progress. This civilization developed not only by virtue of the large measure of freedom that was offered to the talents of its cultural leaders. It was also ready to borrow ideas and techniques on the basis of their inherent attractiveness and merits, rather than discriminate among them based on their provenance.[3] This was a tolerant civilization, open to the outside world. Diversity was tolerated, intellectual and artistic endeavors supported, and distinction recognized and rewarded.

Outside the major urban areas, the high culture or established orthodox teachings on what was or was not permissible in Islam were irrelevant. Educational opportunities were limited, literacy rare, and access to the high culture largely limited to a small urban elite, so its dissemination and the application of its norms was limited. Until the sudden massive shift to urban living that has taken place in the last two decades, Muslims mostly dwelt in a world of rural settlements and villages or nomadic social organization, where people's ability to participate in the life of the community or the tribe was limited not by formal legal norms but by the circumstances of their birth. The only culture most people knew was a local or tribal folk culture. Islam itself showed manifold regional variations and was often as localized and particularized as other aspects of folk culture. As a folk religion it was very different from the Islam that was taught in great religious academies.[4]

Islamic law is currently in the process of expanding its corpus of rules on social and cultural rights. In recent decades governments, Islamic institutions, and individual Muslims have offered interpretations that extend classical Islamic precepts, thereby creating new, ostensibly Islamic rules that deal with questions posed by modern phenomena like mass education, the growth in literacy, the development of modern media and mass communications, and the international influence of Western popular culture. These newly developed Islamic rules do not have the weight of centuries of tradition behind them, however, and their authority is, at best, debatable.

CULTURAL POLITICS
IN CONTEMPORARY MUSLIM COUNTRIES

The rise of powerful, centralized states occurred in the Muslim world much later than it did in the West. When it did, its goals were to reinforce established power, aiming at totally controlling individual thought and action and preventing the development of collective solidarity in the community. This entails subordination of culture to political power, which aims at depriving society of any ethical resources to employ against the state or its transformation into an instrument of oppression. This state preemption of the cultural domain means that culture becomes assimilated to propaganda and ideology, becoming transformed into something frozen, decadent, and, ultimately, inanimate. As culture becomes identified with nationalist power it can no longer function as culture, as a spiritual flowering with the capacity for constant renewal and readaptation to new conditions and change, while at the same time preserving identity.[5]

This pattern of state preemption of culture has not only meant the death of real intellectual life in most Muslim societies but has also produced patterns of human rights violations as states have imposed draconian regimes of censorship. As a renowned modern Arab intellectual has lamented:

> The cult of state led to enslavement: the state as repressive tool or as prison. . . . The cultural effort did away with the role of culture and of the intellectual alike: culture became a mere weapon of the ruling apparatus and the intellectual a mere servant.[6]

NEW ISSUES RAISED BY ISLAMIZATION

Until recently there was little impetus for people in the Muslim world to consider what an alliance of church and state would

mean for the exercise of social and cultural freedoms. But, with
the adoption of Islamization programs in some countries, these
problems must now be faced. The idea underlying Islamization
campaigns is a new one. *Islam* is now defined by states in ways
that serve their political goals and interests, and Islam becomes
just one more instrument of the pattern of repressive cultural
politics.

As one would expect in these circumstances, where Islamic
criteria have been applied by contemporary governments to human rights, they have tended to curtail the exercise of rights. It
is dangerous for Muslim intellectuals to speak out against this. One
eminent Arab intellectual has lamented in an essay entitled "Why
the Reversion to Islamic Archaism?":

> In the Arab world, those who think for themselves and
> are capable of elaborating a criticism of all the sacred or pro-
> fane mystifications come up against the political and religious
> censorship of the present Arab state — a censorship far worse
> than that of the caliphate state. The fact is that the best Arab
> poets and thinkers of the early centuries of Islam would not
> be able to exist in the present-day Arab world. . . .[7]

While intellectuals who oppose official Islamization measures
face censorship, Muslims who support it are able to disseminate
their views without impediment. The concept that Islam requires
placing constraints on the exercise of human rights is found in much
of the new "Islamic human rights" literature, where supposedly
Islamic criteria are applied to set limits on the freedoms that are
set forth in international human rights provisions. It should be noted
that international law does not allow the use of religious criteria
to circumscribe human rights, much less to deny them altogether.
Therefore, the practice of imposing Islamic restrictions on these
rights is in conflict with international human rights principles.

The 1979 Constitution of the Islamic Republic of Iran is a
relevant human rights case in point. "Islamic" standards limit freedom of the press and publication (Article 24), the right of association (Article 25), the right to demonstrate (Article 27), and the
right to choose a profession (Article 28). In Article 20 the constitution guarantees citizens, among other things, human and cultural
rights "according to Islamic standards." "Islamic standards" are

determined by conservative clerics allied with the policies of the regime. The effect is that Islam calls for sharply contracting the affected rights when not denying them altogether.

So-called Islamic limits may also be imposed on rights in Iran where none are expressly provided for in the law. For example, the right to education is not restricted in the Iranian constitution itself (Article 30). In practice, the right to education, and particularly to advanced education, has been restricted subsequently by the regime in the name of Islam.

THE USE OF ISLAM AS A PROPHYLACTIC AGAINST SOCIAL AND CULTURAL WESTERNIZATION

When directed against freedoms in the social and cultural sphere, Islamic criteria have tended to be utilized as screening devices designed to exclude foreign influences and, more particularly, Western cultural influences that are viewed by many Muslims — but certainly not all — as *ipso facto* un-Islamic.

Long years of Western political control and economic exploitation created lasting resentments against the West in the Muslim world and those have been exacerbated by the ongoing Arab-Israeli conflict and Western support for Israel. Modernization has also shattered the stability of traditional institutions, while not bringing about the level of development and prosperity that was hoped for. Disillusionment with the capacity of Western-style development to bring about a better life has led to considerable disenchantment with the Western model of progress generally, and the spread of Western popular culture and the emancipation of women has encouraged an anti-Western reaction. Many Muslims are eager that indigenous values and institutions in the social and cultural areas should be protected from corrosive Western influence.

This anti-Western reaction is linked to the sense of crisis in Muslim cultural identity. Increasingly, they have shown themselves disposed to solve this crisis with a reaffirmation of traditional Islamic cultural identity.[8] But how does one find or impose a cultural identity via a religion?

Many Muslims believe that in Islam religion and culture are

virtually identical. It makes sense, therefore, to speak of "Islamic" architecture, "Islamic" cities, and "Islamic" science in a way that one would not speak of "Christian" architecture, cities, or science. They assert that Islam determined both the flourishing of classical Islamic civilization and the shaping of many features of its constituent parts.[9] If this is true, the canons of Islamic orthodoxy and authenticity can be extended to all the arts and sciences, and a consistent distinction can be drawn between customs and ideas that meet Islamic criteria and ones that violate them. There is a built-in justification for censorship against all culture which they deem "un-Islamic," which does not correspond to models found in classical Islam. Islam is presented as a countermodel to Western society and an expression of authentic national tradition. Muslims' association of traditional values and institutions with Islam does not, however, mean that it is actually Islamic doctrine that is compelling this anti-Western reaction and the censorship that it has led to.

CULTURAL REVOLUTION IN THE NAME OF ISLAM

Ayatollah Khomeini formally announced a cultural revolution in June of 1980, the effects of which are still very much felt in Iran.[10] The dominant Islamic Republican Party adopted a program of eliminating Western influences in food, clothing, architecture, city planning, education, and manners. Dancing was to be prohibited. Universities were to be made Islamic. In an attempt to eliminate from the teaching profession persons imbued with either Western or Eastern ideologies ("alien" ideologies, not just Western ideologies, were the target here), tens of thousands of teachers were purged. A cultural revolution committee with both clerical and lay members was established to redesign educational curricula to serve Islamic values and to rewrite textbooks to bring them in line with Islamic criteria. University faculties were closed, in some cases for several years. When they reopened, it was the technical subjects like engineering that were first permitted to accept students. The curricula had been restricted, but mandatory religious instruction had been added. Sexual segregation in education was imposed, and women were prohibited from studying law. Instruction in foreign languages other than Arabic was sharply curtailed. Music was generally banned, and Western-style popular music was specifically condemned. Proposed theatrical presentations had to be screened by censorship committees, which included members whose task was to ensure that productions of plays did not conflict with official Islamic standards. Writers found that it was difficult to avoid running afoul of the new Islamic guidelines affecting publications and many were arrested. Hundreds of books were banned. After a brief period of freedom immediately after the revolution, most papers and journals were censored or closed down—including the paper published by the then-President of Iran, Bani-Sadr, when it ran afoul of Islamic censorship criteria; the Iranian Writers Union had to abandon its open resistance to the encroachments of censorship and go underground; and opposition writers and intellectuals were forced to flee the country or risk arrest and even execution. Movies could not be shown unless they had subjects that suited the guidelines of the new, official Islamic morality. In the process, *Islam* became effectively associated with a censorship which punished the expression of ideas by those who questioned the regime's policies and which banned all artistic activity that did not suit the tastes and moral sensitivities of the more prudish members of a conservative faction of Islamic clergy.

A prominent Egyptian intellectual, sympathetic to many of Khomeini's ideas, nonetheless saw that Khomeini's rejection of everything Western as part of constructing an Islamic identity meant that

> he leads the Islamic Revolution from action to reaction, from anticolonialism to hostility toward everything Western. He thus dismisses rationalism, the scientific spirit, humanism, in a word, progress.[11]

The experience of Pakistan with cultural control and censorship since President Zia seized power in 1977 and adopted an official policy of Islamization has been quite similar to that of Iran. Because of President Zia's close political alliance with conservative clerics and members of right-wing Islamic fundamentalist groups, the latter have been able to gain considerable control over education and the media. Textbooks and curricula have been re-

vised to eliminate all "un-Islamic" elements, religious instruction
has become mandatory at the university level, and teachers with
"un-Islamic" or "irreverent" ideas have been dismissed or demoted
to jobs in the provinces. Expressions of dissent and criticism have
been deterred and widespread self-censorship or self-exile on the
part of Pakistani writers and intellectuals has resulted.[12]

OFFICIAL STANDARDS OF ISLAMIC DRESS

Islamization presumes an Islamic model of how to dress. The
growing tendency to emulate Western styles of dress — which either
blur gender distinctions or reveal the human form and are sexually provocative — is unacceptable. An Iranian circular of April 21,
1985, provided in Article 102 that women who appeared unveiled
in public were subject to seventy-four lashes, which suggests that
the perceived need for strong disincentives for ignoring the rules
had not diminished in the six years during which the veiling requirement had been in effect. Iranian government officials have
continued in public remarks to insist on the critical nature of this
Islamic dress requirement. In remarks on April 23, 1985, President Khamene'i condemned the West for propagating as part of
its "colonialist policies" in Iran the "deliberate flaunting of immorality, of the nonobservance of Islamic dress, or laxity of ob-
servance of Islamic dress," and attacked Iranian young people who
"wear strange clothes which are manifestations of Western culture and the cultural domination of the West, and the political
domination of our enemies."[13]

The drab and formless chador mandated for Iranian women
is a typical costume for lower-class Iranian women in major urban centers; it has, however, no particular claim to be more au-
thentically Iranian than many other forms of traditional women's
attire, such as the equally modest but at the same time often color-
ful and beautiful clothes worn by Iranian peasant and tribal women
outside the major cities. Nor is wearing the chador necessarily
associated with Islam outside Iran and spheres of Iranian influence. Instead, the chador is in actuality a standardized uniform
that has been effectively imposed on all Iranian women. As such
it symbolizes the ascendancy of a clerical group that happens to

associate this particular type of attire with the preservation of tradition and the morality associated with it — with all the constraints that these mean on women's freedoms. Thus, the law requiring the wearing of the chador symbolizes the clerical appropriation of power in the social and cultural spheres more than it does a reversion to some uncontrovertibly Iranian or Islamic model of how women must dress.

The same clerical group, in contrast, does not find any "Islamic" objections to the sporting of male attire that is in all respects Western and in any color — as long as the attire is of the conventional sort. However, no necktie may be worn by Iranian men, since that particular piece of Western dress has become symbolically associated with enmity toward the revolutionary cause. The results of the regime of dress control in Iran are representative of the intellectual confusion that results when *Islam* is used as a criterion for restricting freedoms.

THE STATUS OF WOMEN

Classical Islamic doctrine does not definitively indicate what the parameters affecting women's participation in the social and cultural domains should be. Instead, it assumes the existence of traditional patriarchal societies, where men and women operate in separate, complementary spheres — men in the public sphere, women in the home and family. Contemporary feminist interpretations of Islamic law, according to which the authentic Islamic message is one that supports women's emancipation, would argue that there can be no Islamic justification for restricting women's social and cultural activities in the modern world. The feminist position is energetically contested by Islamic conservatives, who condemn the expanded role that women have come to play in the wake of modernization. Among the typical contentions of Islamic conservatives are that Islam requires female seclusion, restrictions on women's mobility, sexually segregated education that gears women for their responsibilities as housewives, the exclusion of women from many "masculine" fields of study and work, and elimination of women from the media. Obviously, the implications of these views for women's social and cultural rights are very serious — as they are for culture itself, which is thereby deprived of the contributions of one-half of the total population.

One should consider the question of women's participation in sports. Male sports activities are encouraged and often well financed in the Muslim world, and male Muslim athletes have made their marks internationally in fields like track, soccer, cricket, wrestling, and swimming. In contrast, Islamic sources are currently being interpreted to justify requiring women to be fully veiled when engaged in sports and even denying women the right to participate in sports altogether. Not surprisingly, in Iran television reportage of the Olympics had to be censored; it is difficult to think of any Olympic sport where the accepted dress for women athletes would not be deemed highly indecent by the Islamic standards employed by Iranian guardians of morality. The result was, of course, that Iranian women were deprived of the inspiration of seeing the accomplishments of great female athletes.

In these circumstances it is unlikely that the historic 1984 achievement of the Moroccan Nawal El-Mutawakal (who trained in the United States), the first Arab and first African woman gold medalist in the history of the Olympic Games, was acclaimed in countries where conservative Islamic standards of dress are *de rigueur* for women. Her triumph was, however, celebrated with wild enthusiasm in Morocco, where Muslims seemed disinclined to find an inherent conflict between adherence to Islamic standards of propriety and women's competition in track events.

Athletic activities are an important part of modern society and culture, they promote health and longevity, and they offer opportunities for talented individuals to develop their skills and to win recognition and rewards. Using Islamic criteria to bar one-half of the population from participation in these activities constitutes a significant infringement of social and cultural rights.

RELIGIOUSLY GROUNDED CENSORSHIP OF SCIENCE

Classical Islamic civilization seems to have been largely free of the fear that scientists might disprove the tenets of religion if systematic religious censorship of scientific investigation were not imposed.[14] The denunciations of Galileo and Darwin in the name of Christian doctrine did not have any real counterparts in classical Islam. In recent years, however, Islamic fundamentalists have called for a reformulation of scientific tenets to bring them into line with new interpretations of what does or does not accord with Islamic orthodoxy. Science has become associated with the West, scientific progress in the Muslim world having long since come to a halt, so that Muslim students must now turn to Western scientists for guidance in many fields. The assumption is that science that comes from the West is as tainted as are other parts of Western culture, and that Western science needs to be corrected by the imposition of Islamic criteria which will screen out tenets that conflict with Islamic values.[15] In an essay called "Without Islamic Science, No Islamic Civilization," a proponent of this approach claims:

> There is nothing in Islam which says that knowledge in itself is a virtue; this is a dangerous Aristotelian fallacy. The pursuit of all knowledge is not *ibadah* ("worship"). . . . Islam has always emphasized that certain categories of knowledge are per se evil; and the pursuit of such knowledge can lead Muslim societies away from Islam.[16]

Imitating their Christian fundamentalist counterparts, Muslim fundamentalists have decided that the teaching of Darwinian evolution poses a threat to religion, and, due to their pressures, instruction in Darwinian evolution is being eliminated in some schools and universities in Muslim countries. Christian fundamentalist tracts that expound the notions of "scientific creationism" are being circulated in translation in the Muslim world. This result is strange, since the peculiar problem of reconciling Darwinian evolution with the scriptural account of creation in Genesis, which has led Christian advocates of the idea of scriptural inerrancy to object to Darwin's theory in the West, does not exist in the case of the Islamic sources. Here, as elsewhere, it is possible to see in the censorship of science not something that is entailed by Islamic doctrine but, rather, a manifestation of a fundamental fear of modern science and critical thought that is publicly justified by invoking religion, while actually being prompted by other concerns and motives.

Sheikh Ibn Baz, the Deputy Rector of the Islamic University of Medina, announced in 1966 that the earth was stationary and that the sun revolved around it.[17] To dispute this was, he insisted, heresy. Although he announced that this finding was mandated by texts in the Qur'an and the sayings of the Prophet, his peculiar convictions actually seem to rest more on the influence of the Ptolemaic astronomy and geocentric cosmology that was accepted in traditional Islamic scholarship and his own lack of understanding of modern science. He is not alone, however, among Islamic fundamentalists in charging that the modern astronomical view that the earth moves around the sun is heretical and must be banned.

The parallel between the case of Ibn Baz and the attitude of the Catholic Church in condemning Galileo (1564–1642) is striking. However, there is an important difference: it is highly unlikely that any Vatican official today would be so lacking in a grasp of the basics of astronomy to venture such an outlandish statement or to insist that it had to be treated as a binding religious ruling. It is striking that in recent decades Islam has been converted into an instrument of censorship by an obscurantist clergy that has watched with resentment as religious learning has been eclipsed by the growing.prestige of the modern sciences. Unlike the clerics of classical Islam, who were often accomplished, brilliant polymaths, contemporary clerics are rarely learned outside the religious sciences and tend to be hostile to new fields of knowledge, which they attempt to discredit by the use of religious criteria.

The results of the Iranian dress rules, according to which a concealing dark covering must be thrown about the woman's form, are symbolic of a related manifestation of a nationalist-Islamic reaction to Western science: the hostility on the part of Islamic conservatives toward realistic, scientific inquiry into the nature of human sexuality. What one Muslim intellectual has labeled the "normative, repressive discourses that are unfurled everywhere on 'women in Islam'" is, as he says, just "a mutilation that these societies are inflicting on themselves on the pretext of preserving their being."[18] The consequences will be that Muslim societies will be delayed in confronting a critical dimension of human experience with which modern science in the West has now had many decades to try to come to terms. In contrast, it should be recalled that in classical Islamic civilization great religious scholars exhibited a readiness to examine sexual matters scientifically as well as a sensitive awareness of aspects of human sexuality which was often far in advance of that offered by the work of religious scholars in the contemporaneous West.

A sign of hostility to the scientific methodology itself could be seen in the violent attacks by Muslim clerics in Lebanon on the 1969 work of Sadiq al-'Azm, an eminent Yale-trained philosopher and Muslim intellectual.[19] In a work entitled "A Critique of Religious Thought" he offered a critique of the deficiencies of Islamic religious sciences and proposed the introduction of critical methods of scientific thought that had won international acceptance in the religious domain. Al-'Azm called the traditional education of Muslim clerics inadequate and said that they needed an education that measured up to secular standards in the technical and scientific domains. The reaction of the Sunni Mufti of Lebanon was typical. Al-'Azm, he charged, was following the ideas of world Zionism, which fights religion in order to weaken people and to take their fatherland. Islam guaranteed freedom of the individual, he said, but such freedom had limits. The state had to take action against those who insulted Islam to protect the community from anarchy and trouble. At his trial, the ostensible grounds for which were provoking confessional strife, al-'Azm denied that he had any connection with anti-Islamic causes and he sought to explain his position in the course of a hostile interrogation, which included the following exchange:

> Question: Did you write your book in the spirit of defense of Islam or in your capacity as an atheist?
> Answer: I wrote the book in the spirit of the so-called critical sciences that are concerned with religion — like sociology of religion or the comparative study of religions. I wrote it in the spirit of the critical sciences.[20]

The implicit assumption underlying the question — that there are only two possible positions, either unquestioning acceptance of Islamic doctrines as formulated by traditionally educated clerics, or atheism — is one that appears to be widely shared by Muslim conservatives.

CONCLUSION

The persecution of al-'Azm was just one manifestation of the generally hostile climate which today confronts Muslims who seek to undertake critical analyses of their religion and the functions that it plays in their societies. This climate has discouraged the participation of intellectuals in the difficult processes of reformulating Islamic thought and accommodating it to the challenges of modern life. In the absence of free debate, the forces that support what passes for orthodoxy have facilitated the cooption of Islam by the state and its use to justify denials of human rights — without needing to fear that their manipulations of Islam risk being exposed to the faithful as having no particular Islamic authority behind them.

An encouraging sign in this connection is that a fearless, searching inquiry into the defects of the existing Islamic sciences and methodologies and an attempt to reconstruct Islamic knowledge on a modern, scientifically sound basis are being purused by Professor Mohammed Arkoun at the Sorbonne. In his many distinguished writings and particularly in his book *A Critique of Islamic Reasoning*,[21] Professor Arkoun argues for a fresh, scientific spirit in the study of Islam and is sharply critical of obscurantist tendencies that use *Islam* to impede the acquisition and dissemination of knowledge. As he has noted with regret, there has accumulated within the field of Islamic thought a whole domain of what is treated as unthinkable. To enlarge the thinkable area, he argues that it is necessary to integrate the modern sciences within the Islamic tradition.

It seems that so far we have heard mostly from one side in the debate among Muslims on human rights in the social and cultural spheres — the side that supports policies that mandate what one observer has called the "return to Islamic archaism [that] is part of the process of totalitarian uniformization of all aspects of cultural consumption."[22] There is another side, however, that may yet produce arguments which will convince Muslims that their religion, properly understood, does not call for them to forfeit their social and cultural freedoms and will persuade them to challenge the authority of those who tell them that it does.

NOTES

1. Examples of one tendency in this literature can be found in Sultanhussein Tabandeh, *A Muslim Commentary on the Universal Declaration of Human Rights* (London: Goulding, 1966); Abul A'la Mawdudi, *Human Rights in Islam* (London: Islamic Foundation, 1980) and *Universal Islamic Declaration of Human Rights* (London: Islamic Foundation, 1981). A very different approach can be seen in Abdullahi Ahmed El Naiem, "A Modern Approach to Human Rights in Islam: Foundations and Implications for Africa," in *Human Rights and Development in Africa*, ed. Claude E. Welch, Jr., and Ronald I. Meltzer (Albany, N.Y.: SUNY Press, 1884).

2. Edward Mortimer, "Islam and Human Rights," *Index on Censorship* 12, no. 5 (1983): 5.

3. For an introduction to aspects of classical Islamic civilization, see "Society and Civilization," *Cambridge History of Islam*, ed. P. M. Holt, A. K. S. Lambton, and B. Lewis (Cambridge: At the University Press, 1970), 2, pt. 7, pp. 441–889; and Seyyed Hossein Nasr, *Islamic Life and Thought* (Albany, N.Y.: SUNY Press, 1981).

4. For a modern anthropological investigation of the cultural diversity in Moroccan and Indonesian versions of Islam, see Clifford Geertz, *Islam Observed: Religious Development in Morocco and Indonesia* (Chicago: University of Chicago Press, 1968).

5. This view is expressed cogently in Burhan Ghalioun, "Identité, culture et politique culturelles dans les pays dependents," *Peuples Mediterraneens* 16 (1981): 31–50.

6. Adonis, "From Military Intellectual to Military Faqih," *NAD*, July 7, 1980, quoted in Emmanuel Sivan, *Radical Islam: Medieval Theology and Modern Politics* (New Haven, Conn.: Yale University Press, 1985), p. 157.

7. Lafif Lakhdar, "Why the Reversion to Islamic Archaism?" *Forbidden Agendas: Intolerance and Defiance in the Middle East* (London: Al Saqi, 1984), p. 286.

8. Islam's function in this cultural crisis is thoughtfully analyzed in Bassam Tibi, *Der Islam und das Problem der kulturellen Bewaltigung sozialen Wandels* (Frankfurt: Suhrkamp, 1985).

9. An excellent source of ideas on the complicated subject of the relationship between Islam and the cultural production historically associated with it is the discussions of the nature of Islamic architecture in seminars sponsored by the Aga Khan Award for Architecture. The proceedings of these international seminars have been published periodically

since the first volume, entitled *Toward an Architecture in the Spirit of Islam*, was issued in 1978.

10. Some discussion of the impact of the cultural revolution can be found in Gholam Hoseyn Sa'edi, "Iran under the Party of God," *Index on Censorship* 13, no. 1 (1984): 16–20; Esmail Kho'i, "Khomeini Shoots Writers," *Index on Censorship* 13, no. 5: 36–37, 41; Dilip Hiro, *Iran under the Ayatollahs* (London: Routledge, 1985), pp. 255–57; C. Benard and Z. Khalilzad, "The Government of God," in *Iran's Islamic Republic* (New York: Columbia University Press, 1984), pp. 116–17; and Rouhallah K. Ramazani, "Iran: The 'Islamic Cultural Revolution,'" in *Change in the Muslim World*, ed. Philip H. Stoddard, David C. Cuthell, and Margaret Sullivan (Syracuse: Syracuse University Press, 1981): pp. 40–48.

11. Hassan Hanafi, in his introduction to the Arabic translation of *Khomeini's Islamic Government* (Cairo, 1979), p. 29, quoted in Sivan, *Radical Islam*, p. 179.

12. Some information on the state of censorship in Pakistan can be seen in Maleeha Lodhi, "Deterring Dissent in Education," *Index on Censorship* 14, no. 2 (1985): 28–30; Scriptor (pseud.), "Why the Press is Tame," *Index on Censorship* 14, no. 2 (1985): 31–33; Farhad (pseud.) "Curbing Free Thought," *Index on Censorship* 14, no. 2 (1985): 33–36.

13. BBC Summary of World Broadcasts, April 25, 1985, ME.7934.A.2.

14. A useful summary is provided by Seyyid Hossein Nasr, *Science and Civilization in Islam* (Cambridge, Mass.: Harvard University Press, 1968).

15. Some idea of the kinds of discussions that have occurred on this subject can be gleaned from Ziauddin Sardar, ed., *The Touch of Midas: Science, Values and Environment in Islam and the West* (Manchester: Manchester University Press, 1984); and Isma'il Al Faruqi and Abdullah Omar Nasseef, eds., *Social and Natural Sciences: The Islamic Perspective* (Sevenoaks, Kent: Hodder & Stoughton, 1981).

16. Ziauddin Sardar, "Without Islamic Science, No Islamic Civilization," *Afkar*, July 1984, p. 48.

17. Werner Ende, "Religion, Politik, und Literatur in Saudi-Arabien: Der geistesgeschichtliche Hintergrund der heutigen religiösen und kultur-politischen Situation," *Orient* 22 (1982): 381–82.

18. Mohammed Arkoun, *Pour une critique de la raison islamique* (Paris: Maisonneuve, 1984), p. 218.

19. This incident is discussed in an excellent article by Stefan Wild, "Gott und Mensch im Libanon," *Der Islam* 48 (1972): 206–53.

20. Ibid., p. 234.

21. See note 18.

22. Lakhdar, "Why the Reversion to Islamic Archaism?" p. 300.

PART III

Hinduism and Buddhism

7

Duties and Rights in Hindu Society

JOHN B. CARMAN

A DRAMATIC MOMENT IN Louis Malle's film portrayal of India is the scene of a vast throng at night near the Mylapore temple in Madras City. At the center of the crowd is frenzied activity, for the giant temple car—looking like a small temple on great wooden wheels—is being pulled by ropes drawn by hundreds of devotees. Louis Malle saw this excited crowd milling about in a darkness lit intermittently by bright petromax lanterns as an epitome of the incomprehensible chaos at the heart of Hindu life.

I suggest that the French filmmaker could hardly have been further from the mark in selecting an example of chaos, for a Hindu temple procession consists of a complicated but orderly network of groups. Almost all those hundred thousand or more knew why they were there, what they should do, and when they should do it, as well as do the twenty-two players on a football field—but in the West we are accustomed to having the crowd of a hundred thousand in the stands!

All those participants in the Hindu temple procession give us a clue to the relations of duties and rights in traditional Hindu society and help us understand how it has been possible for Hindus to accept different notions of human rights in modern India.

The giant temple car pulled in these processions had fascinated Western observers from the time more than two hundred years ago when the British East India Company's trading posts started to expand into a veritable empire. Our English word *juggernaut* comes from the temple car of Jagannatha, "Lord of the Universe," the title of Lord Vishnu in the great temple in Puri, in Orissa. Such a huge vehicle was difficult to get moving but then

113

awesome in its motion — a moving temple — and difficult with such momentum to bring to a quick stop. Europeans were told that some Hindus would even commit suicide by jumping in front of those great wooden wheels. This has become a large part of our Western notion of the juggernaut, which is defined in Webster's both as "a belief calling for blind self-sacrifice" and "any massive inexorable force that advances irresistibly, crushing whatever is in its path."

Whether or not such things happened, it is clear that the center of awesome attraction for Hindus was something much smaller — the movable image of the deity enshrined in the temple, usually made of metal. Hindus go to temples to get the blessed sight (*darshan*) of the deity incarnated in image form. During the processions of the temple car, which take place at the major festivals celebrated at a particular temple, the deity is taken through the streets around the temple so that all the people who catch a glimpse of the deity may be blessed. Most importantly, however, the deity is taken to visit various festival halls (*mandapams*) along the route to be worshiped by and to bestow honors upon particular groups of devotees.

I referred to those who pull the cars as devotees, and so in many cases they are, but in the traditional system of South Indian temples existing at the beginning of British East India Company rule in the eighteenth century, the pulling of the car was the traditional duty of particular outcaste groups living near the temple. They would live in separate hamlets at the edge of the town and would have to keep out of the way of Brahmins lest they pollute them with an accidental touch or even with their shadow; in any cases they were not allowed into the temple precincts. They were, however, allowed to see, from a distance, the movable image of the deity on the temple car. Indeed, some of them were not only allowed, but required, to pull that temple on wheels. We may say that the need for their muscle power was greater than the concern about the pollution they might bring. In any case their physical contact with the car was only through the medium of a long rope!

Once in the mid-nineteenth century a group of Brahmins representing the hierarchy of a temple in Tirunelveli, in the extreme south of India, came before the British magistrate with a

serious complaint. The outcastes with the traditional duty of pulling the car had become Christian, and they now refused to pull
the car, with the result that the entire festival could not take place.

It was generally British policy to respect the customs of Hindus and other religious groups, but in this case the British magistrate had a serious problem. How, he asked the Brahmins, could
he compel the outcastes to perform a vital service for a religion
to which they no longer belonged? To this the Brahmins had a
prompt and emphatic reply. It does not matter, they said, what
your personal religious convictions are, or what the personal feelings of the outcaste servants are. The duty to which they were
born, their *dharma*, is to provide physical labor to the rest of the
community, and your duty as a ruler is to force them to do their
duty. Otherwise the procession cannot proceed, and the *dharma*
of the temple will be disregarded. If the ritual order is upset in
this way the deity will be displeased and will withhold the rains.
Your duty as ruler is to ensure the prosperity of the entire people
through the timely arrival of the monsoon rains, and that maintenance of cosmic order depends on the ritual order of the temple,
including the pulling of the temple car.

The British magistrate declined to act on that complaint, but
it was not because British law in India paid no attention to Hindu
notions of law, including moral and religious duties. Indeed, the
British went to a great deal of trouble to seek out manuals of traditional law, both Hindu and Islamic, in some cases to translate
them into English and in a great many cases to adjust British law
to the Indians' own sense of what was fair and just. In this case,
however, the magistrate also felt an obligation to the outcastes,
who by becoming Christians had assumed new religious duties,
including what might be called the negative duty of *not* participating in Hindu festivals. What that magistrate was doing,
whether he realized it or not, was interpreting *dharma* as a self-
imposed obligation by morally free agents aware of and responsible for their own choices. It may well have been impossible for
any British magistrate in the nineteenth century, anywhere in the
world, to do otherwise. Yet this was a profound change from the
traditional notion of *dharma* as a differentiated duty built into
the very nature with which a particular group of beings is born
and related to a vast system of natural duties embracing all classes

of beings in the world. Failure to live according to one's own caste *dharma* would not only produce bad karma that would affect one's station in life in a future birth; it would also upset the present order of nature, leading to floods, or in South India still more frequently, to droughts.

If one wonders whether the failure of the British magistrate to enforce the traditional duties of outcastes at Hindu temples has led to such natural disasters, I can only report that the last century and a half has seen many floods and droughts, but also increasingly successful efforts to avoid famines by the wise use of water resources. This is a policy instituted by the British and greatly expanded by independent India since 1947. Nevertheless, each new natural disaster does raise some traditional voices pointing to the dire consequences of the government's withdrawal from the enforcement of traditional *dharma*. My last visit to India in 1983 came after a prolonged period of drought in much of South India. The reservoirs supplying Madras City were almost empty, and that city of more than four million could do no more, as the hottest weather of the year approached, than supply water through the pipes for less than an hour every other night, taking around truckloads of water to be doled out bucket by bucket to those without access to a tap. It was remarkable to have the avowedly secular and somewhat anti-Brahminical state government of Tamilnad issue an appeal to all religious communities to use every means of worship, sacrifice, or meditation at their disposal to bring rains. Many diverse prayers were uttered — I offered one prayer for rain myself when leading a Sunday service — and I am happy to report that rains began again, in some areas even ahead of the normal June beginning of the rainy season! That particular drought came to an end, but no one in South India can take lightly the threat that decline of *dharma* will lead to natural disaster. The British magistrates and the Indian magistrates who followed have, however, a serious problem in following traditional Hindu *dharma*, since they no longer base their rulings on a cosmic harmony of *dharma*, recognizing instead a variety of conceptions of religious, moral, and political duties — conceptions that sometimes conflict.

Behind the British magistrate's decision, however, there was something else at still greater variance with traditional Indian custom. This was the notion, continually expanded since the Magna

Carta wrested by Anglo-Norman nobles from a weak King John, of the rights of English subjects. By the beginning of the nineteenth century this was a doctrine of universal human rights, even if it was not clear in practice whether it applied to black men as well as white men, and to women as well as men. To force the outcastes to pull the temple car would violate their fundamental right to religious freedom, forcing them to act against their conscience – or so it might have seemed to the magistrate; and this right of the outcastes to withhold their service must take precedence over the principle of upholding the local customs of Her Majesty's subjects.

As in the Western world, the language of duties was rather quickly replaced by the language of rights, and this process was perhaps even speeded up by Indians themselves during the struggle for independence. Certainly the elaborate statement of "Fundamental Rights" in the Indian constitution far exceeds in detail the provisions of the American Bill of Rights. This emphasis is clear from the preamble:

> We, the People of India, having solemnly resolved to constitute India into a Sovereign Democratic Republic and to secure to all its citizens:
> Justice, social, economic, and political;
> Liberty of thought, expression, belief, faith, and worship;
> Equality of status and of opportunity; and to promote among them all
> Fraternity assuring the dignity of the individual and the unity of the Nation;
> In our Constituent Assembly this twenty-sixth day of November, 1949, do hereby Adopt, Enact, and Give to Ourselves this Constitution.

The long Part 3, "Fundamental Rights," contains the following sections: "Right to Equality," "Right to Freedom," "Right against Exploitation," "Right to Freedom of Religion," "Cultural and Educational Rights," "Right to Property," and "Right to Constitutional Remedies." It is under the second section, "Right to Freedom," that the rights equivalent to those in the American Bill of Rights are located, although with some significant provisions for restricting these rights. It is noteworthy how many other kinds of rights are explicitly recognized. The section on "Cultural and Educational Rights," for example, guarantees all linguistic groups and cultural minorities both access to all educational institutions receiving state funds and "the right to establish and administer educational institutions of their choice."

Many of the rights enumerated directly challenge the unequal privileges that are so fundamental to the traditional Hindu system of *varnadharma*, which, in practice, means the caste system. This is still further emphasized by beginning with the "Right to Equality," which includes equality before the law, equal protection of the law, nondiscrimination by the state, and equal access both to public places such as wells and roads and to private places serving the public, such as shops and restaurants. Article 17 states that "'untouchability' is abolished and its practice in any form is forbidden." One qualification of this section, moreover, stipulates that "nothing . . . shall prevent the State from making any special provision for the advancement of any socially or educationally backward classes of citizens or for the Scheduled Caste and Scheduled Tribes," those groups at the under and outer edges of traditional Hindu society. There is a provision against traffic in human beings and forced labor in the section "Right against Exploitation"; and the "Right to Freedom of Religion" is qualified to assure that the state may provide "for social welfare and reform or the throwing open of Hindu religious institutions of a public character to all classes and sections of Hindus" (25.2.b). This provision is the recognition in the constitution of the demand by Gandhi and other Hindu reformers that Hindu temples be open to all Hindus, including those groups traditionally regarded as outcaste or untouchable.

The explicit challenge to all forms of inequality in Hindu society may seem more prominent in the Indian constitution than the issue of "fundamental rights." That may indeed be the case, but the use of the language of rights is also important, not least as signaling a participation of the political leaders of modern India in this shift from the language of duties to the language of rights.

At the end of his *History of Dharmaśāstras* the late P. V. Kane makes some critical comments about the Indian constitution.

The Constitution makes a complete break with our traditional ideas. *Dharmasutras* and *Smṛtis* begin with the *dharmas* ("duties") of the people (*varṇas* and *āśramas*). Prime Minister Padit Nehru himself says in his Azad Memorial Lectures on "India today and tomorrow" (1959, p. 45), "All of us now talk of and demand rights and privileges, but the teaching of the old *dharma* was about duties and obligations. Rights follow duties discharged." Unfortunately this thought finds no place in the Constitution.

One fact of the greatest importance in the life of India is the accession of the masses to power, not only political, but also social, economic, intellectual, and moral. The Constitution engenders a feeling among common people that they have rights and no obligations whatever and that the masses have the right to impose their will and to give the force of law and justice to their own ideas and norms formed in their own cottages and tea shops.

The Constitution of India has no chapter on the duties of the people to the country or to the people as a whole.[1]

Professor Kane also notes with regret

that the directive principles of state policy mostly contain provisions on the economic system for raising people's standards of living (Articles 43, 47, etc.), i.e., it lays emphasis only on the material things for the people. It seems to be assumed that if material prosperity or benefits are assured for all, then there is nothing more to be done by the State. The present author feels that the directive principles should also have put equal or greater emphasis on moral and spiritual values and should have called upon the State to promote among the people high moral standards, self-discipline, cooperation, sense of responsibility, kindliness, high endeavor. Man is a many-sided being. The satisfaction of mere physical needs is not enough. Man has intellectual, spiritual, cultural, and social aspirations also. The socioeconomic pattern for the future must be based on the foundation of the best part of our traditions, the rule of *dharma*, the duties common to all.[2]

This comment may be taken as the overly idealistic and impractical reflection of a retired professor — Kane was then eighty-two — but before that statement Kane had pointed out that

> from 1950 there have been ten amendments [this was written in 1962] while in the U.S.A. there have been only 22 amendments during a period of about 170 years. The very first amendment was made within less than a year and a half from the day the Constitution came into force. It affected about a dozen Articles, among which there were three Articles dealing with fundamental rights, viz., 15, 19, 31. One fails to understand the meaning of the words "fundamental rights" in a constitution which took over two years of deliberations, if they could be changed within a year and a half.[3]

Thus the Indian constitution lists an impressive series of "fundamental rights," but it does not ground them in anything, whether in individual human nature, the requirements of human community, or the creative intention of God. What can be created by legislative fiat can be altered or abrogated in the same way. It has been pointed out in another critical analysis of these fundamental rights that the Indian equivalent of "due process" in American law is legislative enactment. There is therefore no explicit appeal to that which is right (*ius*) beyond the letter of the enacted law (*lex*). This is a point that Professor Kane does not make, but it is not very far away from his major concern, that the constitution does not recognize the fundamental *dharma* affirmed by the Hindu tradition and sets no spiritual obligation for the state itself or for the people.

This is a point on which scholars of the Hindu tradition, both inside and outside it, are likely to agree, even if they have difficulty in agreeing on the content of *dharma*. Yet the shift from outlining duties to listing rights has been done by lawyers, most of whom are Hindu, though it is certainly significant that one of the chief framers, Ambedkar — himself an outcaste Mahar — later formally renounced his Hindu ties and led many of his Mahar community into a mass conversion to Buddhism. This same question — how it was possible so easily and apparently unconsciously to shift from *duties* to *rights* — could be and has been asked about developments in many parts of the world, including the eighteenth-century constitutional developments in the thirteen colonies, when many Calvinists joined with deists in affirming that God created "all men" equal and "endowed them with certain inalienable rights." Our question, however, is about modern India. Are there features in traditional Indian society that could help prepare for a shift in social values from the duties of those with different social roles to universal rights for all citizens of India?

To such a speculative question there may be many answers, and perhaps none that is wholly satisfactory. One obvious approach is to ask what rights are assumed from the listing of duties in the *Dharmaśāstras*. If we include special privileges for particular groups among rights, then there are many rights included in the discussion of duties. Most notable, of course, are the special privileges of the three "twice-born" or "noble" classes (*varṇas*): Brahmins (priests and scholars), Kṣatriyans (rulers and warriors), and Vaiśyas (the Āryan commoners who became farmers and later merchants). With some exceptions there is a sharp hierarchical grading that applied not only to positive rewards but also to punishments meted out by the ruler. The Brahmin is most rewarded and most lightly punished. It is worth noting that our Western notion of rights goes back much further than the affirmation of *equal rights*. What is one's right is what is one's due, whether because of who one is by birth or because of what one has accomplished. It is one's fair share even if it is not an equal share. That notion of right is certainly deeply embedded in the Hindu social system. In the traditional village economy in which very little money changed hands, different laborers and artisans received a prescribed amount or share of the harvest. Their share or "rights" were usually unequal, but they were supposed to be appropriate. The basic right was not a matter of community decision; it was an expression of the particular nature of one's *dharma* as the producer of particular goods (for example, the potter) or the performer of particular services (for example, the washerman). The shares of the harvest had to be supplied by the farmer or landowner who garnered the harvest. But were there any rights owed equally to all in the village? Yes, for there was one person in this traditional system who owed something to all: the ruler. What the ruler owed was protection to all, not only from external enemies but also from violators of *dharma* within the village. The ruler also owed bounty, which is specifically the overflowing of the ruler's wealth, but which is closely connected to maintaining the general conditions for prosperity. This discussion brings us back to that deeply felt connection between the ruler's maintenance of *dharma* and the timely coming of the rains.

Sometimes the ruler was thought to be the owner of the land rather than simply its protector, in which case what the ruler was given, or took, from all others was "rent" rather than tax. In either case everyone had the right to expect protection and some kind of bounty. In practice the bounty went to those at opposite ends of the social scale, to the indigent at the bottom and to the poor Brahmin at the top—that is, ritually at the top but in principle totally dependent economically on the ruler's generosity.

There is, however, another kind of ruler who is a living presence in many Indian cities and towns: the chief deity enshrined in a local temple, in many cases thought to be embodied or "incarnated" in the consecrated images of that temple. It is this divine owner and ruler who should be acknowledged by all inhabitants of the town and by visitors to the temple. That acknowledgement is made by visitation: the bringing of offerings, the circumambulation of the central shrine where the deity resides, and finally a reverent beholding, often accompanied by kneeling or complete prostration. In the presence of the Sovereign of the Universe all must bow, including the human monarch; and this is not less the case when the human monarch, who is the temple's chief human benefactor, is also considered the deity's human representative. In one respect there is a human equality before God, both in the acknowledgment of a vast gulf between human and divine and in the secret knowledge of a profound kinship or an intimate relation between God and the devotee.

Human acknowledgment of God with the presentation of gifts is one side of the relationship. The other side is the divine acknowledgment of the devotee. This is what is known as "temple honors" (*maryāda*). They are distributed according to the prominence of the devotees—sometimes measured by family connections, sometimes by the size of the offering. In some cases these honors are inherited as "rights" specifying the proper share due to the ruler and other important worshippers.

The importance of these honors has been shown in recent

studies of two South Indian temples — one of the Śrī Mīnākṣi Sundaresvarar Temple in Madurai by Carol Appadurai Breckenridge, and the other of the Śrī Pārtasārati Svāmi Temple in the neighborhood of Triplicane, Madras City, by her husband, Arjun Appadurai.[4] Dr. Arjun Appadurai defines the South Indian temple as "a *sacred space* . . . an architectural entity that provides a royal abode for the deity enshrined in it, who is conceived as a paradigmatic sovereign." The temple is also a *process*, which

> has a redistributive role, which . . . consists of a continuous flow of transactions between worshippers and deity, in which resources and services are given *to* the deity and returned *by* the deity to the worshippers in the form of "shares" demarcated by certain kinds of honors.[5]

Dr. Appadurai goes on to say that the gift

> initiates a process of redistribution . . . of a part of the offerings to all those involved in the ritual process: the donor himself, the staff of the temple . . . and the worshippers.[6]

In the case of the daily and festival rites "for the sake of the universe" rather than simply for the donor's benefit, "the offering of edible food to the deity is central" and

> shares in the leavings of the deity accrue to all three categories of participants. The largest garland . . . worn by the deity during a specified ritual period and in some cases the silk vestments of the deity . . . are bestowed on the donor, who is also given a share of the leftover food of the deity (*prasātam*) and priority in drinking the water (*tīrttam*) sanctified by contact with the deity's ablutions or meals.
>   Similarly the staff/courtiers of the deity receive a part . . . of the leavings . . . of the deity. And finally, the worshippers receive a share in the sacred water and holy food left over from feeding the deity. . . .
>   These redistributed leavings of the deity are known as honors (*mariyātai*). . . . Recognized sectarian leaders and political figures are often given some prominent combination of these honors.[7]

In her study of the great temple in Madurai, Dr. Breckenridge has analyzed these honors in great detail, but she has also
shown that the opportunity to award them was multiplied and
the relations between the temple and various caste groups were
enhanced by the construction of *mandapams* ("festival halls") along
the processional route of the temple car carrying the images of
Lord Sundaresvarar (Śiva) and the Goddess Mīnāksi (Pārvatī). At
a time early in British rule when there was no longer a Hindu
monarch to endow the temple and protect it, the different castes
in the city could play that royal role, each in its own miniature
"court" called the *mandapam*. At each stop along the route offerings would be made to the Divine Couple, and those making the
offerings would be honored in a way that displayed and confirmed
their special relationship to the deity. In this way many of the
caste communities making up the city of Madurai and the surrounding district got a regular and dependable share of temple
honors. All of them had their "rights" at the same time that all
of them were sharing in the ancient duties of temple worship, the
dharma in human society that plays its part in maintaining the
regular order of the universe. Here we find human rights directly
correlated with human duties, both duties and rights concerned
with the physical and spiritual welfare of individuals, families,
caste groups, and the whole universe, and at the moving center
of this exchange process the festival images of the Divine Couple,
symbolically accompanied by the divine court.

Rights here are still honors, special privileges, even if so many
receive them, and in a hierarchical society there were and are infinite possibilities for quarreling over rank, over who should receive the honors first. Dr. Appadurai recounts a number of fairly
recent court cases involving complaints that due honor had not
been received—some from Brahmin priests, some from sectarian
leaders, and some from non-Brahmins who complained that the
Brahmins had dishonored them in the sight of God by leaving them
out of such meaningful honors as having the Śathakopan crown
(representing the Lord's feet) placed on their heads and giving them
holy water out of a different vessel from the one with which Brahmins were served, and by sitting down after they had been served
the sacramental food, even though the non-Brahmins had stood
while the Brahmins were served first. Dr. Appadurai notes that

the non-Brahmins did not challenge the Brahmins' monopoly of the "first honors" but bitterly resented the Brahmins' symbolically breaking the unity of the worshipping community by not receiving the divine gifts in the same way as the non-Brahmin members of the community.

The records of these recent court cases and much earlier ones are both funny and sad, filled with human foibles but also with the blurring, or even the blotting out, of a magnificent cosmic vision of divine-human community, with the temple at its center. There is considerable irony in the fact that the concrete edible embodiment of freely offered divine grace — for such is the Tengalai Śrīvaiṣṇava theology of the Triplicane temple — should become the measuring stick for minute distinctions in spiritual rank and the occasion for a disruption of that very community of devotees created and sustained by divine grace.

The South Indian temple has had the role historically of mediating between Brahminical insistence on ranking degrees of purity and the strong South Indian feeling that the divine King and Queen should be given a local home of such a kind that the divine presence touches everyone in the town. The doctrine of divine incarnation in a consecrated image and the practice of "seeing God" in that image is already a considerable broadening of the traditions of *yājña* and yoga, that is, of Vedic sacrifice conducted by learned Brahmins for the benefit of powerful and wealthy patrons, on the one hand, and private meditation guided by the secret instructions of the guru on the other. Taking the deity out of the temple and into the sight of every passerby on the street is still a further opening out, and the *mandapams* along the route assure that concrete physical communication with the divine source of life is possible on a regular basis for at least the leaders of the many caste groups.

This openness had its limits, however. Polluted outcastes did not meet the standards of ritual purity necessary to worship in temples with Brahmin priests, and the outcaste communities were neither financially able nor prestigious enough to construct their own *mandapam*, their meeting place with God, along the street outside the temple. They could, to be sure, see the festival image on the temple car, from afar, but even their service, the pulling of the juggernaut, was not conceived as the privilege of transporting God. The Śūdra bearers of the palenquin Dr. Appadurai describes are temple servants for whom service (*kainkarya*, "what may I do?" eagerness in serving) is a privilege. But for those outcastes in Tirunelveli, pulling the ropes was part of the menial service they and their ancestors had always been required to perform. Neither in their own eyes nor in the eyes of higher-caste Hindus did they have any "share" in the divine worship; they were given no "honors"; certainly they had no "rights." It is not surprising that in the last few centuries some of them have gone into the service of a different Lord, the deity of the foreigners, Lord Jesus.

The constitution's emphasis on ending untouchability and opening temples to all Hindus reflects the work of nineteenth-century Hindu reformers and Gandhi's leadership in the twentieth century. Gandhi did not reject the caste system, and he therefore accepted some kind of social differentiation according to inherited abilities; but he believed that purity had to be treated as a quality of the soul, not as the absence of contact with unpleasant aspects of bodily existence. That is why he insisted that all members of his ashram should clean the latrines themselves and not leave this to outcaste sweepers who thereby confirmed their own pollution and degradation. He applied the gentle pressure of non-violence to Brahmin temple priests as well as to British soldiers. He called the outcastes *Harijans*, ("offspring of Viṣṇu," that is, "children of God").

One reason for the emphasis on rights rather than duties is that recent political documents all over the world, like the eighteenth-century American Declaration of Independence and the French Declaration of the Rights of Man, are manifestos of liberation. There is therefore an insistence that rights previously denied now be recognized. In India, however, there is also the accumulated tradition of the language of the British courts, in which thousands and thousands of litigants sought preservation or restoration of inherited rights and privileges, not least the symbolic honors supposedly awarded, not by the British, but by the Sovereign of the Universe enshrined in the temple.

For Gandhi and other Hindu reformers, both priests and rulers have duties to all that can be the basis of universal rights, and all people have, in addition to their particular occupational duties, a common *dharma* of fundamental duties, of which the most important are truth telling (*satya*) and not harming living beings (*ahiṁsa*). It is no accident that Gandhi, growing up with Jain relatives and neighbors in Gujarat, should uphold the Jain emphasis on these common moral precepts, which Hindus often had previously left largely to those who have withdrawn from the moral ambiguity of life in society. Most educated modern Hindus would agree theoretically with this emphasis on the common *dharma*, not only of Hindus, but of all human beings. But the language of *dharma*, whether traditional or revised, is strangely absent from the Indian constitution.

One reason for the absence is that the chief framer of the constitution, the Minister of Law in Nehru's first cabinet in independent India, was sharply opposed to the structure of Hindu *dharma*. He came from the untouchable community of Mahars and had worked with Gandhi and Nehru in the struggle for independence. But he made a very emotional break with Gandhi because of what he considered Gandhi's very halfhearted support of the effort to get rid of untouchability. In 1935 the Mahars renounced their membership in Hindu society and gave Dr. B. R. Ambedkar the task of choosing a new religious alliance. He had talks with Muslims, Sikhs, and Christians before deciding that the Mahars should become Buddhists. The formal accession to Buddhism came twenty-one years later, in 1956, six years after the new Indian constitution came into force, and only a few months before Dr. Ambedkar's death. He deliberately chose 1956 as the 2500th year of the Buddhist era, and chose the date of October 14 on which the Emperor Ashoka had embraced Buddhism. It is no wonder, then, that universal rights of equality, the special rights of minorities, and the outlawing of untouchability should loom so large in the constitution's statement on fundamental rights.

The fact remains, however, that most educated Hindus not only accepted these fundamental rights but insisted that they expressed age-old Hindu principles. How they could come to such a conclusion is difficult to understand simply on the basis of philosophical analysis. We must instead look at the intricacies of traditional and modern society, including the rights and duties of the throng surrounding the juggernaut temple car, if we are to determine whether in the Indian constitution rights and duties have been dangerously separated or quite profoundly merged.

NOTES

1. P. V. Kane, *History of Dharmaśāstras*, 2d ed., rev. and enl. (Poona: Bhandarkar Oriental Research Institute, 1968), pp. 1664–65.

2. Ibid., p. 1669.

3. Ibid., p. 1665.

4. Professor Appadurai's study has been published: Arjun Appadurai, *Worship and Conflict under Colonial Rule: A South Indian Case* (Cambridge: At the University Press, 1981).

5. Ibid., p. 18.

6. Ibid., p. 35.

7. Ibid., pp. 35–36.

8

Personal Rights and Contemporary Buddhism

TAITETSU UNNO

THE QUESTION OF PERSONAL rights, as understood in the contemporary West, has not been of traditional concern in East Asian societies. The concept of rights, as demanding one's due, arose as part of the adversarial legacy of the West. In East Asia, on the other hand, the consensual model of society prevailed, ruling out any assertions of self against recognized forms of authority, whether secular or religious.[1] In the consensual society molded by Confucian ethics, it was the principle of *duty*, felt and carried out with sincerity, rather than *rights*, that was crucial for what it meant to be human. In fact, sincerity was at the heart of *li*, rites and rituals, that reached heaven (*t'ien*). Likewise, in periods of great Buddhist influence, it was the sense of *gratitude*, rather than *rights*, that was regarded as essential for a truly human life. Gratitude was born from a profound appreciation for all of life and nature, and it was to be expressed in various acts of compassion and thanksgiving.

The fact that the Buddhist tradition in its past history has had little to say about personal rights in the current sense of the term does not mean that Buddhists were not concerned with human well-being, with the dignity and autonomy of the spirit. In fact, throughout its long history, in spite of some dark and unsavory moments, Buddhism has taught the path whereby all forms of existence, animate and inanimate, would be able to radiate and shine in their own natural light. Contemporary Buddhism, if it is to survive in the modern world and especially if it is to establish roots in the West, must clarify what it has to offer to the concept of personal rights and its realization for all people. The first task for Buddhists, then, will be to clarify the meaning and content of the basic teaching of *anātman*, translated variously as "not-self," "non-self," and "non-ego," which forms the essence of personhood.[2]

As a basic teaching or *yana* the realization of not-self is a practical method of liberation from all kinds of delusion, especially self-delusion, which requires that one *live* not-self rather than simply debating its meaning from a purely theoretical and abstract viewpoint. Moreover, "the supreme truth to be realized [not-self] is not a product of 'my' efforts, not a conceptual entity to be visualized or concocted by my mind."[3] It is an awareness that the true self is more than what the self is normally conscious of as self, an awareness that dawns upon the self as it deepens and grows in religious practice. The core of that awareness, born from the repeated realization that "this is not mine, I am not this, this is not myself," produces the power of critical analysis leading to the insight that there is no permanent, abiding entity called the self.

I

The intellectual milieu of India during the time of the Buddha in the sixth century B.C.E. is summarized by the Buddhist logician Dharmakīrti (seventh century C.E.) in the following words:

> The unquestioned authority of the Vedas;
> the belief in a world-creator;
> the quest for purification through ritual bathings;
> the arrogant division into castes;
> the practice of mortification to atone for sin;
> — these five are the marks of the crass stupidity
>   of witless men.[4]

Countering these "five marks" of traditional religion, societal values, and accepted practices were the so-called heterodox (*śrāmana*) religions, among which the surviving ones are Buddhism and Jainism. These originated for the most part far from the center of the Indo-Āryan cultural sphere in northwest India and incorporated indigenous pre-Āryan beliefs, such as yoga, transmigration, karma, and nirvana.

Countering the class or caste system, based on color and born from the mystical depth of the creation myths, Gautama Buddha established the Saṅgha, the community of practitioners, which was a society of equals — regardless of birth or lineage or whether one was rich or poor, man or woman. His fundamental teaching was a radical negation of the ruling Brahmanic religion. The teaching of not-self (anātman) was the cornerstone of a new religion which undermined the absolute authority of Ātman-Brahman and the life characterized by the "five marks." Besides not-self there were other basic teachings which directly countered the supreme values characterizing the Brahman-Ātman unity: permanent being (sat), knowledge (cit), and bliss (ānanda). In contrast, the Buddha's teaching emphasized impermanence (anitya), rather than permanent being, as the universal human condition; radical ignorance (avidyā) as more elemental than knowledge; and suffering (duḥkha, "life does not go according to one's wish") as more fundamental than bliss.

By negating the metaphysical basis of traditional religious values and practices the Buddha affirmed instead the crucial nature of human conduct and virtus as determining what is truly human.[5] He also stressed reliance on the powers of analysis and autonomous reason and rejected revelation, authority, and tradition as sources of knowledge. In the words ascribed to Gautama Buddha:

> Just as the experts test gold by burning it, cutting it and applying it on a touchstone, my statements should be accepted only after critical examination and not out of respect for me.[6]

The new ideal of what should be regarded as desirable in a person is found in the *Dhammapada*, one of the earliest recorded sayings of the Buddha, wherein he infuses new content into the meaning of the high-born priest caste (brāhmaṇa):

> I do not call a man a *brāhmaṇa* because of his origin or of his mother. He is indeed arrogant, and he is wealthy; but the poor man who is free from all attachments, him I call indeed a *brāhmaṇa*.

> Him I call indeed a *brāhmaṇa* whose knowledge is deep, who possesses wisdom, who knows the right way and the wrong, and has attained the highest end.
>
> Him I call indeed a *brāhmaṇa* who, after leaving all bondage to men, has risen above all bondages to the gods, and is free from all and every bondage.
>
> Him I call indeed a *brāhmaṇa,* the manly, the noble, the hero, the great sage, the conqueror, the sinless, the accomplished, the awakened.[7]

The new concept of *high-born,* based on the teaching of not-self and manifested in the mode of personal conduct, meant that the low-born (*śūdra*), depending on his or her actions, could be regarded as a high-born. And similarly a high-born, by ignoble and virtuous living, could become a low-born. Various criticisms are found in Buddhist texts from this early period which reject the caste system. They may be organized into seven kinds of arguments: biological — plants and animals have many different species but humans make up one species; anthropological — the caste system began as divisions of labor and occupational distinctions and has nothing to do with race or color; sociological — the four-class system is not universal, not found among neighboring kingdoms; legal — punishment for crimes crossed class lines (not necessarily true in Hindu law as it is known today); moral — we are all subject to the karmic law; ethical — we are all equally capable of good and evil; and religious — we are all endowed with the potential for enlightenment.[8]

This transformation in traditional values, freeing people from fixed stations determined at birth and enabling them to decide their own destiny, is also evident in other changes. Terms of racial connotation, such as *Āryan,* meaning "noble," were infused with religious significance as evidenced in the doctrines of the Four *Noble* Truths and the *Noble* Eightfold Path. The concept of *middle* contained in the Middle Country, Madhyadeśa, the center of Āryan culture in northwest India, was transformed into the Middle Way, *madhyama-pratipad,* the universal path to supreme enlightenment — a path that was, at the same time, the concrete manifestation in daily life of enlightenment itself. The ultimate goal of such radical changes was to open wide the gates to religious life, such that any person could claim for himself or herself the proclamation made by the Buddha at his birth: "Heavens above, heavens below, I alone am the World-honored One." This legendary affirmation expressed the spirit of a revolutionary age when a new sense of personhood, based on the negation of *ātman*, was born, and people became truly liberated.

The community of the liberated formed the Saṅgha, composed of people from all walks of life, both men and women, who were accorded equal treatment under the aegis of the Three Gems — Buddha, Dharma, and Saṅgha. A remarkable degree of democratic practice was observed, especially in the rules and regulations set forth in the *Vinaya*, which were formulated to protect the individual rights of monks and nuns. Inheriting the liberal atmosphere of northeast India, the Saṅgha was modeled after the elected councils and the assembly forum. Hierarchy was based on the character and quality of the person. The *Vinaya* places a premium on the rights of the individual members of the Saṅgha. An example would be the treatment of someone accused of an alleged crime or a violation of precepts. Evidence had to be presented and confession of guilt made together with repentance and a vow to correct one's errors.[9]

Having established the historical context in which the teaching of not-self arose, we will explore its evolution in China as manifested in Hua-yen thought and in Japan as expressed in the Shin Buddhism of the Japanese Pure Land tradition. Before proceeding, several crucial points about this teaching should be made. While not-self is to be manifested in a mode of action, it is nevertheless deeply rooted in meditative practices whose primary aim is the radical transformation of the ego-self to the egoless self. Without this transformation (*parāvṛitti*) at the base of the mind system, focusing on the deep-rooted source of self-centeredness, not-self has yet to be fully realized and meditative absorption remains nothing more than another form of delusion. In the history of Buddhism the teaching of *śūnyatā* ("emptiness" or "voidness") evolved into the Mādhyamika philosophy in third-century India and deepened and expanded the awareness of not-self to include the negation of all fixations on substantial being, whether within the self or without in the external world. Second, not-self does not mean the loss of personality, individuality, or moral responsibility but a realization of an egoless personhood that is truly human. In accomplishing the true act of giving (*dāna-pāramitā*), for example, there is no attachment to the giver, the gift, or the receiver. This is so because each exists not in isolation but in interdependence and interconnectedness with all existence, and no one should make an exclusive claim as to giver, gift, or receiver. This interdependence, transcending the bounds of the human world and involving all sentient and insentient existence, including nature, is regarded as a more elemental relationship than anything rationally conceivable. Crucial to this interdependence is the egoless self which, properly understood, rules out any kind of self-centeredness which would destroy it. The content of interdependence will be clarified in its most developed form as articulated by the Hua-yen School. However, the immense difficulty of eliminating the deep roots of self-centeredness was realized from the very beginning of Mahāyāna Buddhism in the first century B.C.E., an awareness that led to the evolution of the Pure Land tradition. This tradition, which had always gathered a large lay following in East Asia, reached its heights in thirteenth-century Japan and opened the way for the establishment of the new schools of Japanese Buddhism — the various forms of Pure Land, of Zen Buddhism, and of the Nichiren schools. We shall focus on the Pure Land tradition and see how the problem of self-centeredness relates to the realization of not-self.

II

The teaching of not-self is not simply a matter of following the dictum "This is not mine, I am not this, this is not myself" as a guide to becoming free of the fictive self. It also has a positive aspect. The true *dharma*-nature is brought to full realization in a person, manifesting fundamental reality (*tattva*) itself. What hinders this realization is the deep-rooted self-centeredness that arises from a depth below the reach of ordinary consciousness. In the analysis of Yasuo Yuasa, a Japanese philosopher who has done extensive research into the mind-body relationship from both the Western and the Eastern perspectives, there are two levels of consciousness in meditative experience. One is a bright, disembodied, surface self-consciousness. The other is a basic structure of con-sciousness which is dark, hidden below the bright glance of sur-face consciousness, and one with the body. Conventional thinking is pursued in the surface consciousness which is light and quick, but our affective life is bound to the base structure of conscious-ness which is dark and heavy. Until the latter is dealt with prop-erly, we lack true awareness of self, we are not fully integrated, and we are not completely free.[10]

Meditative practices are directed to the base structure of con-sciousness, to what Buddhists traditionally call the "darkness of ignorance" (*avidyā*), the source of inexhaustible self-enclosure, which weaves the net of delusion into which we unknowingly throw ourselves. When the transformation called *parāvṛitti* occurs at the base structure of consciousness, then the darkness of igno-rance is illuminated, its power and energy are properly channeled, and the body becomes light and free to work in consonance with surface consciousness. Meditative practice is more than a mere subjective, psychological experience, for it involves the whole be-ing, including the base structure of consciousness, which realizes *dharma*-nature, the fundamental reality, in the transformation of ego-self to egoless self.

When the Buddha proclaims in the *Dhammapada* that "self is the lord of self, who else could be the lord? With self well-subdued, a man finds a lord as few can find," he is referring to such an egoless personhood, liberated from the bondage of subtle self-centeredness. Such also is the self to which the Buddha makes reference in his farewell sermon to his lifelong companion and disciple:

> Therefore, O Ananda, be ye lamps unto yourselves. Rely on yourselves, and do not rely on external help. Hold fast to the truth as a lamp. Seek salvation alone in the truth. Look not for assistance to any one besides yourselves.[11]

Reliance on "self as a lamp" and on "truth as a lamp" suggests that the reference is not to the conventional self but to the egoless self manifesting *dharma*, translated here as truth.

The optimum functioning of the realized self, the integra-tion of thinking and feeling, the unity of surface and base con-sciousness, is a prerequisite to realizing the goal of Buddhist life:

seeing things, including the self, as they are (*yathābhūtaṃ*), freed
from any self-centered distortions. The stopping of external stim-
uli (*śamatha*) in meditative practice is a mere preliminary to the
insight into reality (*vipaśyanā*) which is possible only when things,
including the self, are seen as they truly are — that is, from their
own centers, rather than from the perspective of the individual
or the ego-self. This radical form of seeing, beyond any subject-
object dichotomy, is true wisdom (*prajñā*), which is simultaneously
true compassion (*karuṇa*). When both are active, they bring to
life all things, including nature, as they truly are. Each reality is
then affirmed just as it is in its nonobjective mode of being.

In the history of Buddhism this standpoint of not-self (*nai-
rātmya*) was expanded to include not only the human self (*pud-
gala*) but all things (*dharma*), negating the existence of any permanent, substantial entity in the world. With the rise of Mahāyāna
Buddhism this evolved into the teaching of *śūnyatā* ("emptiness"
or "voidness"), that which makes all phenomenal things possible.
The basic meaning of emptiness is succinctly stated in the *Heart
Sutra*: "Form is none other than emptiness; emptiness is none
other than form." The negation of that which has form — persons,
things, objects — by emptiness has two connotations: first, it ne-
gates a permanent, substantial form grasped conceptually; and
second, it restores form in its essential mode of existence, manifesting emptiness.

The form thus affirmed is *dharma*, the product of dependent
coorigination (*pratītyasamutpāda*). As the reality of each mode
of existence, including not only humanity but all things in life and
nature, *dharma* is clearly real, but it is also temporary and passing. Each *dharma* at its elemental source, then, is both real and
unreal, appearing in double exposure. This is expressed in the classic Mahāyāna statement, "True emptiness is miraculous being";
and in T'ien-t'ai Buddhism reality is grasped in the "middle" mode
of being, as the unity of "emptiness" and "provisional being."
Dharma thus realized is the suchness (*tathatā*) of things, including the self, in the world and nature. On the field of emptiness,
devoid even of the re-presentation of emptiness, each existence
realizes its suchness, its *dharma*-nature. Life is then seen not from
the human standpoint but from the nonobjective mode of each
being as it is.

What this means is that each reality, *dharma*, cannot be denoted as either subject or object, nor can it be subsumed under any category of discursive thinking. Keiji Nishitani, the contemporary Japanese philosopher, denotes such a reality as an "in-itself" (*jitai*) — also called "selfness," "be-ification," "*samādhi*-being," etc. — to differentiate it from the notion of substance (*jittai* — "grasped objectively") which has been standard since the time of Aristotle in Western philosophy, and from the subject (*shutai*) which is central to the critical philosophy of Kant. Both are established on the field of dichotomous consciousness which contains within it the paradox of representation. This occurs when a thing is lifted up from the elemental mode of being and transformed into an object re-presented to the subject. A thing thus known in re-presentation is grasped conceptually and abstractly but never as it is.[12] What all this implies is that true appreciation for a person, other living things, or inanimate objects in nature means seeing each in its own nonobjective mode of being, from its own center, and not from an anthropocentric or egocentric standpoint. Such a realization in Zen is exemplified in Lin-ch'i's "True Person of No Rank."

When not-self is manifested, when each reality reveals itself in suchness, one realizes the interdependence and interconnectedness of all life, the true form of existence more real and elemental than anything conceivable by human consciousness alone. In this understanding human beings are *not* the center of the universe; each existing reality as *dharma* is the center, a center of a circle without a circumference. Such an understanding inevitably leads to the realization that what we call "rights" inheres not only in people but equally in all sentient beings, as well as in nature itself.

The understanding of the vast interdependence and interconnectedness of life and nature, based on dependent coorigination (*pratītyasamutpāda*), received its fullest theoretical formulation in the Hua-yen School. In brief, in the words of D. T. Suzuki this school teaches that "each individual reality, besides being itself, reflects in it something of the universal, and at the same time, it is itself because of other individuals."[13] As we have already pointed out, "individual reality" refers not only to human beings but to everything in existence, including nature. Religiously speaking, this is the basis for affirming the universality of Buddha-nature, found in both sentient and insentient existence. Its logical conclusion appears in the assertion of Chan-jan of the T'ien-t'ai School, who was strongly influenced by Hua-yen thought: "A single grass, a single tree, a single dust particle, each contains Buddha-nature."[14] The Shingon School develops this even further and proclaims the Buddhahood of mountains, rivers, grass, and trees.

The traditional explication of interpenetration is found in the Fourfold Realms of Reality (*dharmadhātu*) of Ch'eng-kuan (738–839), the fourth patriarch of the Hua-yen School. The first is the realm of things (*shih*), including the self. This is the realm of ordinary experience, the world of naive realism. The second is the realm of the universal principle (*li*), suggesting an underlying order according to some transcendent reality. This "principle" in Buddhism is *śūnyatā* or emptiness which is one with dependent coorigination. The third is the realm of the unhindered interrelationship between the universal principle and phenomenal things (*li-shih*). Illustrative of this is the statement discussed earlier, "Form is none other than emptiness, emptiness is none other than form." What has form and shape is the result of multiple causes and conditions, nothing in the world being static and permanent and hence empty of "own being" (*svabhāva*); but that very emptiness makes possible the origination of countless things, including self and nature. The underlying principle—emptiness and dependent coorigination—upholds the phenomenal world. Finally, the fourth is unique to Hua-yen: the realm of the unhindered interrelationship among phenomenal things (*shih-shih*). Here any notion of an absolute or universal principle has disappeared, for it is now contained in its totality in each phenomenal thing. That is, what is absolute or universal cannot be divided up into bits and pieces to be connected with multiple things; it must relate to each thing in its totality, being contained wholly within it. Thus, each phenomenal thing is both absolute, complete in itself, and relative, related to all things, making possible "interdependence." In this way emptiness and dependent coorigination constitute the structure of interdependence, such that when A is affirmed, B, C, and D are negated, only to come alive in A; simultaneously, when B is affirmed, A, C, and D are negated, but they too come alive in B. This mutual negation and affirmation, taking place endlessly and inexhaustibly, is the interdependence that is found in the fourth and ultimate realm of existence.[15]

A more technical exposition of interdependence may be seen in two basic concepts in Hua-yen: *mutual identification* and *interpenetration*. They are made possible by the fact that in dependent coorigination each phenomenal thing simultaneously manifests emptiness (without "own being," *svabhāva*) and provisional being (real and true, although passing and temporary).

According to Fa-tsang (643–712), the third patriarch of Hua-yen, mutual identification is understood as follows: When, for example, A is the focus as provisional being, B is empty of own being and is identified with A; but when B is the focus, A is empty and identified with B. Since A and B cannot both be being or empty at the same time, everything in the world is in the relationship of mutual identification. This is not the same as mere oneness or unity, since the world of distinctions and individual uniquenesses is affirmed. Each *dharmic* reality exists in mutual negation and affirmation with all other *dharmic* realities. The concept of interpenetration is based upon a similar structure. That is, when A has the power to affect B, B is devoid of power and enters A. But when B has the power to affect A, A is devoid of power and enters B. Since A and B cannot both be with power or without power at the same time, there is nothing that does not interpenetrate with the other. Here again the world of distinctions and individual uniquenesses is affirmed as the basis of dynamic interpenetration.[16]

One of the favorite metaphors used to illustrate interdependence is that of master and servant. When one thing is master — a metaphor for the absolute uniqueness of a thing — all other things become its subordinate; but simultaneously a subordinate can become the master and all other things, including the master, become its servant. Nothing is static in the world of flux and emptiness; hence, the positions of master and servant are instantaneously interchangeable. This relationship of master and servant includes not only humanity but all sentient existence, animate and inanimate, including nature. What has to be underscored is that the world of interdependence is realized only on the basis of emptiness, where self-centeredness cannot exist. Lacking this basis of emptiness, selfishness will abound, arrogance become rampant, and violence to life and nature ensue.

In the historical context this interpenetration is understood as the relationship of one and many. One and many are contradictory opposites, but they are also interdependent, the one entering the many and the many entering the one. First, the one entering the many means that a person is a historical product, being born, living, and dying in the world, including nature. Second, however, the many entering the one is also a reality; that is, the historical world and nature are affected by the creative powers of the individual. In sum, each person is molded by historical forces, but he or she is also responsible for the world and nature. Such a one is no longer one among the many, but one as the absolute subject, the negation of the many; and the many is not simply a collection of ones, but many as the common good, the negation of separate ones going their different ways. Here we find the absolute affirmation of the individual, irreplaceable and unique, but at the same time subservient to all things for the good of the many.[17]

In this way respect for the individual and the recognition of rights is not a static but a dynamic fact which makes it imperative that as we affirm our own individual rights we must also be willing to give up ourselves in order to affirm the rights of others. When, however, we affirm only our own rights at the expense of the rights of others — including the rights of humanity over nature, one nation or one race over another, one belief or view over others — we become tyrannical and oppressive. The proper understanding of interdependence, as the elemental form of relationship, would exclude such self-righteousness and would create a truly global society of equals.

The reality of interdependence is at the heart of the bodhisattva ideal that places the needs of others before one's own. Yet in essence there is no one who is placed above the other, for as found in the classical formulation, there exists absolute equality of self and other (parātmasamatā) and interchangeability of self and other (parātmaparivarta). Again, it should be noted that "self and other" is not limited to the human nexus; this understanding embraces the world of nature, including animate and inanimate existence.

The average person in traditional East Asia, of course, does not have such an intellectual understanding of interdependence, but he or she does live the life of gratitude which is its practical, everyday expression. The Japanese idiomatic expression "Okage-

sama" is a case in point. The expression is impossible to translate into English, but it may be rendered loosely as "How grateful I am." The phrase consists of the word *kage*, meaning "shade," implying protection, beneficence, kindness, assistance, and so on, with two honorifics, *o* and *sama*. It is the recognition that whatever one's present circumstances, fortunate or unfortunate, one lives by virtue of the working and sacrifices of countless others, including the blessings of nature. Whether in good times or in bad, the Japanese preface their greetings, opening remarks, and responses with "*Okage-sama*," for just to be here, to be alive, is a blessing and a gift. The sense of gratitude nurtures humility, and humility expresses a deeper appreciation for the gifts that make life possible. One is then motivated to repay society and work for the common good. Humility and gratitude are boundless.

We have discussed the teaching of not-self and the meaning of interdependence, both of which are meant to uproot the deep source of self-centeredness. But human nature is such that not everyone will undertake the discipline truly to manifest not-self or live according to the principle of interdependence founded on emptiness and dependent coorigination. In fact, history seems to be a chronicle of those who asserted their egocentric needs and exploited the powerless for their own selfish ends. Ancient people were fully aware of this human reality, as shown by the emergence of the Pure Land tradition simultaneous with the rise of Mahāyāna Buddhism in the first century B.C.E.

Historically, the Pure Land path had been an adjunct to mainstream Buddhism throughout history, and even in China the Pure Land tradition never became an independent movement. This had to await the revolutionary epoch of thirteenth-century Japan, when Honen (1133–1212) proclaimed the founding of the Jodo School. He and his disciple, Shinran (1173–1262), wrought a radical change by opening the path to enlightenment to those who had hitherto been denied access for being "evildoers"— those who had failed in meditative practices, those who had violated the precepts, those who made a living by taking life (hunters, fishermen, traders, peasants), and women from all walks of life.

The Pure Land teaching proclaimed that true compassion was directed solely to the beings of karmic evil, the infinite burden of self-enclosure without beginning and without end. But through the power of the Primal Vow of Buddha Amida, those so hope-lessly lost in the darkness of ignorance (*avidyā*) could entrust them-selves to the Primal Vow and thus be liberated. This entrusting to the Primal Vow of Other Power, itself the working of true com-passion, is the fullest manifestation of not-self: the abandonment of reliance on the powers and accomplishments of self.

Just as the crucial point about meditative practice is transfor-mation (*parāvṛitti*) from ego-self to egoless self, so also in true en-trusting there occurs a fundamental transformation (*ten*) from a being of karmic evil (ego-self) to a being of highest good (egoless self). Through the power of the Primal Vow, "karmic evil, with-out being nullified or eradicated, is made into the highest good."[18] In the words of Shinran,

> Having gained true entrusting majestic and profound
> By virtue of Amida's Unhindered Light,
> The ice of blind desire melts without fail
> To become the water of enlightenment.
>
> Evil hindrance becomes the substance of virtue
> As is the case of ice and water;
> The more the ice, the more the water;
> The more the hindrance, the more the virtue.[19]

The roots of self-centeredness in the unfathomable depths of karmic evil require the working of the Primal Vow. Neither hu-man awareness nor human effort can reach the bottomless depth; only the working of true compassion can have any effect. Such is the thought expressed by a disciple of Shinran, writing several years after the death of his teacher: "How grateful I am that Shin-ran expressed this in his own person to make us realize that we do not know the depth of karmic evil and that we do not know the height of Tathāgata's benevolence, all of which cause us to live in utter confusion."[20] Such a realization led Shinran to assert: "Even a good man attains birth in the Pure Land, how much more so the evil person."[21]

This "evil person" is the existential realization of the finite being that Shinran is, but having realized it from the very bottom of his existence, reality is manifested in him and a personhood that no one can deny or take away is attained. The self truly and really becomes itself. In his own words:

> When I ponder on the compassionate vow of Amida, established through five kalpas of profound thought, it was for myself, Shinran, alone. Because I am a being burdened so heavily with karma, I feel even more deeply grateful to the Primal Vow which is decisively made to save me.[22]

This radical affirmation of personhood echoes the proclamation of the Buddha at the beginning of Buddhist history: "Heavens above, heavens below, I alone am the World-Honored One." The manner of awakening to true personhood is also reminiscent of the salvific process described in early literature. *Magga*, in the following quotation, means "path" but also the moment of spiritual transformation from ego-self to egoless self:

> This insight [arises and] subsides, as if signalling to *magga*: "Now be born!" and *magga* too, as if not failing the given signal, follows on that flash of insight and arises, penetrating and breaking through the mass of greed and ill-will and delusion that hitherto was unpierced. . . .
> This *magga* not only breaks through the mass of greed and ill-will . . . but also dries up the ocean of ill in the round of existences . . . brings the seven noble treasures into one's presence . . . quietens all enmities and fears, leads one to the cherished sonship of the supremely perfect Buddha. . . .[23]

The working of *magga* parallels the working of the Primal Vow breaking through the darkness of ignorance, melting the ice of blind passion into the water of enlightenment.

III

When we apply some of the principles discussed above to the traditional understanding of personal rights, we gain a new meaning of and a fresh appreciation for this concept.

First, the question arises whether it is sufficient to speak of personal rights from a strictly human standpoint alone. Of course *personal* implies the human, but when *rights* are seen from a purely anthropocentric or egocentric perspective, can we ever do justice to other forms of existence, animate and inanimate? Even more problematic, however, is that such a self-centered viewpoint, which is already a distortion, blinds us to true reality, both the reality of our own self and that of the external world. In short, it is nothing more than subjectivism. If we are ever to go beyond self-delusion, we must break through our self-enclosure and affirm all things, including the self, as they are from the field of emptiness wherein each mode of existence may radiate in its own natural light. All things deserve to be affirmed not from the standpoint of the "darkness of ignorance" (*avidyā*), which is subjectivity at its worst, but from that of enlightenment, which makes possible the radical objectivity that gives life to all things, including the self.

Second, as a natural corollary of the above, shouldn't the concept of *rights* also be extended to nature? We can no longer treat nature purely objectively and continue to exploit it simply as a source of human sustenance. We are already aware of the tenuous ecological balance that threatens life on earth. Can we correct the imbalance simply with the understanding and efforts of people of good will? Or with the power of scientific know-how and technology? Is it not time to undertake a fundamental shift in our basic attitude toward nature, a shift so drastic as to appreciate nature from the standpoint of nature, rather than from the human standpoint? This does not devalue the human place in the universe; it simply puts it in the proper perspective and enhances the capacity for wisdom and compassion of human beings. In sum, only by a radical change in our relationship with nature can we reverse the acceleration toward ecological self-destruction, the ultimate denaturalization of nature, as well as the complete dehumanization of humanity.

Third, the most difficult problem in considering the nature of personal rights is the ego-centeredness that lurks in its background. Unless this is properly dealt with, it can easily lead to another form of subtle oppression. This implicit self-centeredness also appears frequently in disguised form in the name of a higher principle—whether social, political, ethical, or religious. Our life may be dedicated to some significant social cause, political ideology, or ethical and religious movement in which we are expected to curb, and even negate, our selfish concerns. Yet, too frequently in the course of events do we find self-centeredness resurfacing in some noble guise.

The most subtle forms of disguised self-centeredness appear in all world religions; we see it in sectarianism and triumphalism, classism and sexism, and the idea of the religious elite, whether individuals or nations. How can we root out this radical egocentricity, all the more difficult because it is affirmed in noble language? How can we affirm plurality, cherishing our own beliefs without negating those of others? Good will and tolerance have been inadequate as evidenced in the world today. What is necessary is a new understanding of reality, a new vision of the ideal community, based on the interdependence and interconnectedness of life, such that each reality becomes simultaneously master and servant to all others. When this is realized on an elemental level, there is no room for any form of ego or self-assertion — one claiming superiority over all others — for that goes against the true nature of reality and spells self-destruction.

Finally, having raised these questions, I feel that it is necessary for contemporary Buddhism to come forth with a clear and unequivocal statement on personal rights, incorporating some of the issues raised here. It has the necessary foundation and ample examples demonstrating respect for all life, including individual — in Buddha's own history, in the lives of the countless bodhisattvas, in the taming of people's passions, in the politics of compassion, and in countless other ways. More concretely, if we take Japanese Buddhism as an example, even a cursory review reveals the advancements in human welfare that Buddhists contributed to in various ways.

Beginning in the sixth century C.E., the teaching of not-self not only inspired great art and architecture, but its representatives transmitted knowledge of astronomy, medicine, and calendars; taught people irrigation methods, agriculture, and sericulture; built bridges, dams, and roads; dug wells; founded infirmaries, orphanages, leprosariums, and public bathhouses; cared for the elderly, beggars, and abandoned domestic animals; planted trees and built way-stations; held special ceremonies to release captured animals, fowl, and fish; and taught people to respect all life and to give proper burial rites to the dead. Whenever Buddhist influence was pronounced, it made a distinct contribution to a more civilized society. During the Heian Period (794–1185), for example, not a single case of capital punishment was recorded; and during the Tokugawa Period (1600–1868), in areas of strong Shin Buddhist faith the crime rates were lower than in any other provinces.

But in the complexity of our modern world in which the advancements in technology and communication have brought greater efficiency in denying personal rights, and in causing wanton death and destruction, what has contemporary Buddhism to offer? The answer remains to be seen; but an interesting historical phenomenon is emerging as Buddhism, with its teaching of not-self and universal compassion, nurtured in consensual society, begins to take root in the adversarial legacy of the West, which has increasingly stressed individual rights—personal, human, and civil. In the Buddhism growing in the United States, for example—much more than in the Asian forms where it is an establishment religion—we see greater concern with social issues, such as the role of women (*Kahawai: Journal of Women and Zen*), the question of poverty and hunger, the desire for peace (the Buddhist Peace Fellowship), and respect for animals (Buddhists Concerned for Animals). Although these movements are youthful and small in number, they struggle to encounter these problems from the classical Buddhist standpoints of not-self, compassion, and enlightenment.

NOTES

1. James C. Hsiung, ed., *Human Rights in East Asia: A Cultural Perspective* (New York: Paragon House, 1985), pp. 3–30.
2. For the most recent study on Buddhist "not-self," see Steven Collins, *Selfless Persons* (Cambridge: At the University Press, 1982).
3. Mahinda Paliwahadana, "A Theravada Buddhist Idea of Grace," *Christian Faith in a Religiously Plural World*, ed. Donald G. Dawe and John B. Carman (New York: Orbis Books, 1978), p. 193.
4. Padmanah S. Jaini, "*Śrāmaṇas*: The Conflict of Brahmanical Society," in *Chapters in Indian Civilization*, vol. 2, ed. Joseph Elder (Dubuque, Iowa: Kendell/Hunt, 1970), p. 41.
5. For an illuminating article on the subject see Keiji Nishitani,

"The Awakening of Self in Buddhism," in *The Buddha Eye*, ed. Frederick Franck (New York: Crossroad, 1982), pp. 22–30.

6. V. Krishnamacharya, ed., *Tattvasaṃgraha* (Baroda: Gaekwad Oriental Series, 1926), v. 3588.

7. Edwin Burtt, ed., *The Teachings of the Compassionate Buddha* (New York: New American Library, 1955), pp. 71–73.

8. K. N. Jayatilleke, *The Principles of International Law in Buddhist Doctrine* (Leiden: A. W. Sijthoff, n.d.), pp. 516–17.

9. For examples see ibid., pp. 519–33.

10. Yasuo Yuasa, *The Body: Toward a Japanese Mind-Body Theory* (Albany, N.Y.: SUNY Press, forthcoming).

11. Burtt, *Teachings of the Compassionate Buddha*, p. 49.

12. Keiji Nishitani, *Religion and Nothingness* (Berkeley, Calif.: University of California Press, 1982), pp. 113–18, 131–40.

13. D. T. Suzuki, "The Gandavyuha," in *On Indian Mahāyāna Buddhism*, ed. Edward Conze (New York: Harper & Row, 1968), p. 62.

14. Taitetsu Unno, "The Buddhata Theory of Fa-tsang," in Transactions of the International Conference of Orientalists in Japan, no. 8 (1963), p. 40.

15. Historically, the usurper empress Wu Chao in China (reign 690–705) and Emperor Shomu in Japan (reign 724–49) attempted to establish their empires based on Hua-yen ideology.

16. *Hua-yen i-ch'eng-chiao-i fen-ch'i-chang, Taisho Daizokyo* (Tokyo, 1927), 45:503b.

17. Yoshifumi Ueda, "The Status of the Individual in Mahāyāna Buddhist Philosophy," in *The Japanese Mind*, ed. Charles A. Moore (Honolulu: University of Hawaii Press, 1967), pp. 164–78.

18. Yoshifumi Ueda, ed., *Notes on "Essentials of Faith Alone,"* (Kyoto: Hongwaji International Center, 1979), p. 32.

19. Shoho Takemura, ed., *The Koso Wasan: The Hymns on the Patriarchs by Shinran*, Ryukoku Translation Series, no. 6 (Kyoto: Ryukoku University, 1974), pp. 62–66.

20. Taitetsu Unno, trans., *Tannisho: A Shin Buddhist Classic* (Honolulu: Buddhist Study Center, 1982), p. 36.

21. Ibid., p. 8.

22. Ibid., p. 35.

23. Quoted in Paliwahadana, "Theravada Buddhist Idea of Grace," pp. 190–91.

9

Social and Cultural Rights in Buddhism

ROBERT A. F. THURMAN

WE CANNOT ISOLATE THE legal/political/economic level of human rights discourse from the metaphysical level and the sociocultural level.[1] A particular culture's notion of rights is not understandable without understanding what it thinks an individual is, what a society is, in what sort of universe. And it is not evaluable without knowing their social "habits of the heart," in Bellah's nice phrase.[2] So, I begin with the Buddhist universe, and I will try to convey the essence of Buddhist habits of behavior; only then will I summarize some Buddhist teachings on human society.

It is important to acknowledge at the outset that Buddhist elements never had much success in affecting the political/legal/ economic level in the highly stratified, hierarchical, premodern Asian civilizations. The principles of human rights were all there in the Buddha's earliest teachings, and he embodied them in the constitution of his *Aryasamgha* "Holy Community" within the society. These principles often influenced the good among monarchs and other individuals to moderate or even temporarily suspend the oppressiveness of existing social practices, but they never led to any sort of institutional democracy until modern times, which only happened then with outside help. Though my scholarship focuses on the Buddhist traditions, I want to avoid the danger of romanticizing the social realities of ancient times, and I do not agree with those advocates of traditional cultures who in my opinion underestimate the unprecedented value of the modern human rights tradition. However, the Western revolutionary trumpeting of the "rights of man" is not merely the discovery of human dignity, as if no one had ever thought of it before. It can also be seen as a desperate, perhaps ultimately ineffective, band-aid that we moderns, self-styled "homo rationalis," try to plaster over the mortal wound to human dignity inflicted by modernity's metaphysical materialism, psychological reductionism, and nihilistic ethical relativism. From this point of view I can definitely sympathize with those advocates of traditional cultures who feel that modern liberal human rights pietists are missing many important things in their missionary zeal for modernity.

The Buddhist vision of reality in the *Flower Ornament Scripture*[3] is supposedly that closest to the Buddhas' own vision. In it there are innumerable, incalculable universes in infinite expanse, all filled with sentient beings, hellions, hungry ghosts, beasts, humans, titans, and the many gods in the desire, form, and formless realm heavens. The Buddhas' opening into omniscient awareness of all this somehow turns into a power of love which becomes light which then solidifies into living bodies which teach — turn the wheel of truth — in whatever way is appropriate to the beings in each realm. Thus, although the Buddhas do not themselves create these universes, they enter all of them in this transforming way, turning them into environments perfectly adapted to the cultivation of sentient beings' evolution, liberation, and enlightenment. The inconceivability is that the Buddhas simultaneously perceive both the ultimate reality of pure bliss, light, emptiness, and freedom and the historical reality of living beings caught in delusion and suffering. The Buddhas' calm and blissful knowledge is thus simultaneously limitlessly energetic interaction with these worlds through appropriate incarnations.

Thus our world is uniquely itself at any moment in history, yet the Buddha-force is omnicompetently present, engaged in our history to see that it becomes our ideal opportunity to develop and to become free. The "turning of the wheel of truth"— teaching — indicates, of course, the limits of the power of that Buddha-force. As the Buddhas are not creator-gods, are not omnipotent in a theistic sense, they cannot simply propel beings into bliss and freedom, like machines. Each being has to earn its own perfection and realize its own bliss by its own merit and its own understanding.

Within the matrix of this optimistic vision, let us turn to our critical questions. What is an individual being in the Buddhist view? Based on that, what is a society? What is a culture? Based on what these are, what are the individual's rights and responsibilities? And what are the ways of trying to secure them or achieve them?

THE BUDDHIST INDIVIDUAL

A. Selflessness and Individualism

The Buddhist "individual," as a living, relative, social, conventional being emerges as the center of the Buddha's Teaching since there is no such thing as an unchanging, ultimate, isolated, intrinsically identifiable "individual." The realization of the ultimate insubstantiality of all possible things coincides with the understanding of all relative things as conditional constructions. According to Buddhist psychology the individual who truly confronts his or her intrinsic lack of identity thereby takes full responsibility for creating his or her living individuality and manifesting it in the interactions of relativity.

Absolute individualism was rejected by the Buddha, and its absence was presented as the ground of a powerful claim of social individualism.[4] On the social level the doctrine of "selflessness" (anatmata) was a powerful critical tool that enabled many persons in those role-ridden, hierarchical ancient societies to awaken to their unique individualities beyond social, cultural, and religious stereotypes. It was also the cornerstone for the society-transforming institutional innovation of monasticism, which effectively created a free space beyond role requirements and social obligations wherein individuals might pursue their self-realization.

The source of the common misunderstanding of this crucial doctrine, and the key to its accurate understanding, lies in the distinction between the "empirical self" (vyavahārikatma) and the "absolute self" (paramarthikatma). Thus, selflessness refers only to the absence of an absolute self in the empirical self. Never and in no way does it deny the existence of empirical selves. Empirical selves change, grow, decay, perfect themselves and destroy themselves, do good and do evil. Absolute self is merely an incoherent notion, a misuse of language, that nevertheless is often used to reinforce the false idea that growth, change, and transcendence are either impossible or unnecessary. Thus empirical selves become liberated when they critically transcend habitual adherence to their hypothetical absolute selves. And that liberation is simultaneously an assumption of responsibility for their presence in relativity.

B. The Relative, Biological Individual

The Buddha taught that the causality which produced human beings is a process of evolution (karma) from a beginning-less past. This evolution is quite mechanical, just like modern biological evolution. Thus, a human being, just as in biology, is the product of an inconceivably long process of evolutionary action and represents an amazing achievement due to a process of successful adaptations.

But there is an immense difference between the Buddhist and the Darwinian evolutionary theory. The Buddhist evolution is not only a physical process. It is also linguistic and mental. Therefore a human being is not just the product of countless previous generations. We are the product of countless previous generations *of our own selfhood.* Therefore the magnificent evolutionary achievement of human embodiment is the individual human being's own personal achievement. Every person has earned his or her own humanity.

The Buddhist "inner scientists" adapted the Indian lineage concept *gotra* to capture this sense of the individual's being literally "self-created" in part.[5] They described the act of conception of a living being as involving three sets of genes: those of the mother, those of the father, and those of the person being born. This is symbolically expressed in the tantric literature by the image of conception as the union of three drops (*bindu*): the red drop of the mother mingles with the white drop of the father and then the blue drop of the child unites with them both.[6]

By the same token, according to the theory, the mental, verbal, and physical actions committed by a human being shape the spiritual gene they take with them through death into their own next individual generation. No god or nation can damn or save them, and they cannot count on an automatic anesthesia after death. They are thoroughly embedded in an endless relativity of causes and effects, and they must take responsibility first of all for their own destinies.

This biological theory of the Buddha's, while hotly disputed by both theists and atheists, provides a metaphysical base for a responsible individualism. One cannot belong totally to one's parents, tribe, nation, or even culture. One must evaluate every compulsion from family or priest or king in terms of what the actions they demand of him or her will produce by way of effects he or she alone must experience in the future. Not even a god can change those effects.

Hence if the orders of the god through the priest, or of the king through the general, conflict with my own understanding of what I should do, I am rationally serving my self-interest by obeying the evolutionary causal (karmic) law, expressed as moral injunctions, instead of the social or political regulations. The theory describes in great detail how one comes to be human, rising up from the wretched states of hells, the grotesque limbo hunger realms of the *pretas*, the vicious realms of the beasts, the realms of power, jealousy, and violence of the titans, and realms of corrupting pleasures in the lavishly manifold heavens. One's human state was slowly evolved, through transcending aggression by expressing love, transcending greed by expressing generosity, and transcending delusive stupidity by expressing intelligence and wisdom. These are called the three positive mental evolutionary paths. This whole theory is replete with dreadfully vivid depictions of actual results of actions in experiential states which, if contemplated by the imaginative, generate a healthy terror that energizes compliance with these evolutionary laws.[7] This terror and this ambition become the motivating drives for enlightenment, which itself is actually the tenth positive path, that of cultivating intelligence or wisdom to the transcendent degree. And one finds that the Buddha's *dharma* teaches that the supreme value of the human life lies in its closeness to enlightenment; hence its supreme use is in the quest of enlightenment. Evolution can be negative as well as positive, descent as well as ascent, so human life can be wasted by living for the aims of this life only, as one can throw away a diamond. The terror of experiencing another hellish devolution thus becomes a powerful motive for self-transcendence.

In sum, the individual human who possesses rights is presented as a spiritual as well as physical being of unique accomplishments and valuable opportunities. We have earned our rights through suffering and transcending egotism in the sea of evolution, and no one can deprive us of them, since no one conferred them upon us. Societies cease to be truly human when they cease to acknowledge that each individual's fulfillment is the purpose of the whole. And humans are free also to give away their rights in furtherance of the fulfillment of others. Indeed it is by the supreme generosity of giving even one's life that one evolved into a human out of lower forms. Thus talk of rights quickly passes over into talk of responsibilities, as the self-fulfilled (that is, enlightened as to selflessness) individual automatically wills to share that happiness of release with others by aiding them in their own quest of enlightenment. Morality becomes a matter of evolutionary causality, reason and enlightened will having come into harmony, and there is no longer need of unreasoned obedience or rational expedience.

THE BUDDHIST SOCIETY

The Buddha was clearly rejecting his own society when he renounced his family and throne and departed to attain enlightenment. The society that places its collective interest ahead of the interests of its individuals is considered not helpful to human beings in achieving their real purposes. But the Buddha, after enlightenment, returned to his society and instituted key changes that made it truly beneficial to its members, making it recognize their individual interests as its paramount concern. Therefore, there are societies that are worthwhile from a Buddhist perspective.

The major change here was the Buddha's introduction of the institution of monasticism, the transcendentalist, educational institution *par excellence*. Monasticism institutionalizes the development of individuals toward freedom and enlightenment. Production or service for the good of society on whatever level is secondary. The jewel of a Buddhist society's institutions therefore is one which serves no utilitarian purpose for the collective as a whole.[8] Thus, in theory, a society wherein all lay men and women were ordained in the Buddhist precepts would itself become an

instance of the Community Jewel, an object of worship of humans
and gods. Such has never been the case throughout the history of
Buddhism in Asia, however. So the Buddhist community and the
larger society were always in tension, sometimes creative and balanced, sometimes out of balance and destructive.

In considering the problem of culture in Asia there is a similar dualism from the Buddhist perspective. From the most general
point of view human culture is an essential attribute of humanity,
a great karmic evolutionary good which sentient beings gain along
with their human embodiment. Combining ideologies, languages,
habitual forms of perception and behavior, culture allows individual humans to interact much more intimately and widely than
other animals. Language is especially valued, in that it enables
communication and sharing of understanding over space and
through generations in time.

In a sense, Sanskrit *dharma* can be translated "culture," as
it can mean "that which holds" ideas or actions in meaningful
patterns. The pre-Buddhist meaning of *dharma* was along those
lines, conveyed as "pattern of being—phenomenon," "thing," "law,"
"tradition," "duty," "custom," "principle," "religion," and so forth.
Actually, Buddha was radical in his rebellion against the *dharma*
of his day, the *dharma* of his race, class, ritual duties, ideologies.
Therefore, a "culture" that holds humans in patterns of ignorance,
conflict, harmful behavior, is rejected from the Buddhist perspective. However, after his enlightenment, the Buddha redefined
dharma as "teaching," "truth," even "nirvana," the reality that makes
freedom and enlightenment possible, that "holds" one safe from
suffering. Under this definition, a "culture" that encourages humans to transcend egotism, greed, and harmfulness, and achieve
insight and liberation, is itself a primary technique of the Buddha
work. Again, in actual Buddhist history, no Asian culture ever became a fully "Buddhist culture." Of all of them, Tibet perhaps
came closest, but even it failed, so far—though it was a very instructive failure.

The *Theravada Discipline (Vinaya)* of the monastic orders
contains the blueprint of this new transcultural culture. It contains hundreds of rules, moral as well as social, practical rules about
economic interactions and rules of etiquette. These rules are designed to restrain by deconditioning negative habits of behavior

and speech, and to encourage transcendence-oriented behavior and speech. Important here were the democratic authority and decision-making structures the Buddha designed, based on his admiration for the republican governing customs of the Shakyas, Vajjians, Licchavis, and other preimperial Indian peoples. As in philosophy, so in legislation for the community, the Buddha elevated reason over authority and individual freedom over hierarchy. In a culture where this institution thrives, the lay society's behavior is automatically affected by the presence of such orders of systematic self-transcenders in its midst. This is where the "habits of the heart," as well as habits of body and tongue, are cultivated.

As for habits of mind, the monastic institution from the beginning focused on intellectual education as well as meditation. The study and recitation of the *Sutras* were major activities of the monks and nuns, which spilled out into the larger society. The monasteries became the first schools open to students from all castes and both sexes. Finally, the intellectual cultivation of *prajñā* ("genius" or "wisdom" or "insight") through systematic education in the *Abhidharma* sciences became central to the monasteries' function.

The Buddha's enlightenment awakened him to the discrepancy between his metaphysical view of the individual and the social capacity of human beings on the one hand, and the ideological confusions and political habits of his contemporaries on the other. Correspondingly, his teachings aimed not only to help the individual transform him- or herself but also were concerned with the methods of the transformation of societies of such individuals. He led a nonviolent revolution by founding his "Holy Community" (*Aryasamgha*) as a distinct social world within the larger society. And he planted other seeds of social evolution through his direct instructions to the laity, inciting trends in ideology, religion, literature, art, and, most importantly, personal "habits of the heart."

ELEMENTS OF A BUDDHIST SOCIAL PHILOSOPHY

Buddhists never challenged the institution of kingship. Aryasanga, in the *Stages of the Bodhisattva*,[9] sanctions revolution against a miserly and oppressive king, stating as an exception to the precept of "not taking the not given" (not stealing) that a bodhisattva must revolt against such a king, deprive him of his hoarded treasury, and share it back out among the people. Yet even here, Aryasanga seems to assume that eventually a just and generous king will take over rule. That the system itself is wrong, as our American founders insisted, never occurs in Buddhist literature, even though the monastic community is structured democratically and the Buddha himself conspicuously praised the parliamentary decision making of the Vajjians.

Having accepted the inevitability of kings and emperors, Buddhists did not stint in giving them advice. The Buddha himself gave advice to Bimbisara, Prasenajit, his father Suddhodhana, Ajatasatru, and other kings of his era. The stone-carved edicts of Emperor Ashoka (third century B.C.E.) reflect extensive advice under the headings of five principles of Buddhist politics: (1) individualistic transcendentalism, (2) nonviolent pacifism, (3) religious pluralism with an educational emphasis, (4) compassionate welfare paternalism, and (5) reliance on a powerful central authority to affirm the rights of individuals over claims of intermediate groups.[10]

The next important source of royal advice is the sage Nāgārjuna, whose *Friendly Epistle* and *Jewel Rosary of Royal Advice*, written to the Satavahana King Udayi (second century C.E.) contain far-reaching prescriptions for running the kingdom according to Buddhist principles.[11]

The fact that the majority of the *Garland* is devoted to transcendent selflessness, the door of the liberation and enlightenment of the individual, is clear evidence that the heart of Buddhist social activism is individualistic transcendentalism. The attainment of nirvana is everyone's ultimate good, and the good of each single person is always more important that any good of any putative whole or collective. Thus, the Individual Vehicle, the Buddha's "original" teaching, remains indispensable, the essence of the Universal Vehicle as well.

The second major strand in Nāgārjuna's *Counsels* is that of self-restraint, which he analyzes as detachment and pacifism. The king will not be able to act selflessly without a basis of intuitive wisdom which understands the critique of the "I" and the "objective self," realizing their ultimate nonexistence and conventional relativity. Likewise, he will not be able to resist the temptations of consumption, food, possessions, sex, if he does not understand the reality of the objects of his passions. Therefore Nāgārjuna dwells extensively on the timeworn and effective meditation on "unloveliness" (asubhatva) to help the king free himself from passion. The themes collected under this principle of pacifism — namely, revulsion from lusts, restraint of aggressions, vanity of possessions and power — may seem to lead to a drab puritanism, but here is where Buddhist social action shows its realism, its hard-nosed acceptance of the facts of life, grounding the heroism of transcendent virtue in the effective calmness of a deglamorized awareness.

Next Nāgārjuna turns to the third principle of Buddhist social activism, that of transformative universalism. This is expressed specifically in the complete commitment to a pluralistic, enlightenment-oriented educational effort, considered the major business of the whole nation. The Buddha image is not, as Westerners have assumed, merely an object of devotion. Its main function is inspirational. The Buddha is the image of each individual's own perfection. Once the image of perfection is everywhere to act as inspiration, there are the actual teachings themselves (dharma), the teachings individuals may use to develop and liberate themselves. Finally, to put these teachings into practice, teachers are required, who must also be exemplary practitioners, both of which functions were fulfilled by the monastic communities (Samgha).

The fourth principle of Buddhist activism, compassionate socialism, concerns the economic and legal administration of society. Here Nāgārjuna describes a welfare state, millennia ahead of its time, a rule of compassionate socialism based on a psychology of abundance, achieved by generosity. "To dispel the sufferings of children, the elderly, and the sick, please fix farm revenues for doctors and barbers throughout the land" (Nāgārjuna, Friendly Epistle and Jewel Rosary of Royal Advice, v. 240). This is a concise description of a socially supported universal health care delivery system. "Please have a kind intelligence and set up hostels, parks, canals, irrigation ponds, rest houses, wells, beds, food, grass, and firewood" (Nāgārjuna, Friendly Epistle and Jewel Rosary of Royal Advice, v. 241). A policy of total care of all citizens is plainly recommended, including care for travelers, even strangers passing through, and special shelters for beggars, cripples, and wandering ascetics. He

even recommends that a special custodian be appointed to provide food, water, sugar, and piles of grain to all anthills, caring
also for dogs and birds, showing that his ecological concern is wider
than just for human society.

These general counsels to the king just give him the broad
outlines of an individualistic, transcendentalist, pacifist, univer-
salist, socialist society. The emphasis throughout is on the king's
own self-cultivation. We have very little physical evidence as to
how successful King Udayi was in enacting these counsels, although
the picture of the Southern kingdoms that emerges from sources
like the *Gandavyuha* section of the *Flower Ornament*, the non-
Sanskrit literatures of South India, the art of Ajanta and Amara-
vati, the accounts of the Chinese pilgrims, and the Tibetan histories is certainly idyllic. They depict a civilization of wealthy
cities, luxurious courts of great sensuous refinement, widespread
scholarship and intense asceticism, prosperous farmers and peasants, relatively long-lasting peace and political stability. This picture represents a considerable advance over the India of the
Mauryas, reflected in Megasthenes' accounts or in the *Arthaśāstra*.

A third source of Buddhist social thought is a Mahāyāna Scripture called *The Teaching of the Manifestations of Liberative Strategies in the Repertoire of the Bodhisattvas*, a Scripture dating from
around the time of Nāgārjuna.[12] This Scripture survives only in
Tibetan and Chinese translations.[13] It develops a fairly thorough
picture of good government in the teachings of the sage Satyavadi.
Satyavadi's discourse on society begins with a critique of any ex-
cessively unequal distribution of wealth as the source of much strife
and suffering. Interestingly, the state's right to intervene in the realm
of private affairs to forestall bankruptcy or mismanagement is out-
lined. Most surprising is Satyavadi's discussion of the proper method
of conducting a war, most unusual in the Buddhist literature. War
should only be for self-defence. There are three stages: before, during, and after. In the first, all diplomatic efforts must be made
to avoid bloodshed, through compromises, compensations, even
threats and demonstrations. If all fails, then preparations should
be made as for an act of self-sacrifice. One should not wage war
if the outcome seems hopeless, and one should plan so as to mini-
mize loss of lives on both sides. In the third stage one seeks a swift

resolution, with minimal destruction, and one does not seek to punish the enemy vindictively after victory.

Another Scripture, the *Universal Vehicle Scripture of Kshitigarbha Bodhisattva, the Ten Wheels of Government*,[14] describes a whole society from the Buddhist point of view. In this Scripture, which some scholars think of as much later in date, the Buddha himself speaks, beginning with the statement that the state is essential to the welfare of individuals, as without it there is chaos. This fits with the well-known myth of origin given in the *Aggannya Sutta*, already so aptly elucidated by Tambiah,[15] where the first king is elected (he is called *Mahasammata*, the "Great Elected One") by popular demand to protect the citizens from one another, from a war of all against all.

CONCLUSION

I have argued that human rights in theory and reality must be investigated in the metaphysical and social realms, as well as in the political. I have sketched the Buddhist vision of reality and the concomitant institutional strategy of addressing the social "habits of the heart." I have acknowledged the failure of either the Buddhist theory or the Buddhist practices of individual and social transformation to transform the political reality of any Asian society in a structural way. And finally I have sketched the social philosophy of the Buddhists, used as principles of counseling rulers in order to make the best of the autocratic systems of government accepted as inevitable. Finally I want to refer to the one nation where Buddhist principles seemed to dominate the ideology, society, and politics up until the modern period, namely, the presently "lost" nation of Tibet.

I have written previously about what I called the "interior modernity" of Tibet.[16] I consider that achievement to have resulted from the application of three out of four of the Buddhist principles for organizing a society. Only the universalism became stunted, due to Tibet's isolation and consequent internal ossification. However, some elements of what Tibet achieved still recommend its case to our attention, since our "exterior modernity" stands in grave need of balance from an interiority that we could employ without having to succumb wholesale to some kind of traditionalist atavistic worldview.

During the seventh century Tibet emerged as a powerful nation, feared by the T'ang emperors, Bengali and Nepali kings, and other Inner Asian princes. Tibet was the only nation with which the Caliph Harun al-Rashid ever made peace on equal terms, when he was unable to defeat the Tibetan armies in Khotan along the silk route. In the seventh century Songzen Gampo introduced Buddhism over the strenuous objections of his feudal vassals, and it took his dynasty almost two hundred years to build the first monastery. The *dharma* of nonviolence, renunciation, love, and wisdom does not sit well right away with bloodthirsty, tribal warriors. And a nation's support of a monastery, a nonutilitarian sacred space for the individual, is the threshold of its entry into the sphere of Buddhism as a way to enlightenment.

In the tenth through the fourteenth centuries Tibet was slowly monasticized, as the nation's warrior energies turned more and more inward to the conquest of ignorance, lust, and hate. The power of the feudal nobles still remained great, however, and the fortunes of the monastic orders teetered in a precarious balance during conflict with various dynasties and foreign powers, especially the as-yet-untamed Mongols.[17]

Then in the fifteenth through the seventeenth centuries something remarkable happened that did not happen anywhere else on the planet. The monastic, spiritually centered institutions became the secular power. They gradually assumed responsibility for government, took over management of resources, and developed a skillful bureaucracy. During these same centuries in northern Europe, the merchant classes backed secular kings to suppress the feudal nobles; the Protestant ideology destroyed the role of the monasteries by making "interior industry" irrelevant to a predetermined salvation by faith alone and hence irrational; and the unification of the sacred/secular duality was accomplished by the collapse of the sacred into the secular. Max Weber has analyzed this process of "exterior" modernization in *The Protestant Ethic and the Spirit of Capitalism* (1905). In Tibet the monastic orders employed Messianic and Apocalyptic Buddhist ideas to produce a Sacred King to control the feudal nobles, depriving them of much of their land and of all feudal claims over their serfs. The new monastic government absorbed their power into a bureaucratic state under which serfs became "commoners" (*mi ser*), that is, free agents with only economic obligations to other individuals and taxpaying obligations to the state. The monasteries became the seats of the national industry, the inner perfection of minds and souls through education and contemplation. And the Apocalyptic Buddhist ideology encouraged a sense of millennial immediacy of ultimate spiritual fruition that led to the sacred/secular nonduality being focused on the sacred, the exact reverse of the Western secularistic "nonduality." Although rough and tough individuals still roamed free, especially in the east of Tibet, the national policy was nonviolence. There was no army and few police. There was total access to learning and wide social mobility through the universal monastic education system. The central government protected the lower classes from the greatly weakened nobility, whose landholding was now dependent on their service to the government; and there was a new avenue of ennoblement through having the merit or good fortune to receive a reincarnate saint in the family by birth. Above all, the whole nation lived for the enlightenment of each individual, within a multilife time frame, with a messianic and apocalyptic sense of the immanence of the divine benefactors of the world. It is impossible to describe in more detail here this unheard-of emergence of a more-than-half Buddhicized culture.[18] As a Buddhist effort in furthering human social and cultural rights it is an example of what one long-term Buddhist experiment actually did produce.

   I want to see more thinking and discussion about Tibet's unique "interior modernity," its "conquest" of the realms of the individual mind through a refined technology of spiritual education, and its "industrial revolution" of producing powerful and beautiful enlightened human beings. I mean to open a path of insight toward this social possibility, to bring us to conceive of something as important, useful, essential to us as an alternative modernity: a way of becoming modern which is equal and yet opposite to the one Europe chose; a way of modernity that may complement our own in such a way as to help us stay modern and also stay alive, enjoying the comforts of environmental technology while recovering inner spiritual values.

NOTES

1. In my essay "Human Rights and Responsibilities in the Buddhist Civilizations," in *Human Rights and the World Religions*, ed. I. Bloom (New York: Columbia University Press, forthcoming), I developed a scheme of the interconnectedness of worldview, political rights, and social habits. As a precursor to the present effort, that essay was my first formulation of many of the arguments addressed here from a new angle.

2. Robert N. Bellah et al., *Habits of the Heart: Individualism and Commitment in American Life* (Berkeley, Calif.: University of California Press, 1985).

3. *The Flower Ornament Scripture*, trans. Thomas Cleary (Boston: Shambhala, 1984), pp. 55–56.

4. See my essay, "Buddhist Ethics: Whose Essence Is Emptiness and Compassion?" *Religious Traditions*, November 1981.

5. We translate *gotra* in the Mahāyāna context as "spiritual gene."

6. For a vivid description of these biological notions, see Lati Rinbochay and Jeffrey Hopkins, trans., *Death, Intermediate State, and Rebirth in Tibetan Buddhism* (London: Rider, 1979).

7. For example, the malicious liar eventually ends up in a hell for liars, in which he or she is born as a small bulbous globe of consciousness attached to a giant tongue of great sensitivity, spread over many acres of burning iron ground, with little horned devils merrily running red-hot iron plows back and forth through its nerves from dawn to dusk of a multimillion-year day. Or on a less fantastic note, one who kills other beings, especially human beings, will be killed one time in a future life in a similar way, one for each being one kills.

8. Actually the "Community Jewel" (*Samgharatna*) includes ordained lay men and women with monks and nuns, so it is a little larger than just the monastic orders themselves.

9. Aryasanga, *The Stages of the Bodhisattva*, trans. Jampel Thardod et al. (American Institute of Buddhist Studies, manuscript translation), chap. 10, pp. 84ff.

10. See Robert A. F. Thurman, "The Politics of Enlightenment," *Lindisfarne Letter* (1975).

11. See Robert A. F. Thurman, "Buddhist Social Activism," *Eastern Buddhist* (1983).

12. The date is controversial. My colleague, the Ven. Losang Jamspal, is doing a study of this text, and he claims that by evidence of its mode of reference to the Buddha Bodies it should be dated close to the *Lotus Scripture*.

13. My account comes from the Tibetan version, Kanjur, Ladakh Tog Palace edition, *mdo sna tsogs*, la 77:2–166; reprinted Delhi, 1980. I am also indebted to the Ven. Samdong Rinpoche, for his article "Social and Political Strata in Buddhist Thought," in Samdong Rinpoche, *Social Philosophy of Buddhism* (Sarnath, 1972).

14. Also mentioned in Rinpoche, "Social and Political Strata in Buddhist Thought."

15. S. J. Tambiah, *World Conqueror and World Renouncer* (Cambridge: At the University Press, 1976).

16. Robert A. F. Thurman, "Tibet: Mystic Nation in Exile," *Parabola, Exile* (1985).

17. This was the period of the "feudal, medieval Tibetan society" so many think still existed until recently, due to the combination of Tibet's lack of "exterior modernity," Chinese propaganda, ignorance, and a lack of even a concept for a form of personality and society that existed nowhere else, a form we call "interior modernity."

18. The best recent source on the innovative government formed by the Dalai Lamas is Franz Michael, *Rule by Incarnation: Tibetan Buddhism and Its Role in Society and State* (Boulder: Westview, 1982).

PART IV

Confucianism

10
Why Take Rights Seriously?
A Confucian Critique

HENRY ROSEMONT, JR.

It is a bedrock presupposition of our moral, social, and political thinking that human beings have rights, solely by virtue of being human. Which rights are basic, how conflicting rights claims are to be adjudicated, whether rights should be the foundation of moral and/or political theory are, among others, issues in dispute. But with a very few notable exceptions, the concept of human beings as rights-bearers is not itself in serious question in contemporary Western moral, social, and political philosophy.

Every one of us, however, has a definite sex, a color, an age, an ethnic background, certain abilities; and we all live in a specific time and a specific place. From these facts some disturbing considerations follow. The first is that if rights are borne by human beings regardless of these differentiations, then those rights must obtain for human beings altogether independently of their culture. But then it becomes extremely difficult to imagine actual bearers of rights, because there are no culturally independent human beings.[1] And if our culture has no concept of rights, or has concepts incompatible with that concept, then how could we imagine what it would be like to have rights, or that it would be right and good and proper for us to so imagine?

A second disturbing consideration is related to the first. Our concept of human rights is closely related to our view of human beings as freely choosing autonomous individuals, a view which is at least as old as Descartes and which is reaffirmed in the 1948 United Nations Declaration of Human Rights.[2] But this concept is overwhelmingly drawn from the culture of the Western industrial democracies and is concerned to propose a particular moral and political perspective, an ideal, appropriate to that culture.

At least 75 percent of the world's peoples, however, have no intimate acquaintance with the culture of the Western industrial democracies. Thus we seem forced to embrace a form of relativism.[3] On the one hand, we might wish simply to cease believing that our philosophical efforts can find a purchase beyond our Western cultural heritage. On the other hand, we can simply insist that all human beings do have rights even if they are not recognized in other cultures.

The first extreme has the aura of tolerance about it but leaves us nothing to say ethically about the activities of such people as the Marquis de Sade, Aztec ritual cannibals, or Nazi storm troopers. Pessimism, cynicism, and nihilism are all predictable outgrowths of this position. The other extreme has the virtue of arguing for a moral ground from which culturally and historically independent judgments might be rendered but invites chauvinism, imperialism, and, increasingly, irrelevance for the two billion people who do not share our culture.

I wish to suggest that it may be possible to work out a conceptual framework—what I will call a *concept cluster*—within which both ethical statements and an ethical theory can be articulated which can be applicable to, and appreciated by, all of the world's peoples. Before such a concept cluster can be worked out by philosophers, however, the Western philosophical tradition will have to incorporate more non-Western philosophy than it has in the past.

If my alternative is to be made at all attractive, I shall have to talk more about rights within the context of our culture, and then partially decontextualize—*not* deconstruct—those concepts and simultaneously recontextualize them by contrasting them with another cluster, in this case, that of the early Confucian philosophies.

Many people today are subject to a host of physical and psychological indignities: incarcerated and tortured because of their color, their nationality, their political beliefs, or their religious and social convictions. We are angry at these circumstances and events, indignant that they continue to take place, and frustrated that we are personally able to do so little to bring an end to such heinous practices.

Consider, now, the accounts we would typically give to describe and explain our feelings and beliefs about these practices. They are unjust, we say; no one should be imprisoned, tortured, or held hostage because of their color, nationality, or political or religious beliefs, because all human beings have basic *rights* which are clearly being violated in these instances. They have lost the self-governing autonomy which makes them uniquely human.

Such an account is sufficiently straightforward that virtually every reflective citizen of the English-speaking countries would accede to it. It is the same perspective incorporated in the United Nations Declaration. I want to suggest, however, that the concept of the individual as a self-governing, autonomous self, which underlies this account, may not be the most appropriate way to characterize human beings. Nor is it the account the vast majority of the human race would give.

Moreover, within the Western industrial democracies, especially in America, the concept of rights is central to national moral issues. The abortion controversy, for example, asks whether fetuses have rights, and if so, whether those rights take precedence over the rights of women to control their own bodies.[4] Problems of suicide and the treatment of terminally ill patients are commonly analyzed by asking when, if ever, the rights of the individual to decide matters affecting his or her own life and death may be overridden by doctors or others.[5]

Ecologists also commonly defend their positions by appealing to the rights of our descendants to inherit a maximally healthy and genetically diversified natural world.[6] Further, a number of philosophers are asking whether or not animals may be seen to have rights solely in virtue of their being living things, and they would place sharp constraints on our right to manipulate them and the natural environments in which they live.[7] Finally, a number of domestic political issues — such as welfare, tax reform, capital punishment, and affirmative action — reduce to a fundamental moral tension between individual rights and social justice.[8]

In short, ours is largely a rights-based morality. To be sure, once we move from the general public arena to the narrower domain of ethical philosophy there is much less uniformity. Here we might speak of goal-based and duty-based moralities as well. Thinkers working in the Kantian tradition, for example, accord rights a more basic place in their theories than do the adherents of any of the several forms of utilitarianism; and a few philosophers, such as MacIntyre, are turning away from contemporary moral theories altogether, arguing instead for the reintroduction of a virtue-based moral philosophy inspired by an updated Aristotle.[9]

But MacIntyre's work remains on the periphery of current ethical debate; and however differently Lockeans, Kantians, Benthamites, and others wish to ground their moral principles, the concept of rights is crucial to all of their views.

Most foundational is Robert Nozick, who opens his *Anarchy, State, and Utopia* with the statement that

> individuals have rights, and there are things no person or group may do to them (without violating their rights).[10]

In his influential book *A Theory of Justice* John Rawls formulates his First Principle as follows:

> Each person is to have an equal right to the most extensive total system of equal basic liberties compatible with a similar system of liberty for all.[11]

And on behalf of the modern British tradition, the following passage from R. M. Hare's recent *Moral Thinking* is fairly typical:

> It should be clear by now how lacking in substance is the common objection to utilitarianism, which might be advanced against my own theory of moral reasoning too, though it can give no place to rights, and can ride rough-shod over them in the interests of utility. . . . If we take [rights] seriously enough to inquire what they are and what their status is, we shall discover that they are, indeed, an immensely important element in our moral thinking . . . but that this provides no argument at all against utilitarians. For utilitarianism is better able to secure this status than are intuitionist theories.[12]

From these illustrations it is clear that the concept of rights thoroughly permeates contemporary Western moral and political thinking. And just because it permeates our thinking, we should not be surprised that the term *rights* is seldom fully defined by those who employ the term most frequently.

The best example of this is the well-known, tightly argued work *Taking Rights Seriously,* in which Ronald Dworkin reflects this point.

> Principles are propositions that describe rights; policies are propositions that describe goals. But what are rights and goals and what is the difference? It is hard to supply any definition that does not beg the question. It seems natural to say, for example, that freedom of speech is a right, not a goal, because citizens are entitled to that freedom as a matter of political morality, and that increased munitions manufacture is a goal, not a right, because it contributes to collective welfare, but no particular manufacturer is entitled to a government contract. This does not improve our understanding, however, because the concept of entitlement uses rather than explains the concept of a right.[13]

In a not unrelated way Patricia Werhane, in attempting to ground her views on moral rights, begins with:

> I shall assume that all human beings, and in particular rational adults, have inherent value. Because human beings have inherent value they have certain rights. These rights are moral rights. . . . [14]

Werhane's statement illustrates the question-begging problem mentioned by Dworkin, for one could certainly hold that human beings have inherent value without having the concept of rights at all.

If a definition of rights is not ready to hand, how are rights distinguished? The right to life is taken to be a passive right — because it requires recognition by others — while the right of freedom is an active right because one must do something in order to exercise it. Rights are also distinguished as positive and negative, for example, the right to security as opposed to the right not to be tortured. The most common division is between *prima facie* and absolute rights, or, as they are also described, defeasible and indefeasible rights. There is little agreement among philosophers about which rights are absolute, if indeed there are any, but the following have been defended as the most basic rights of all:

H. L. A. Hart[15] and others have argued for the primacy of the right to freedom; Henry Shue,[16] for the primacy of the right to security and subsistence. Many philosophers consider the right to life as the most basic,[17] but Dworkin argues that the right to equal consideration (*not* equal treatment) underlies all of the others.[18]

The differing positions in contemporary Western moral philosophies are distinct from early Confucianism in that it is not a moral philosophy at all. To show why this is so, and why it is important, and at the same time to avoid moral relativism, let us consider one of the sets of arguments commonly given on behalf of moral relativism based on examinations of other cultures. These are the arguments from anthropological evidence.[19]

All languages have terms for the approval and disapproval of human conduct, and terms for concepts employed in the evaluation of that conduct; but many of the world's languages have no words for a set of actions ostensibly circumscribed by the pair *moral/immoral* as against the nonmoral. Yet the *moral*, like rights, is a foundational concept in Western philosophical thinking and, like rights, is almost never given a clear definition.

The simplicity of this linguistic fact should not obscure its philosophical significance. Speakers of languages having no term corresponding to *moral* cannot logically have any *moral* principles or theories. It follows that they cannot have any moral principles incompatible with other moral principles, our own or anyone else's.

Put another way *we* might disapprove of an action which members of another culture approve. But if our disapproval rests on criteria essentially involving the concept cluster of contemporary rights-based morality, a concept cluster absent in their culture; and if their approval rests on criteria involving a concept cluster absent in our culture; then it is simply a question-begging, logical mistake to say that the members of the two cultures are in basic *moral* disagreement. The term is ours, defined contextually, not theirs. The ethnographic argument for moral relativism gains force only if it can be shown that two different people evaluated human conduct in the same way — invoking similar criteria grounded and exhibited in the same or very similar concept clusters — and that one approved the action and the other disapproved.

But why not simply find the closest approximation to the English *moral* in the culture under investigation, and proceed with the analysis from there? This is exactly what most anthropologists, and not a few philosophers and linguists, have done. But now consider specifically the classical Chinese language in which the early Confucians wrote their philosophical views. That language not only contains no lexical item for *moral*; it also has no terms, for example, corresponding to *freedom, liberty, autonomy, individual, utility, principles, rationality, rational agent, action, objective, subjective, choice, dilemma, duty*, or *rights*; and, probably most eerie of all for a moralist, classical Chinese has no lexical item corresponding to *ought* — prudential or obligatory.

No, it is not only a term corresponding to *moral* that must be sought in other languages if we are to speak cross-culturally about morals, for the sphere of contemporary Western moral philosophy is designated only roughly by the single term itself. A clear delimitation requires the full concept cluster of terms just adumbrated, plus a few others. Now if contemporary Western moral philosophers cannot talk about moral issues without using these terms, and if none of the terms occurs in classical Chinese, it follows that the early Confucians could not be moral philosophers in our sense. We will consequently be guaranteed to miss what they might have to tell us about human conduct, and what it is to be a human being, if we insist upon imposing on their writings the conceptual framework constitutive of our modern moral discourse.

For this reason I should like to distinguish *morals* from *ethics;* if the full and rich history of Western ethical thought and its variants in other cultures is to be fully intelligible to us, the subject must be defined so as to be inclusive of the ancient Greeks, their Christian successors, modern Western moral theorists, the early Confucians, and the relevant concept clusters of many other non-Western peoples as well.

I define ethics as the systematic study of the basic terms employed in the description, analysis, and evaluation of human conduct. It is also the employment of these basic terms in the evaluation of human conduct.

It might be objected that this definition is too broad. Under it, one might decide to study, for example, the descriptions, analyses, and evaluations of such actions as slurping soup, wearing inappropriate dress, the improper performance of rituals, or making crude sexual advances; and surely we must distinguish rudeness from immoral conduct? Of course we must, if we are committed in advance to contemporary rights-based moralities as the be-all and end-all of *ethical* thinking. Unfortunately, such commitment, common though it may be, begs a large cultural question; for without the vocabulary of the concept cluster of contemporary Western moral philosophy it is fairly difficult to state clearly the purported distinction between *boorishness* and *immorality*, as everyone who has contemplated the meaning and significance of the Chinese idea of *li* knows full well. The above definition allows greater room for comparative studies than contemporary Western philosophical usage would encourage. It also, not irrelevantly, approximates fairly closely the more ordinary usages of *ethics* as found in standard dictionaries of English and simultaneously reflects the linguistic fact that whereas even philosophers speak of social ethics, medical ethics, professional ethics, and so forth, they do not — nor does anyone else — speak of social morals or professional morals.

If contemporary Western moral philosophy is correctly seen as only one among many possible ethical positions, we must reflect on a number of consequences which follow. The distinction between morals and ethics does not completely vitiate the arguments for ethical relativism, but it does question a number of their premises. The "moral" counterarguments given here are not confined to the ancient Chinese language. Ethical relativism may be true, but it does not necessarily require moral relativism.

Second, this distinction shows that non-Western materials continue to be approached from a strongly Western perspective. To be sure, no comparative scholar can come to another culture as a *tabula rasa*. Pure culture-free objectivity is indeed a myth. Physicists and physicians, scholars and scolds, plain men and philosopher-queens are one and all influenced by their cultural and historical circumstances. But there are degrees of culture-boundedness which are in principle capable of being measured by all. Anthropologists of the late nineteenth century, for instance, made intelligence the determining characteristic of culture, and it was certainly a step toward reducing the Victorian English chauvinism underlying that concept when the focus shifted to learning as the determining characteristic.[20]

Still another consequence of distinguishing different concept clusters is that the most common method of working with non-Western materials has been to ask: How do these texts answer philosophical questions which vex us? The moral of the "moral" illustration, however, is that the basic question needs to be reformulated to ask: To what extent do these texts suggest that we could be asking very different philosophical questions?

This approach may appear to rest on a conceptual confusion. It would seem that Confucian ethics cannot be all that different from contemporary Western moral philosophy, or else we could not understand accounts of it in English as ethical thinking. That is to say, in order to make a case for the Confucian persuasion, isn't it necessary to employ some at least of the English-language concept cluster comprising contemporary Western moral philosophy? And if so, then isn't Confucian ethics after all not so very different therefrom?

I maintain that the concept cluster of early Confucian ethics is very different indeed from the concept cluster of contemporary Western moral philosophy. The vocabulary of English for making normative judgments and discussing ethics, however, is far richer than is found in contemporary Western moral philosophy. The most fundamental challenge raised by early Confucian ethics is that contemporary moral philosophy has become increasingly irrelevant to concrete ethical concerns, utilizing an impoverished — and largely bureaucratic[21] — technical vocabulary emphasizing law, abstract logic, and the formation of policy statements. Contemporary moral philosophy, the Confucian texts suggest, is no longer grounded in the real hopes, fears, joys, sorrows, ideas, and attitudes of flesh-and-blood human beings. Since the time of Descartes Western philosophy — not alone moral philosophy — has increasingly abstracted a purely cognizing activity away from persons. It has determined that this use of logical reasoning in a disembodied "mind" is the choosing, autonomous essence of individuals, which is philosophically more foundational than are actual persons, the latter being only contingently who they are and therefore of no great philosophical significance.

What the early Confucian writings reflect, however, is that there are no disembodied minds, nor autonomous individuals; unless there are at least two human beings, there can be no human beings.[22] By their lights, the writings of virtually every Western philosopher from Descartes to the present can only be seen as incantations for exorcising the human ghost from the calculating machine, to the current extreme that we cannot any longer even be certain that we are not brains in vats. But to advance this challenge on behalf of the early Confucians is not to decry the Western cultural tradition, nor to applaud raw feeling, nor to claim that irrationality is somehow more human than rationality — all of which would be fairly difficult claims to establish on the basis of rational argumentation given in a language central to the Western cultural tradition. Rather it is to suggest that the contemporary philosophical stereotype of a disembodied, purely logical and calculating autonomous individual is simply too far removed from what we feel and think human beings to be. It has raised problems that seem incapable of solution, and it is therefore becoming increasingly difficult for moral or political philosophies embodying this stereotype to have much purchase even on ourselves, not to mention the peoples who do not live as inheritors of the Western philosophical tradition.

Take only one small example: John Rawls's very rich and influential concept of the veil of ignorance. Confucius would have to interpret it, I believe, as an insistence that the conceptual ground laying of a decent society should be entrusted to thoroughgoing amnesiacs; and he would be rather bewildered by that.

By now, the "What else?" question is sufficiently pressing that it must be addressed. Describing the early Confucian lexicon[23] — their concept cluster — would take us too far afield sinologically, but this much should be said: the Chinese philosophical terms focus attention on qualities of persons, and on the kinds of persons who have or do not have these qualities. Where we would speak of choice, they speak of will, resolve; where we invoke abstract principles, they invoke concrete roles, and attitudes toward those roles. Moreover, if the early Confucian writings are to be interpreted consistently, they must be read as insisting on the altogether social nature of human life, for the qualities of persons, the kinds of persons they are, and the attitudes they have, are exhibited not in actions but only in human interactions.

Against this background, let me attempt to sketch briefly the early Confucian view of what it is to be a human being. If I could ask the shade of Confucius "Who am I?" his reply, I believe, would run roughly as follows: "Given that you are Henry Rosemont, Jr., you are obviously the son of Henry, Sr., and Sally Rosemont. You are thus first, foremost, and most basically a *son;* you stand in a relationship to your parents that began at birth, has had a profound influence on your later development and has had a profound effect on their later lives as well, and it is a relationship that is diminished only in part at their death."

Of course, now I am many other things besides a son. I am husband to my wife, father of our children, grandfather to their children; I am a brother, my friend's friend, my neighbor's neighbor; I am teacher of my students, student of my teachers, and colleague of my colleagues.

Now all of this is obvious, but note how different it is from focusing on me as an autonomous, freely choosing individual self. For the early Confucians there can be no *me* in isolation, to be considered abstractly: I am the totality of roles I live in relation to specific others. I do not *play* or *perform* these roles; I *am* these roles. When they have all been specified I have been defined uniquely, fully, and altogether, with no remainder with which to piece together a free, autonomous self.

Moreover, seen in this socially contextualized way, it is clear that in an important sense I do not achieve my own identity, become my own person. Of course, a great deal of personal effort is required to become a good person. But nevertheless, most of who and what I am is determined by the others with whom I interact, just as my efforts determine in part who and what they are at the same time. Personhood, in this sense, is conferred on us, just as we confer it on others. Again, the point is obvious, but the Confucian persuasion suggests that we state it in another tone of voice: my life as a teacher can only be made significant by my students, my life as a scholar only by other scholars.

All of the specific human relations of which we are a part, with the dead as well as the living, will be mediated by the *li,* that is, the courtesy, customs, and traditions we come to share as our inextricably linked histories unfold; and by fulfilling the obligations defined by these relationships we are, for the early Confucians, following the human Way. It is a comprehensive way. By the manner in which we interact with others our lives will clearly have an ethical dimension infusing *all*, not just some, of our conduct. By the ways in which this ethical interpersonal conduct is effected, with reciprocity, and governed by civility, respect, affection, custom, and tradition, our lives will also have an aesthetic dimension for ourselves and for others. And by specifically meeting our defining traditional obligations to our elders and ancestors on the one hand, and to our contemporaries and descendants on the other, the early Confucians offer an uncommon form of transcendence. This human capacity to go beyond the specific spatiotemporal circumstances in which we exist gives our personhood the sense of humanity shared in common, and thereby a sense of strong continuity with what has gone before and what will come later. To borrow an incisive distinction first put forth by Kurt Baier: though the early Confucians did not question the meaning *of* life, we may nevertheless see that their view of what it is to be a human being provided that everyone could find meaning *in* life.

This is a brief account of a reconstructed early Confucian view of what it is to be a human being.[24] A host of philosophical objections leap immediately to mind. Where is there room for freedom and creativity within this concept cluster? If relations are all this personal, have we no obligations to those unknown to us? Aren't we being asked, on behalf of the early Confucians, to *choose* their concept cluster, their view of human beings?

A fuller account of the early Confucian ethical alternative to rights-based moralities will not only assist our efforts in establishing a closer international community, it can be of direct and immediate relevance to many of the issues which currently divide the members of our own culture. It would be correct to endorse moral relativism only where it could be shown that two peoples employed the same or similar evaluative concepts and criteria, and that one approved a particular human action, and the other disapproved.

Unfortunately we do not have to trek to exotic lands to find just such examples of *moral* relativism; they are in abundance in contemporary American society. Abortion is a prime example.[25] Within the modern concept cluster of morals, it may not be possible to resolve the issue of abortion. One might want to argue that abortion is fundamentally a legal and not a moral issue, but for good or ill the vocabulary utilized in discussing the issue is the concept cluster of modern morals. It is difficult to see how the matter could be otherwise, for when one side says that basic human rights are at stake, and with rights being at the center of our concept cluster of morals, then we cannot but have a paradigmatic moral issue. Nor can it be objected that abortion is an instance of moral conflict rather than moral relativism, for this objection misses the point. An abortion is a human action tolerated by a large group of people and loathed by another large group. This is precisely the same situation described in all ostensible instances of moral relativism based on anthropological evidence.

The examples can be multiplied, as at the outset: animal rights, euthanasia, the rights of the not-yet-born to a healthy and genetically diversified natural environment, and others. More generally, where the moral and the political spheres are seen to overlap — justice and fairness — there is a good deal of *prima facie* evidence for relativism in recent philosophical writings, especially in the works of Rawls and Nozick and their numerous commentators; individual rights and social justice may not be altogether compatible concepts.[26]

Perhaps all of these ethical and related issues can be well settled within the concept cluster of modern morals without alteration. That framework has been deeply ingrained in Western thinking for a long time and has surely served humankind well. It was an integral element of the ideology undergirding the American and French revolutions. But perhaps that framework now needs to be modified in order to help the continuing human search for how better to live, and how to live with one another in this complex world.

I do not wish to imply that the early Confucian writings are the be-all and end-all for finding answers to the multiplicity of questions I have posed. I do want to suggest that they are a highly salutary beginning; for just as Ptolemaic astronomers could not consider seriously that there were fundamental problems with their view of the heavens until the Copernican view had been articulated, just so we cannot seriously question our concepts of rights, of ethics as morals, and of what it is to be a human being, until there are alternatives to contemplate. Is it possible to have an ethical and/or political theory that does not employ the concepts of autonomous individuals, or choice, or freedom, or rights, and does not invoke abstract principles? Could there be such a theory, grounded in a view of human nature as *essentially* involving interpersonal relations, a theory that accords both with our own moral sentiments and with those of the two billion human beings who do not live in the Western industrial democracies? If there were such a theory, could it conceivably be conflict-free?

I do not know the answers to these questions. I do know, however, that if the early Confucian ethical alternative can genuinely alter our perspectives it will not only have made a contribution to ethics; it will have made an important contribution toward reconstituting the entire discipline of philosophy.

Some Western philosophical concepts will, and should, remain with us; some others will have to be stretched significantly in order to represent more accurately non-Western concepts and concept clusters. Still other Western philosophical concepts may have to be abandoned altogether in favor of others not yet extant. If we are reluctant to participate in the requiem mass currently being offered for philosophy, if we wish instead to seek new perspectives that might enable the discipline to become as truly all-encompassing in the future as it has mistakenly been assumed to have been in the past, we must begin to develop a more international philosophical language which incorporates the insights of all of the worldwide historical tradition of thinkers who addressed the questions of who and what we are, and why and how we should lead our all-too-human lives.

NOTES

1. A. J. M. Milne, *Human Rights and Human Diversity* (Albany, N.Y.: SUNY Press, 1985), pp. 3–6.

2. As cited in ibid., p. 2.

3. For further discussion see Henry Rosemont, Jr., "Against Relativism," in *Interpreting across Boundaries*, ed. Gerald Larson and Eliot Deutsch (forthcoming).

4. See Judith Thomson, "A Defense of Abortion," *Philosophy and Public Affairs* 1 (1972); Mary Anne Warren, "On the Moral and Legal Status of Abortion," *Monist* 57 (1973); L. W. Sumner, *Abortion and Moral Theory* (Princeton, N.J.: Princeton University Press, 1981), and David B.

Wong, *Moral Relativity* (Berkeley, Calif.: University of California Press, 1984).

5. See, for example, James Rachels, "Active and Passive Euthanasia," *New England Journal of Medicine* 292, no. 2 (1975).

6. This major and diverse field of study had its philosophical beginnings with John Passmore, *Man's Responsibility for Nature* (New York: Scribner's, 1978).

7. See, for example, Tom Regan and Peter Singer, eds., *Animal Rights and Human Obligation* (Englewood Cliffs, N.J.: Prentice-Hall, 1976), and many more recent books.

8. See Alasdair MacIntyre, *After Virtue* (Notre Dame, Ind.: University of Notre Dame Press, 1981), esp. pp. 229–33.

9. This is the major thrust of MacIntyre, *After Virtue.*

10. Robert Nozick, *Anarchy, State, and Utopia* (New York: Basic Books, 1974), p. ix.

11. John Rawls, *A Theory of Justice* (Cambridge, Mass.: Belknap Press of Harvard University Press, 1971), p. 302.

12. R. M. Hare, *Moral Thinking* (Oxford: Clarendon Press, 1981), pp. 154–55.

13. Ronald Dworkin, *Taking Rights Seriously* (Cambridge, Mass.: Harvard University Press, 1971), p. 90.

14. Patricia Werhane, *Persons, Rights, and Corporations* (Englewood Cliffs, N.J.: Prentice-Hall, 1985), p. 3.

15. H. L. A. Hart, "Are There Any Natural Rights?" *Philosophical Review* 64 (1955).

16. Henry Shue, *Basic Rights* (Princeton, N.J.: Princeton University Press, 1980).

17. See Milne, *Human Rights and Human Diversity,* p. 139.

18. Dworkin, *Taking Rights Seriously,* pp. 180–83.

19. See George W. Stocking, *Race, Culture, and Evolution: Essays in the History of Anthropology* (New York: Free Press, 1968); Elvin Hatch, *Culture and Morality* (New York: Columbia University Press, 1983); Bryan Wilson, ed., *Rationality* (Oxford: Basil Blackwell, 1973); Martin Hollis and Steven Lukes, eds., *Rationality and Relativism* (Cambridge, Mass.: MIT Press, 1982); Michael Krausz and Jack W. Meiland, eds., *Relativism: Cognitive and Moral* (Notre Dame, Ind.: University of Notre Dame Press, 1982); Clifford Geertz, "Anti-Relativism," *American Anthropologist* 86, no. 2 (1984), and Wong, *Moral Relativity.*

20. For the history of this development in anthropology, see Stocking, *Race, Culture, and Evolution,* and Hatch, *Culture and Morality.*

21. The expression "bureaucratic rationality" is from B. A. O. Wil-

liams, *Ethics and the Limits of Philosophy* (Cambridge, Mass.: Harvard University Press, 1985), p. 206.

22. This point is cogently argued in Herbert Fingarette, "The Music of Humanity in the Conversations of Confucius," *Journal of Chinese Philosophy* 10 (1983). See also Herbert Fingarette, *Confucius: The Secular as Sacred* (New York: Harper & Row, 1972); Henry Rosemont, Jr., "Review of *Confucius: The Secular as Sacred*," *Philosophy East and West* 26, no. 4 (1976); and an exchange between us in *Philosophy East and West* 28, no. 4 (1978).

23. Categories of persons I have endeavored to describe briefly in Henry Rosemont, Jr., "Kierkegaard and Confucius: On Following the Way," *Philosophy East and West* 36, no. 3 (1986). For fuller discussion, and citations of philological sources, see Henry Rosemont, Jr., *Confucianism and Contemporary Ethics* (forthcoming).

24. A fuller account may be found in Rosemont, *Confucianism and Contemporary Ethics.*

25. See note 4.

26. In his recent writings Rawls has been narrowing the applicability of his concept of "justice as fairness" to the modern industrial democracies; there is a distinctively relativistic flavor in these writings that is absent in *A Theory of Justice.* It is doubtful, however, that this narrowing of applicability will convince convinced Nozickians. See John Rawls, "Kantian Constructivism in Moral Theory," *Journal of Philosophy* 77, no. 9, and "Justice as Fairness: Political Not Metaphysical," *Philosophy and Public Affairs* 14, no. 3, where Rawls maintains that his concept of a self is political only. In Henry Rosemont, Jr., "State and Society in the *Hsun Tzu*," and Fingarette, *Confucius: The Secular as Sacred*, cases are made for societies which provide most of the benefits that Rawls wishes to provide for citizens, with less government than Nozick would allow.

11

Neo-Confucianism and Human Rights

W. THEODORE DE BARY

SOME MODERN PERSPECTIVES

As a matter of conscious advocacy the concept of *human rights* is a relatively recent Western invention, yet it is also understood to be the product of a long evolution in Western thought having its own distinctive features. From this the conclusion is often reached that human rights are peculiarly Western. Whether this is so or not, however, depends on how one interprets *human rights*. The people of East Asia in the nineteenth century had to face this problem when they put Chinese characters together to form new compounds expressing "human rights" in such terms as the Japanese *jinken* or Chinese *jen-ch'üan*, or "peoples' rights" in *minken* and *min-ch'üan*. Similarly they assimilated such concepts as "liberty" or "freedom" (J — *jiyu*; C — *tzu-yu*) or "liberalism" (*jiyu shugi/tzu-yu chu-i*), where the translation put special emphasis on the importance of the individual and the principle of voluntarism. Though neologisms, intended to convey the special quality of Western ideas, these new terms also had, for Chinese, Japanese, and Koreans, traditional associations attaching to their component parts. Old coins were being recast into new currency. Thus the component for human (*jin/jen*) had strong associations with the central value of "humaneness" or "humanity" in Confucian culture. The term for "rights," *ken/ch'üan* in this compound, while expressing the idea of authority or discretionary power, also had some connotations of "subject to discretion or qualification," hence "provisional," "accommodative," and even "expedient," rather than "constant" or "unvarying" as one might think of "inalienable human rights."

Despite these differences, in my opinion nothing is gained by arguing for the distinctively Western character of human rights. If you win the argument you lose the battle. That is, if you claim some special distinction for the West in this respect, or assert some inherent lack on the part of Asians, you are probably defining human rights in such narrow terms as to render them unrecognizable or inoperable for others. If, however, you view *human rights* as an evolving conception, expressing imperfectly the aspirations of many peoples, East and West, it may be that, learning from the experience of others, one can arrive at a deeper understanding of human rights problems in different cultural settings.

Here the setting for my discussion of the problem is China — Confucianism and especially its later, more highly developed form, Neo-Confucianism. There is one aspect of this cultural setting, however, which requires some clarification at the outset — Confucianism as serving functions which in other cultures have been identified with religion. For my purposes it should suffice to say that I do not consider Confucianism a religion by conventional Western standards, but the religious dimensions of human experience have always held great importance for Confucians. Moreover, because religious attitudes and practices have tended to find expression in this as in other established teachings or ideologies, there is much to be learned about religion from the study of the historical development of Confucianism.

RELIGIOUS DIMENSIONS OF CLASSICAL HUMANISM

What I have just said is especially true of those religious attitudes often thought to underlie human rights questions in other traditions. I have in mind such concepts as the "inherent dignity of man or of the individual," "human equality," the "natural rights of man," and so forth. One can point to the central importance in Confucianism of the concept of "humaneness" or "humanity," and one can see this as constituting the essential basis of Confucian humanism. One can even argue, from the primary attention given to the study of humankind and present human needs, that Confucianism is the most distinctly humanistic of the world's major traditions. But since so much of what Confucius has to say about being truly human also involves a deeply reverential attitude, expressed in the term *ching*, one might well call this a religious humanism.

Much of the Confucian *Analects* is concerned with the virtue of reverence and with the practice of ritual, both religious and civil. Respect for life in the present, to which Confucius gave a high priority, was linked to a reverence for life and for the sources of life, often identified with heaven or one's ancestors. So thoroughly integrated were those two spheres — the heavenly and the human — that one often has difficulty in judging whether the Chinese word *ching* should be translated as "reverence" or "respect." This attitude is not concerned with an afterlife, however, and to render *ching* as "worship," as in the expression "ancestor worship," has no warrant in the Confucian context since Confucius explicitly disavowed any need for placating the spirits of the dead or for abasing oneself before heaven.

Many of the religious traditions Confucius respected were rooted in a clan and family system undergoing change even in his time. In the *Analects* there is an increasing focus on the individual, as compared to the more social character of earlier classics. But for Confucius it was important to reaffirm these earlier roots, even while recognizing that the natural processes of growth led upward from the individual and outward from the family toward participation in a larger community and wider world. Much of Confucius' discussion of the nature of the individual, as represented by the ideal of the "gentleman" or "noble man" (*chün-tzu*), stresses this organic rootedness, this essential particularism, while also drawing out its implications for a universal ethic. Thus: "Let the noble man never fail reverently to order his own conduct, let him be respectful to others and observant of ritual (decorum); then all within the four seas will be his brothers." (*Analects* 12:5).

A distinctive feature of this approach was that it linked the reverential attitude toward human life with forms of respect for others to be expressed in concrete relationships. The treatment one was entitled to, instead of being guaranteed by some contractual arrangement or being enforced by some legal sanction, was defined in relation to the whole network of responsibilities which the members of a family or community owed to one another. Here the emphasis was on loving, affective relations, not on impersonal, legalistic ones. These obligations had a certain objective, formal definition, as in the rules of decorum or rites; but, in contrast to a strict contractual *quid pro quo* or legal requirement, they were considered to depend for their fulfillment on a spirit of good will and mutual regard that could not be measured in quantitative terms alone. Being grounded in natural human affections, this system had a dynamic all its own and did not require external intervention or the threat of force to make it operative.

Another distinctive feature of the system was its emphasis on equity rather than equality in social relations. Confucians accepted social distinctions as an inevitable fact of life and believed that differences in age, sex, social status, and political position had to be taken into account if equity were to be achieved in relations among unequals. In such cases reciprocity would not be won through the exchange of identical goods. A child, for instance, could not in infancy or youth be expected to render to parents the same kind of care and guidance which they, as adults, were obliged to provide for him or her. Hence the virtue appropriate to the parent-child relation was defined not in terms of obedience or service, but of loving care on the part of each, differentiable according to their respective capabilities, and sometimes returnable at a later stage of life. Likewise the virtue appropriate to the relation of ruler and minister was not unconditional loyalty or unquestioning obedience, but *i*, moral propriety in the performance of the shared duties of rulership, again differentiable according to their respective functions.

In this way the underlying principles of reciprocity (*shu*) and equity or propriety (*i*) were blended to serve a moral equality among persons understood to derive from heaven, the common source of human life and of the human order which fostered that life. This, in turn, represented an order of values to which Mencius gave priority over the social and political order in the following memorable passage:

> Heaven confers titles of nobility as well as man. Man's titles of nobility are duke, chancellor, great officer. Those of Heaven are humaneness, righteousness, true-heartedness and good faith. . . . Men of old cultivated the nobility of Heaven and the nobility of man followed naturally from this. Men

today cultivate the nobility of Heaven only with an eye to achieving the nobility of man, and when that has been gained, they cast away the other. But this is the height of delusion, for in the end they must surely lose the nobility of man as well. (*Mencius* 6A:16)

Such at least was the Confucian way of thinking which tended to express human rights in terms of *rites* and reciprocal relations, not in terms of *laws*. Recourse to the law in cases of conflict was, for Confucians, only a last resort, something identified with official interference in the normal processes of community life and associated with the violence or coercion of externally imposed rule. The sanctions of law might indeed be invoked against recalcitrant members of a community, who by their own violent actions put themselves beyond the pale of familial or neighborly sympathy; thus Confucians accepted the need for something like our criminal law in a very limited sphere. But in the conduct of human relations generally they looked on litigation or recourse to the courts as something to be avoided if at all possible. Chinese "courts," indeed, were not independent bodies entrusted with the impartial exercise of judicial functions but simply another aspect of administration from above, rarely kept separate from the political and fiscal interests of the state. Similarly "law," in Confucian eyes, served as an instrument of state power, frequently indeed of exploitation; it was therefore most often viewed as a hostile force, rather than as a covenant or contract among consenting persons, or as a body of principles and precedents expressing a consensus among the people as to how their common interests and rights might be protected.

After the long ascendancy of Buddhism, from the third to the tenth centuries, the Confucian revival in the Sung (from the tenth century on) brought several developments in Chinese thought of potential significance for human rights. Reform movements in the eleventh century drew attention to potential and social needs which it was alleged Buddhism and Taoism had ignored. In reaffirming Confucian ethical principles as a basis for reform, Sung philosophers also elaborated new theories of human nature. Many of these doctrines were drawn from classical Confucianism, especially the book of *Mencius*, but they also took into account relevant Buddhist views concerning "the nature," *hsing*, understood by Neo-Confucians primarily as "human nature" or "the moral nature." In the Ch'eng-Chu school this "nature" was seen as one aspect of a larger cosmic infrastructure of natural or heavenly principles (*t'ien-li*) inherent in all things. Innate in human minds-and-hearts were all the principles needed to understand and deal with the affairs of the world, principles manifested above all through human value judgments and empathetic responses in human relations. Neo-Confucians called these principles "real," "substantial," or "solid" (*shih*), in contrast to the Buddhist view of things as "empty" (*k'ung*), that is, insubstantial, having no nature of their own, no "own-nature." Neo-Confucian principles were constant and enduring; they could be conceptualized in rational and moral terms so as to be of service in dealing with practical problems of everyday life. The nature in Buddhism, on the other hand, as expressed in the prevailing form of Ch'an Buddhism, could only be "pointed to" and intuited within one's own mind-and-heart; it could not be expressed in words (*pu-li wen-tzu*). Neo-Confucians, denying that universal change could only be accounted for in terms of impermanence, evanescence, and unpredictability, characterized reality as a process of growth, governed by constant norms or patterns. Among these the most essential for Neo-Confucians was the ineradicable moral sense in all human persons which Mencius had characterized as "the goodness of human nature."

It is this concept of the inherent goodness of the human moral nature which provided Neo-Confucian thought with a premise somewhat akin to the "inherent dignity of man" or the "intrinsic worth of the individual" as a basis for its social doctrines. In the *Mean* (*Chung-yung*), one of the favorite texts of the Neo-Confucians, the opening lines spoke of this nature as having been ordained by heaven, and Chu Hsi's explanation of this text emphasized the reality of the nature as differentiated in each individual.[1] "Honoring the moral nature" was indeed the starting point of all learning and the foundation for all political and social action. Moreover, Mencius had spoken of what was ordained by heaven as written in the consciences of human beings so that they were impelled to right injustices and were even justified in overthrowing rulers who violated the ordinances of heaven.[2] Writers today often refer to this doctrine as the "right of revolution." Admittedly this is putting it in modern terms; revolution is not exactly what Mencius had in mind. But if the Mandate of Heaven is seen to confer on human beings an authority or justification for acting in accordance with their moral nature, we may be entitled to ask whether this Neo-Confucian doctrine of the innate moral imperative does not provide a basis for asserting certain human rights.

Part of the answer, at least, appears especially in the Neo-Confucian reaffirmation of the responsibilities to each other of persons engaged in the paradigmatic human relations: parent/child, ruler/minister, husband/wife, elder/junior, friend/friend. In these reciprocal relations one was entitled to a certain kind of treatment attaching to these constant human relationships. Chu Hsi, in his discussions with his friends and students, tended to speak of these reciprocal obligations and correlative responsibilities in the context of Confucian "rites," not legal rights. Throughout his life he devoted much study to the traditional rites or rules of decorum appropriate for members of the political and cultural elite, believing like the ancients that these social forms set the norm for all and thus were the key to social harmony. Herein he showed his deep consciousness of the special responsibilities of the educated person. It is significant, however, that this concern did not extend to the study of laws, still a comparatively neglected subject among Confucian scholars, but rather focused attention on developing the individual's capability in responsible leadership, to be accomplished through self-cultivation in the context of rites.

As Chu explained in his commentary on the *Great Learning*, the noble have a responsibility first to cultivate their own person, their own moral nature, and then to assist all in fulfilling their own natures.[3] Chu's preface to the same text upholds as an ideal the system of universal education which he believed had obtained under the sage-kings, strongly implying that the innate moral nature in each person entitled him or her to whatever help the ruler could give in developing his or her natural capabilities.[4]

Inadequate though the preceding is as an account of Chu Hsi's view on ritual and popular education, it may at least offset the tendency to think of Chu as addressing himself exclusively to the needs of the educated elite or to the elite's control over the uneducated. In fact, even among his writings addressed to the latter audience, few fail to stress ritual and popular education as the base on which higher culture rests, and it is probably only the greater difficulty of dealing with the historical details of times remote from our own which has made us slow to study and evaluate adequately the influence of Chu's views on ritual and education at the grassroots level.

RITES, PRINCIPLES, AND LAWS

At this point a few observations should be made concerning the significance of the foregoing for our understanding of human rights in the Neo-Confucian context. Chu Hsi thought of the ritual order as the embodiment in human society of principles inherent in the universe, principles which had both a static and dynamic aspect — that is, they represented a basic structure or pattern in the universe (*li*), as well as a vital process of change and renewal (*sheng-sheng*). In addressing the problems of twelfth-century China, Chu felt a need to restructure society on a humane basis, avoiding, on the one hand, the moral relativism and pragmatism fostered by Ch'an Buddhism and Taoism, and, on the other, the absolutism identified with an increasingly autocratic state. Ritual would provide a flexible structure for a humane social order, but to accomplish this the traditional ritual would have to be adapted to the changed conditions of Sung China. For both the *Family Ritual* and the community compact Chu Hsi took as his models earlier Sung examples or experiments adumbrated by the Ch'eng brothers, Chang Tsai, Ssu-ma Kuang, and Lü Ta-chun. These he then amended to incorporate elements from the classic rituals. In so doing Chu recognized that the economic, social, and political circumstances of the Sung literati varied greatly from those of the old Chou aristocracy, so that even he himself, poor scholar that he was, could not dream of performing the elaborate and costly rituals prescribed for the elite of an earlier time.[5] Without being a social leveler, he wanted to bring the ritual down to the level of the common person in a form adjusted to the latter's condition.

A follower of Chu Hsi's, one generation removed in time, was Chen Te-hsiu (1178–1235). Like Chu, Chen gave much attention to administration on the local level, hoping thereby to achieve "humane government." In the process he often invoked Neo-Confucian principles on behalf of fairness and justice in the treatment of the people. He gave instructions to subordinate officials in the prefecture of Ch'uan-chou in 1232, asking them to "govern the people with humaneness," "clean up the penal system," "be fair in administering tax collections," and "establish charitable granaries" to relieve the distress of landless peasants.[6]

A. Humaneness in Governing

As Chu Hsi said, even scholars of low rank, if they have a mind to love the people, can benefit them. The same is true for those who only keep records or perform police duties, and how much more for those in higher positions. The greater the impact of their actions on others, the greater their need to be sensitive to the sufferings of the people, especially when it comes to inflicting torture and punishment on them.[7] Thus incorruptibility is based on the principles of reciprocity and humaneness. Impartiality, according to Chen, is grounded in the universal principles of heaven, which are fixed and not subject to manipulation for the sake of selfish gain or partiality.

B. Cleaning Up the Penal System

Imprisonment involves precious human life. No one should be imprisoned except through statutory procedures, and the local magistrates should personally see to this; they should not leave investigation and interrogation up to clerks, who often extract involuntary confessions and use these to extort money from the families of those so accused. Torture is often used in the process. Prisoners, kept without enough food, clothing, and covering, often starve or die of cold. Those locked in cangues get blisters on their necks which then become festered. Conditions in prison cells are crowded and unsanitary. Chen gives a long recital of these evils, but even so, he says, it is far from complete. Local magistrates should hold human life dear and see that these abuses cease, making personal inspections of prison conditions and punishing those guilty of violations.

Recognizing that local magistrates are fully occupied with many duties, Chen as prefect has allowed their assistants to handle interrogations and approved the appointment of separate judicial officers. Nevertheless, this has led in some cases to a complete delegation and dereliction of the magistrate's responsibility, which Chen now wishes to correct.[8]

C. Fairness in Taxation

In this section Chen expresses his concern over, and intention to stop, prevalent abuses in the collection of taxes: demands for payment of taxes well in advance of the official due date; the use of irregular grain measures other than the taxpayer's own; holding the heads of collective security (*pao-chia*) units responsible for the collection of back taxes; failure to keep an accurate record of taxes collected or to give certified receipts to the payer; the imposition of surcharges on various illegitimate pretexts. Chen's policies reflect a concern for fairness, humane treatment, and strict legality.

Chen has prohibited the payment of fines in lieu of the statutory punishment because it allows the rich to go unpunished and discriminates unfairly against the poor. He reiterates this position now. He also finds that there are violations of his order to allow households to subdivide as they wish. Instead special offices have been set up in some subprefectures to enforce registration of subdivisions and collect illicit fees for same. Another abuse is the repeated imposition of new responsibilities on the heads of *pao-chia* units, burdening them intolerably.[9] Sympathy for and fair treatment of *pao-chia* heads is a theme running through this set of public policy declarations.

D. Establishment of Charitable Granaries (I-lin)

It has occurred to Chen that although local granaries exist which loan grain to the people, these are only available to those who own land as security for the loans. He wishes to set up a program whereby the well-to-do would contribute grain through the Ever-normal Granary System, so that, by a combination of public and private efforts, loans of grain could be made available to landless peasants.

Chen urges that this be done on the grounds of both principle and practicality. For principle he draws on Chang Tsai's Western Inscription (*Hsi-ming*) and its doctrine of the unity of humankind as offspring of heaven-and-earth, sharing one body composed of the same physical substance and sensitivity of feelings. Humans should act for the mind-and-heart of heaven-and-earth, which cares equally for all. Moreover this charitable granary would, by improving the lot of the landless, ease their distress, obviate conflict, and ensure social peace. Since Chen's proposal is for entirely voluntary donations, and the system is to be operated by local people, without official interference, it avoids the coercive and exploitative features which often vitiate government programs.

As regards the theoretical basis of his work, it is noteworthy that Chen draws on the specific concepts and doctrines of Neo-Confucian thinkers in arguing the case for the reforms he advocates. The Ch'eng Chu doctrine of heaven's principles, the human moral nature, and human physical endowment are cited as the basis for the universal principles underlying his concepts of justice and equity in the application of the law; and Chang Tsai's doctrine of the unity of humanity, based on the parenthood of heaven-and-earth, is the theoretical ground cited for his social welfare principles.

This distinctly reformist use of Neo-Confucian principles stands in contrast to a prevalent modern view that the Neo-Confucian philosophy of principle was inherently authoritarian, conservative, and protective of the status quo. Of course from a modern revolutionary point of view even reformism has been seen as essentially conservative, because it is meliorative rather than radically corrective of the old order; but having seen the reactionary purposes to which revolutionary ideals themselves have been put in the twentieth century, we may question whether the revolutionary claim serves as an adequate criterion of evaluation.

A further point is illustrated by a follower of Chu Hsi in the Ming period, Ch'iu Chün (1420–95), who, in his *Supplement to the Extended Meaning of the Great Learning (Ta-hsüeh yen-i pu)*, discussed institutional reforms needed to provide for the people's physical well-being and moral health. Ch'iu asserted the ruler's responsibility to protect and sustain human life as a duty ordained by heaven. The conditions for achieving self-fulfillment are something to which human beings are entitled in principle by their very nature — the moral nature which heaven has ordained to be cultivated and perfected in every person. In this light the ruler was obliged to serve the common good of all (*kung*) and not any private or selfish interest (*ssu*), a distinction which did not preclude one's having legitimate individual interests and entitlements as long as they were not pursued at the expense of others. On this basis, then, Ch'iu proceeded to anathematize all enactments of the ruler which were in violation of such principles. He called both "contrary to ritual" (*fei li*) and "contrary to law" (*fei fa*).[10] One can see from this that ritual had for him all the validity of law — without the force — and indeed even claimed a higher authority insofar as, in his eyes, ritual should be the first resort and law the last. Here one could say that Ch'iu was making a case for human *rites* in terms that came close to what we call human *rights*.

If these developments seem promising from a modern point of view, they nevertheless fell short of producing anything like the advocacy of human rights by significant numbers of people. For one thing, there was a certain organizational weakness in the schools, scholarly associations, and community groups which supported such discussion but proved unable to sustain themselves in the midst of official repressions, economic difficulties, and civil disturbances at the end of the Ming. For another and perhaps more fundamental reason, the heavy emphasis on self-cultivation and self-fulfillment often led more toward individual spiritual liberation than toward institutional or social reform, or to a reliance on converting individual rulers to the Way of the Sages rather than to the establishment of laws and institutions protective of people's rights.

After the collapse of the Ming dynasty, Neo-Confucian scholars who had experienced the Manchu conquest as a crisis for Chinese civilization reexamined many of the fundamental assumptions of the Confucian faith. One such scholar was Lü Liu-liang (1629–83), who became the vanguard of the orthodox Cheng-Chu school in the late seventeenth century, remained unreconciled to Manchu rule, and put forth a radical critique of dynastic institutions. For this critique he drew on the Neo-Confucian doctrine of human nature. Here Heaven's Imperative (*T'ien-ming*), politically the Mandate of Heaven, is conceived primarily in terms of the human moral nature. It is the moral imperatives inherent in every human mind-and-heart that must be answered to for the validation of any regime's claimed legitimacy. There can be no mandate from heaven for any ruler or regime that violates the basic life-giving principles constitutive of human nature. Indeed government exists only to advance and enhance those human values, and not to serve the interests of the ruler or ruling house.[11]

Elsewhere Lü identifies rulership with heaven in order to emphasize both the overarching responsibility of the ruler to the people and the universality of the principles that should govern the ruler's conduct: "The Son of Heaven occupies Heaven's Position (t'ien-wei) in order to bring together the common human family within the Four Seas, not just to serve the self-interest of one family. . . ."[12] Lü explains that during the Three Dynasties the throne was passed on to others with the idea of sharing responsibility, of doing what was best for the people. "Heaven's Imperative and the minds-and-hearts of the people weighed heavily on them, and the world lightly. [Such being the case, as Mencius said] the sages would not commit even one unrighteous deed or kill even one person, though to do so might gain them the whole world."[13]

Yet after the Three Dynasties this attitude of shared concern disappeared. Social mores became utilitarian and the conception of ministership, as well as rulership, was corrupted when heaven's authority was no longer recognized.

Lü resists the idea that fundamental institutions should be thought of in terms of law, preferring to stay with the traditional Confucian view of them as rites, and of law as only a last, coercive recourse when the possibility of voluntary cooperation through rites no longer exists. He speaks of existing institutions in Mencian terms as "rites that are not rite" (fei-li chih li) and "rightness that is not right" (fei-i chih i). Commenting on Mencius 4B6, Lü asserts an intrinsic link between rites, rightness, and principles:

> Rites represent the principles of things and affairs. Rightness represents what is appropriate to the time. As to their source, although they are there in our minds-and-hearts, rites and rightness have no pertinence apart from given matters or specific instances in time. Once there is a matter at hand and the time comes, then rites and rightness are there. If one

does not analyze this correctly, saying for example that the
rite follows upon the matter-at-hand or rightness upon the
time, one has already bifurcated them beforehand.

Here one sees that Lü uses *rite* to mean a formulation of principle directly in relation to facts and circumstances. It combines
the constancy and universality of principle with its differentiated
application to all human affairs, while *right* or *rightness* pertains
particularly to the appropriateness of an action in time. Both are
indispensable to the employment and fulfillment of principle in
the mind. Hence Lü speaks of rites as the substance or embodiment (*t'i*) of the Way. They are not mere residual excrescences of
some hidden virtue, as Lao Tzu and Chuang Tzu would have it,
or momentary and ephemeral traces of an inconceivable Truth,
as the Buddhists would see them, but are indeed the very reality
of the Way.[14]

A secondary implication is that *rite*, as the formal definition
and concrete embodiment of principle, covers some of the same
ground as our rational and moral conception of *rights*, expressing
the principles of propriety and respect toward others in the broadest sense — that is, respect not only for other human beings but
also for things and affairs in the world at large, including the entire natural order.

If the universal moral nature is the most fundamental principle of the social order, and rites are the embodiment or substance
of the Way governing human affairs, it establishes a certain basic
human equality as the touchstone of government. Speaking to the
Ch'eng-Chu doctrine of renewing the people, Lü says:

> Both the common man and the Son of Heaven are rooted
> in the same principle. Speaking of it in terms of rank from
> the top down, the *Great Learning* says "from the Son of
> Heaven down to the common man," but in terms of princi-
> ple, in reality, it goes from the common man up to the Son
> of Heaven. The Son of Heaven's renewing of the people should
> proceed on the same principle, and conform to the common
> man's regulation of his own family.[15]

Although the matter is discussed in terms of responsibilities
rather than entitlements, it is clear that each thing's having its

own norm to follow confers on it a certain irreducible autonomy, which governance must take into account and respect. The structure of authority, which in Lü's mind derives from the imperative of heaven, is based on the moral nature as expressed through the minds and hearts of the common people, and it works upward from them, not downward from the Son of Heaven.

Finally I mention an alternative view by a contemporary of Lü, Huang Tsung-hsi (1610–95), who was more identified with the Wang Yang-ming than the Ch'eng Chu school. Huang and Lü had much in common in their antidynastic views, but Huang clearly abandoned the traditional Confucian hostility to law and reliance on ritual. While rejecting dynastic law as truly unlawful, he insisted that the people's welfare could only be guaranteed by legitimate laws and institutions. Huang was not alone among seventeenth-century scholars in recognizing the crucial importance of institutions in a more and more complex society, but he was certainly the most outspoken in attacking the despotic state and asserting a new concept of law as essential to the protection of the people against arbitrary rule.

In so doing, Huang Tsung-hsi minimized the power of the individual to effect political and social reform simply by personal example or by practice of rites. In place of the earlier Neo-Confucian slogan, "self-cultivation (or self-discipline) for the governance of men" (hsiu-chi chih-jen),[16] he said, "Only when the laws are well ordered can men be well governed" (yu chih-fa erh hou yu chih jen), meaning that only then can individual efforts and the power of personal example be made effective.

Huang was careful, however, not to go to the other extreme of subordinating the individual to the state. Nor did he deprecate the earlier contributions of Sung and Ming philosophers to the understanding of human nature, the inherent worth of the individual, or the essential voluntarism of the political and social order. Indeed, unable actively to pursue his reformist goals, he made it his life's work to preserve the record of Neo-Confucian thought in the Sung, Yuan, and Ming periods. Under the Manchus his anti-authoritarian views were politically repressed and philosophically out of style, only to be resurrected in the late nineteenth century. But his works still bear witness to the fact that an authentic Confucian, speaking for his tradition after surveying the long experience of the Chinese people, could conceive of a better human state in which the rights of all would be protected by an adequate system of laws. This was not an idea which could only have come from the West.

NOTES

1. Chu Hsi, *Ssu-chu chi-chü* (Taipei: Chung-kuo tzu-hsüeh ming-chu chi-ch'eng No. 018 reprint of Ming edition, 1979), pp. 39–41.
2. *Mencius* 1B8, in *Sources of Chinese Tradition*, ed. W. T. de Bary et al. (New York: Columbia University Press, 1960): 1:95–97.
3. Chu Hsi, *Ssu-shu chi-chü*, pp. 7–8. Ta-hsüeh chang-chü.
4. Ibid., pp. 1–6. Ta-hsüeh chang-chü hsü.
5. See Ueyama Shumpei, "Shu shi no Karei to," *Girei keiden tsu kai, Tōhō gakuhō* (1982): 173–256, esp. pp. 221–22.
6. *Cheng Ching* (Taipei: Ming reprint of original Sung edition of 1241 in National Central Library), pp. 36a–57a.
7. Ibid., p. 36a.
8. Ibid., p. 41b.
9. Ibid., pp. 46a–47b.
10. Ch'iu Chün, *Ta-hsüeh yen-i pu* (Taipei: 160 chüan ed. of Chia ching 38 [1559], reprint of Hung chih [1488 ed.], preserved in the National Central Library), 13:5b.
11. Lu Liu-liang (*Ssu-shu chiang-i* 1686 ed.; 29:10ab on *Chung-yung* 32.
12. Ibid., 26:4a on *Chung-yung* 17.
13. Ibid., 11:1ab on *Lun-yü* 8.
14. Ibid., 29:1b–2b on *Chung-yung* 27.
15. Ibid., 1:19ab on *Ta-hsüeh* 1.
16. Huang Tsung-hsi, *Ming-i tai-fang lu* (Wu-kuei lou ed., 1879), 8a. Yüan fa.

12

Rites as Rights:
The Confucian Alternative

ROGER T. AMES

I. INSIDE *LI*

THE CONCEPT OF *li* ("rites/ritual practice") is extremely broad, embracing everything from manners to mediums of communication to social and political institutions. It is the determinate fabric of Chinese culture and, further, defines sociopolitical order. Ritual practice is not, of course, a purely Chinese innovation, but its prominence as an apparatus for ordering society, and its dominance over formal legal institutions, give the Chinese *li* a somewhat unique definition.[1]

Contemporary Chinese attitudes toward human rights, influenced by the Western model, tend to be state-centered and political. As an alternative I want to examine *li*, the traditional, primarily social mechanism for constituting community and generating its sociopolitical order. I then will show ways in which *li* has done some of the work expected from human rights notions, and how it has influenced the way in which contemporary Chinese society has entertained our doctrine of universal human rights.

The character *li*, generally translated "rites," "ritual practice," and "propriety," has strong religious implications in the sense of "bonding." *Li* is cognate with the character *t'i*, which means "to embody," "to constitute a shape," and, by extension, "organic form." Ritual practices, then, are "per-formances": social practices that effect relationships through prescribed forms. The etymology of the English "rites" and "ritual" is suggestive. In Latin *rītus* derives from the base *ri ("to count," "to enumerate"), which in turn is an enlargement of the base *ar ("to join" as in "arithmetic" or "rhyme"). Ritual practice is the rhyme and rhythm of society.

The translation of li as "propriety" also has its justification. It indicates the proprietorial implications of ritual practice: making community one's own. To perform ritual is, on the one hand, to be incorporated as integral to the society it defines, and hence to be shaped and socialized by it. On the other hand, it is to contribute oneself to the pattern of relationships which ritual entails, and thereby to have determinative effect on society. Because of this contributory and participatory emphasis, li does not carry the pejorative connotations such as superficiality, formalism, and irrationality often associated with the Western understanding of ritual. Li is not passive deference to external patterns. It is a making of society that requires the investment of oneself and one's own sense of importance.

Ritual practices initially lure the performer into authorized and established social relationships, but these are not simply standards of appropriateness rigidly embedded in cultural tradition. Ritual practices have a creative dimension. They exhort more than they prohibit. Rituals inform the participant of what may be properly performed by him or her. Beyond the formal social patterning is an open texture of ritual that is personalized and accommodates the uniqueness of each participant. Ritual is a pliant body of practices for registering one's importance. It is a vehicle for establishing the insights of the cultivating person, enabling one ultimately to leave one's own mark on the tradition.

There are variable degrees of personalization in ritual practices, and the roles they establish are hierarchical. These roles form a kind of social syntax that generates meaning through coordinating patterns of deference. The process of extending and deepening these roles brings with it a greater felt significance. It follows, then, that individual autonomy is anathema to a ritually constituted society, suggesting idiocy or immorality. To be socially unresponsive is to be irresponsible. A community's cultural memory is therefore an inherited repertoire of formalized actions showing the meaning and importance (yi) of the tradition of one's cultural predecessors. Ritual preserves and transmits culture. Ritual socializes a person and makes one a member of a community. It informs

one of shared values. It provides an opportunity to integrate oneself into the community in a way which maintains and enriches
community life.

Confucius declares that the project of ritual practice is to effect social harmony: "The exemplary person (*chün tzu*) seeks harmony (*ho*) rather than agreement (*t'ung*); the small person does
the opposite."[2] Ritual action is a necessary condition for Confucius'
vision of social harmony because, by definition, it not only permits but actually requires personalization. This harmony assumes
that people are unique and must be orchestrated into relationships
which permit expression of this uniqueness.[3] A formal ceremony
without this kind of personal commitment is hollow, meaningless,
and antisocial; on the other hand, a ceremony that coordinates
and expresses the genuineness of its participants is a source of social cohesion and enjoyment. Ritual actions are unique because
they display the specific quality of the performers.[4]

Throughout the *Analects* the truly harmonious community,
relying as it does upon quality people to refine themselves in ritual
action and to assume the internal perspective entailed by a sense
of shame, is defined as fundamentally self-ordering.[5] Where the
definition of the community, constituted by an internal network
of interpersonal patterns of deference, is immanent and emergent
rather than imposed, the "ruler" does not rule.[6] The community
is a project of disclosure. This inseparability of personal integrity
and social integration collapses the means/end distinction, render-
ing each person both an end in himself or herself and a condition
or means for everyone else in the community to be what they are.
The model is one of mutuality.

In ritual-ordered community, particular persons stand in relationships defined by creativity rather than power. This distinction between power and creativity is essential for an understanding of community constituted by ritual action.[7] Community is
programmatic — a future goal that is constantly pursued rather than
an immediate reality or fixed ideal. It is an open-ended aesthetic
achievement, contingent upon particular ingredients and inspiration like a work of art, not the product of formula or blueprint.

I stress the role of self-cultivation and personalization in the
capacity of ritual practice to constitute community. Implicit in
self-cultivation and communal deference to its achievements is cul-

tural elitism. The greater one's excellence, the more outstanding
and determinate one becomes. The converse is also true. In the
absence of self-cultivation and participation, one does not emerge
as either culturally determinate or determinative.

In the Chinese tradition humanity itself is not essentialisti-
cally defined. It is understood as a progressive cultural achievement. There is a qualitative ascendancy from brute (*ch'in shou*)
to indeterminate masses (*min*) to determinate person (*jen*) and
ultimately to authoritative person (*jen**) which reveals the degree
of one's refinement through ritual actions. Those who violate social relations and the values they embody are truly brutes. Humanity is open-ended and can be ever increasingly refined.[8]

Because ritual action can only take account of a person to
the extent that he or she is differentiated and distinguished, the
indeterminate masses (*min*) necessarily have a more passive and
deferential role.[9] This means also that the achieved community
will in some important respect always be local. It thus falls to those
who are the fullest participants in ritual practice to formulate and
shape a future for their particular community.

The relationship between exhortative ritual action (*li*) and
prohibitive penal law (*hsing*) in the tradition defined by Confucius is correlative. The conceptual content and function of penal
law can only be understood against an appreciation for the way
in which ritual practice works to constitute a person in society.[10]
Penal law establishes a minimum standard for what it means to
be human and draws the external perimeter on what is acceptable
at any time within the jurisdiction of ritual practice.[11] Ritual provides a direction for refinement and aspiration. Law instructs with
deterrent force in what is minimally acceptable. Where ritual action prompts creative cultural adventure and reifies what is most
significant in cultural achievement, law secures the society, sets
constraints on the existing social order, and surgically eliminates
what is incorrigible.[12]

Although Confucius aspires to a state that is free of litigation,[13] he is keenly aware of the distance between present reality
and the need for law.[14] On the other hand, several reasons can
be given for Confucius' reluctance to entertain "disorder" (*luan*)
as a topic for discussion, perhaps the most important being his
preoccupation with the ritual structure of society.

II. OUTSIDE RIGHTS

The concepts of *human rights* and *ritual action* are both social practices which establish and define the limits of relationships among persons and between a person and the state. The English term *ritual* is often negative and formal while the Chinese counterpart, *li*, is generally not. *Ch'üan*, or "rights," has generally denoted "power," not in the positive sense of legitimated authority but as a provisional advantage that derives from exceptional circumstances.

When in the nineteenth century this expression, *ch'üan-li**, was employed in translation of the notion of *human rights*, the initial Chinese response to it must have been one of considerable bemusement.[15] Nonetheless, this oblique approximation of *rights* made its formal entry into the Chinese world and has even achieved a technical prominence in the many constitutions promulgated in this century. Even so, the rhetoric of rights which dominates Western political discussion is still very foreign in popular Chinese culture. This Chinese resistance to the notion of human rights is due to factors far more fundamental than bad translation. Rights as defined in the classical Western tradition entail assumptions that are in many ways incompatible with Chinese social considerations.

Historically, our conception of human rights has been influenced by the rupture between the small familial community, in which custom and tradition guaranteed fundamental dignities, and the modern nation-state, in which mobile and atomized populations must claim their humanity from an impersonal and often oppressive governmental machine. A persuasive argument can be made that the industrial revolution has altered our concept of community so that human rights is a reasonable response for protecting personal worth. This same argument can be reversed to explain why the Chinese have not been under the same compulsion to develop a scheme of individual rights.

The classical Chinese formulation of human nature, *jen hsing**, elaborated throughout the tradition, belongs to Mencius. For Mencius, strictly speaking, a human is not a sort of being, but a kind of doing — an achievement. The concept *hsing**, generally translated as "nature," is derived from and a refinement on *sheng*, meaning the whole process of birth, growth, and the ultimate demise of a living creature. In the human context it perhaps comes closer to "character," "personality," or "constitution" than what we generally understand by "nature"— either as *physis* or as *natura*.[16]

This human nature is not innate — in Chinese, "prior to nature" (*hsien t'ien te*). Donald Munro, having translated a classical passage in precisely these terms, concludes: "This means that a person's nature being so decreed, cannot be altered through human action; it is a 'given' that exists from birth."[17] T'ang Chün-i, however, has more appropriately understood *t'ien ming* to be the relationship that obtains between heaven (*t'ien*) and humankind, emphasizing the mutuality of the relationship and shying away from importing the very Western notion of irrevocable fate or destiny to the Chinese tradition.[18]

Mencius suggests that the human being emerges in the world as a spontaneously arising and ever-changing matrix of relationships through which, over a lifetime, one defines one's nature. This initial disposition is "good" in the sense that these bonds are elicited responses to the already formed dispositions of family and community. These bonds are then nurturable with varying degrees of deftness and style (*shan*). Nurturing these primordial ties sustains one as a human being and elevates one above the animal world.

Given this conception of human nature, Mencius is not moved to establish a distinction between nature as the actual process of being a human being and nature as some capacity that underlies the process of becoming human. One device for understanding this relational conception of human nature (*hsing**) is to reflect on the shared implications between it and its cognate, *hsing*** *, which denotes "family or clan name." Like the concept of human nature, one's family name is a generalization shared by a group of people that both defines them and is defined by them. It signifies a set of conditions suggesting both shared tendency and the opportunity for cultivation in particular ways by each member — an opportunity to attach one's personal name (*ming**) to it, as it were. Neither one's family name nor one's nature is an essential or innate faculty; both are a focus of relationships in which one participates.

The fact that the Chinese tradition has been largely persuaded by the Mencian-based definition of human nature described above rather than by any notion of discrete individuality has profound implications for the way in which the soil of China has responded to the human rights transplant.

First, there is no philosophical basis that will justify self as a locus of interests independent of and prior to society. Under the sway of a relational understanding of human nature, the mutuality of personal, societal, and political realization has been generally assumed.[19]

Much if not most of the commentary available on Chinese attitudes toward human rights has reinterpreted this fundamental presupposition as a kind of self-abnegation or "selflessness," a modern echo of Hegel's "hollow men" interpretation of Chinese culture.[20] Attributing selflessness to the Chinese tradition, however, sneaks both the public/private and individual/society distinctions in by the back door, and vitiates our claim that *person* in the Chinese tradition is irreducibly social. To be "selfless" in the sense that Munro presupposes requires first that an individual self exist, and then that it be sacrificed for some higher interest. The suggestion that there are "higher interests" on the part of either person or society covertly establishes a boundary between them that justifies an adversarial relationship.

This attribution of selflessness to the Chinese tradition, both ancient and modern, arises out of an equivocation between *selfish* and *selfless*. The Confucian position is that because self-realization is fundamentally a social undertaking, individualistic "selfish" concerns are an impediment to self-realization.[21] A central issue in Chinese philosophy that has spanned the centuries has been the possible opposition between selfish advantage (*li**) and that which is appropriate and meaningful to all concerned (*yi*), including oneself. The former is associated with retarded personal development (*hsiao jen*) while the latter is the mainstay of the self-realized and exemplary person (*chün tzu*).

Western commentators, in imposing a "selfless" ideal on the Chinese tradition, are appealing to a contest between state and individual that has separated liberal democratic and collectivist thinkers in our own experience but has only limited applicability to the Chinese model. Self-realization for the Chinese requires neither a high degree of individual autonomy nor capitulation to the general will. Rather, it involves benefiting and being benefited by membership in a world of reciprocal loyalties and obligations which surround and stimulate a person and which define his or her own worth.

Having questioned this notion that selflessness is and has been a Chinese ideal, it is further necessary to examine the corollary assertion that the project of self-realization is in fact to be pursued through "obedience . . . to the chief relevant authority," where each higher level of authority takes precedence over the one below it, until reaching the emperor in imperial China and the Party leadership today.[22] Such a combination of "selflessness" and obedience if true would bring this model perilously close to Hegel's characterization of a Chinese totalitarianism.

This "top-down" interpretation is encouraged by the relative absence of the adversarial tensions introduced by separating private from public interests, and by the basic trust that colors the relationship between person and state in what Tu Wei-ming describes as the "fiduciary" community.[23] The coterminous relationship between strong person and strong state presumed in the Chinese model contrasts with the liberal Western concern to limit state powers.

In China, the traditional assumption has been that public order and personal order entail each other, with the broader configuration always emerging out of the more immediate and concrete.[24] When the country succumbs to a disintegration of order, the exemplary person returns to his or her home or community to begin again to shape an appropriate order.[25] Confucius himself, on being asked why he did not have a formal position in government, replied that the achievement of order in the home is itself the basis on which any broader attainment of order depends.[26] The central doctrine of graduated love in which family plays such a vital role is predicated on the priority of the immediate and concrete over universal principles and ideals.

This traditional Chinese prejudice for the immediate and substantive tends to preclude any concept of universal human rights. At the same time, it does not permit the sanctioning of absolute state power. In the classical political rhetoric, a symbiosis between government and people is presumed in which the people have been construed as the more dominant value: "the people as root" (*min pen*). The participation and tolerance characteristic of a bottom-up emergent order provides an internal check on totalitarianism.

In China, from ancient times to the present, conflicts have almóst invariably been settled through informal mechanisms for mediation and conciliation as close to the dispute as possible.[27] Society has largely been self-regulating and has thus required only minimal government. It is this same communal harmony that defines and dispenses order at the most immediate level which is also relied upon to define and express authoritative consensus without more obvious formal provisions for effecting popular sovereignty.

In China, political directives appear to take the form of broad and abstract slogans promulgated in the public institutions and the press. What is not apparent is the degree to which such directives require interpretation and application as they ramify back down through society. Communication and consensus are, in fact, arrived at by a much less abstract mechanism than would be characteristic of a society constituted of strictly autonomous individuals. This is true in large measure because the Chinese conception of humanness does not presuppose any notion of a moral order transcending the consensual order which could justify either demagogic appeals or appeals to individual conscience, and which might disrupt the consensus.

In the Chinese tradition morality is a cultural product that derives from the ethos or character of the society and is embodied in its ritual patterns of conduct. In place of a metaphysics of morals guaranteeing a concept of natural rights, there is a marketplace of morals where what is natural is open to negotiation. Given that order is defined from the bottom up, and concrete conditions temper generalizations to yield varying degrees of appropriateness, the notion of universalizability is certainly problematic. In fact, the Chinese have approached doctrines of *universals* with the caution of a culture fundamentally reluctant to leave the security of immediate experience for the more tentative reaches of transcendent principles. Evidence for this prejudice is everywhere in the culture: a mythology that evolves out of concrete historical events, a concept of divinity as a direct extension of the spirituality of particular human beings,[28] a concept of *reason* emerging out of and defended by appeal to concrete historical instances of reasonableness, a concept of morality articulated through analogy with particular historical exemplars,[29] a conception of knowledge inseparably bound to practical efficacy, a self-originating

cultural identity that is inward-looking to the point of being xeno-
phobic, and so on.

A final and most important illustration of this Chinese reluctance to universalize is a difficulty in accommodating the notion
of equality as we understand it. It is our concept of *individual* as
unit measure that permits the quantitative sense of equality on
which we rely — the possession of an equivalent degree of some essential quality or attribute that entitles one to be regarded and
treated as an equal. Equality thus understood tends to make qualitative ("better than") assessments suspect if not even abhorrent,
leading as they will to egoism, sexism, nationalism, racism, and
so on. It is against an essential equality that we allow that people
have differences in rank, dignity, power, ability, and excellence.

The Chinese conception of person as a specific matrix of roles
will not tolerate our assertion of natural equality. There is another
sense of equality, however, that is relevant. Although persons stand
in hierarchical relationships that reflect fundamental differences
among them, ritual practice serves the notion of qualitative parity in several ways. First, the dynamic nature of roles means that
privileges and duties within one's community tend to even up across
a lifetime. One's duties as a child are balanced by one's privileges
as a parent. One's field of relationships over time produce a degree of parity in what is perceived as the most vital source of
humanity — one's human relations.

Second, the notion of equality, like identity, is equivocal: it
can be used to mean sameness between two or more things or,
when applied to one thing, it can mean forbearance on the part
of other things to allow it to be itself and not something else. Accommodation is thus a kind of equality. The first sense of equality
proceeds from empathy with perceptible sameness; the second from
tolerance and enjoyment of perceptible difference. There is an important sense of equality in the assertion that all things are different, and yet all ought to be allowed to realize their own premise.
This sense of equality, or perhaps parity, is not entirely altruistic;
in fact, it is decidedly self-serving in that diverse elements in one's
environment contribute to one's own creative possibilities. Where
rights-based order strives to guarantee a minimum and yet vital
sameness, ritual-based order seeks to guarantee tolerance. For it
is the basic nature of harmony, the aspiration of ritual practice,

that it is enhanced by a coordinated diversity among its elements.[30] Given this long-standing preference for the substantive over the abstract and the immediate over the generalized, there is an in-built resistance to what must be perceived as the vagaries of the universal human rights rhetoric.

III. CONSTITUTION OR RITUAL CODE?

Andrew J. Nathan, whose work on the Chinese constitution figures prominently in my analysis, observes that a comparison of the American and Chinese constitutions reveals the "challenging combination of broad rhetorical similarities with deep differences in values and practices."[31] These deep differences suggest that the Chinese are still in some important measure looking to ritual practice (li) to do the work reserved in our society for principles guaranteeing human rights.

Since the turn of the century China has promulgated nothing short of twelve official constitutions and numerous constitutional drafts of one kind or another.[32] Since in the Chinese tradition neither human nature nor the social order it defines is static, the constitution must remain open and be adaptable to its particular constituents in their particular circumstances.

A related feature of the adaptable Chinese constitutions is that they not only define an existing sociopolitical order but, further, are "programmatic" in looking ahead to some goals yet to be realized.[33] Like ritual practice, they do not seek to settle universally valid ideals but pursue changing configurations of harmony and refinement in more concrete terms. Any constitution is only the most recent manifesto of Party policies and aspirations. Changes are substantive and are not simply amendments that seek to clarify unalterable principles. Given the resistance to any universalization of order in the ritual community, the constitutionally guaranteed rights do not, as in our case, fix a boundary on the enactment of laws ("no law shall be enacted that . . ."). Rather, the changing social order in China requires that law and Party policy have a free hand in articulating the changing rights and duties of the community.

The Chinese constitution is more a social than a political

document in that its primary function is to promote social harmony rather than to mediate disputes and resolve conflicts. Jerome
Cohen in his discussion of the 1978 People's Republic of China Constitution, for example, asserts that it is not even what we mean
by the term *constitution*, "for it is a formalization of existing power
configurations rather than an authentic institutional framework
for adjusting political forces that compete for power."[34] Where
the American constitution is a basis for establishing laws, the Chinese constitution primarily establishes rituals. That is to say, the
Chinese constitution formalizes status and defines privilege and
obligation on the assumption of coterminous interests between person and community. There is no assumption that strengthening
the authority of the community weakens the options of the particular persons that constitute it. Because the constitution is primarily a compact of cooperation formulated on a premise of trust
between person and community, rather than a contract between
potential adversaries, there are no independent provisions for the
formal enforcement of rights claims against the state. The assumption is that order will be effected and guaranteed by informal community pressures that are more immediate to the circumstances
and allow greater popular participation. As a last resort the constitution does provide for appeal to state organs, but, like appeal
to law in traditional China, this is a no-win course of action. That
is, one's very appearance in such circumstances almost in itself constitutes a tacit assumption of guilt.

Finally, another peculiar characteristic of the Chinese constitution is that rights derive solely from one's ongoing membership in society. While in our tradition the concept of the individual
and his or her attendant rights serves to ground the notion of the
individual's social and political relations, in the Chinese context
humanity exists solely within the bounds of community. Rights
are socially derived *proprieties* rather than individual *properties*.
These proprieties, not unexpectedly, are primarily articulated as
social welfare entitlements rather than individual political rights.
Given that only social beings are human beings, it is thus conceivable in the Chinese case to disqualify oneself from rights considerations by withdrawing from community participation. This
radically social definition of person is reflected in the inseparability of rights and duties in the Chinese document, where even

a positive right such as the right to education is both a personal right and a social duty.

Constitutions, as isolated documents, are formal and abstract. But even at the level of abstraction required by our comparison of the Chinese and American constitutions, it is clear that these documents serve different worlds.

There is much truth in Nathan's conclusion that "modern Chinese political thinkers . . . have modified foreign ideas to fit familiar patterns of thought."[35] In fact, many of these same deep differences between the Chinese and American constitutions could be arrived at by contrasting the language and function of formalized ritual codes in the imperial Chinese tradition with the same American constitution. To the extent that this is so, the contemporary Chinese constitutions can be shown to be a combination of traditional Chinese strategies for effecting social order and the rhetoric of Western law.

In fact, David McMullen has been doing some important work on one of these traditional ritual codes: the T'ang dynasty *K'ai-yüan* ritual code of 732.[36] The basic overlap in the form and function of the *K'ai-yüan* ritual code and the twentieth-century constitutions can be summarized as follows.

A changing society required that the formal documents defining it be a source of continuity and, at the same time, adaptable in line with practical administrative policies. The *K'ai-yüan* code, named for one particular dynastic reign period, was the third in one hundred years and contained both continuities with the past and innovations reflecting the changing dispositions of society. For example, by generally including correlative T'ang recipients of offerings along with the traditional figures they gave the rituals both an antique and a specifically T'ang identity.

Again, the *K'ai-yüan* code was programmatic. For example, the elevation of the ancient military teacher Ch'i T'ai-kung to the same status as Confucius was a concrete innovation that signaled the T'ang determination to develop and legitimate its military capacities.

This *K'ai-yüan* code, although a formal court document, had primarily a social function. Many of the prescribed rituals were repeated throughout the existing hierarchies, both modeling the grand court example and reflecting local variations of their own.

This ritual method of drawing upon the participation of members at all levels of society was a means of reinforcing personal and community correlativity. In such a way the *K'ai-yüan* code, although dealing in the currency of abstract formalisms, sought its content from the specific membership of the community that it served to "constitute."

IV. A CULTURE-CENTERED PROGRAM
OF PERSONAL RIGHTS

The campaign in China to forestall "bourgeois liberal" influences seems a clear condemnation of our human rights values. Yet their rejection of "bourgeois liberalism" is aimed at sustaining the direction and the momentum of *their own* social and economic development.

The Chinese are also taking Western ideas seriously. It is not clear that the reverse is true. I want now to leave the Chinese to their own devices and return to our conception of human rights to see if it cannot be strengthened in some way by appeal to the Chinese model.

It is not necessary to rehearse the many benefits that we derive from our commitment to human rights. In our world today these benefits are as obvious as they are important. I want rather to focus on certain of the weaknesses of rights theory.

A primary issue is the definition of the individual that grounds much rights theory. Henry Rosemont, Jr., has discussed this definition in his essay for this volume. There is much in the Confucian tradition that might be a resource for rethinking our notion of *autonomous individuality*, especially that aspect of the individual which, given its priority over society and environment, effectively renders context a means to individual ends. An obvious weakness here is the priority of individual freedoms over communal and environmental duties.

Corollary to a more contextual definition of person would be to reflect on the temptation to use individual rights to insist on always having all that is one's due. Individual autonomy does not necessarily enhance human dignity. In fact, if dignity is felt worth, the exaggeration of individuality might be anathema to the ultimate project of human rights, which is precisely to protect and foster human dignity. The Chinese concept of person is useful in making a distinction between individual autonomy and self-fulfillment.

In this same vein, the inordinate emotive importance that we are inclined to focus on human rights requires a better sense of proportion. The celebration of human rights as a means of realizing human dignity is of course overstated, unless by human dignity we mean the barest possible existence. To use human rights as a measure for the quality of life possible within community is like using minimum health standards as a universal index on the quality of restaurants. Human rights as law is ultimately a minimum standard, a last resort, the invocation of which signals a gross failure in the community.

The Confucian alternative suggests that almost all the actual rights and duties which define the sociopolitical order are sustained by extralegal institutions and practices and are enforced by social pressures rather than punishments. In fact, reliance upon the application of law and human rights as a subset of law, far from being a means of realizing human dignity, is fundamentally dehumanizing, impoverishing as it does the possibilities of mutual accommodation and compromising our *particular* responsibility to define what would be appropriate conduct. The introduction of obligation mediates and constricts the creative possibilities of a relationship. The emphasis on ritual, by contrast, is an effort toward the optimization of these same possibilities. The Chinese model suggests alternative nonlegal mechanisms for resolving conflicts. It tempers the readiness of the individual to pursue legal measures by providing reasonable alternatives. Movement away from formal procedures is also a movement toward a greater practicability.

The basically Marxian criticism that rights select out only particular aspects of human existence could be blunted by recognizing the immediate and inseparable relationship between cultural conditions and the variable content of abstractly defined human rights. A given right is constantly being redefined by factors that intrude upon it, including every manner of social and political pressure. A variable definition of human rights is only realistic and serves not only our own cultural development but our understanding of cultural differences.

China's resort to the Western model is enabling it to establish more formal and clearly defined guidelines for its changing socio-political order. Our recourse to the Chinese model can stimulate a clearer recognition of the ritual basis of human rights and provide us with a greater tolerance for cultural diversity: the capacity to recognize our own parochialisms and to cherish them as the actual substance of our human rights.

NOTES

1. Herbert Fingarette in his *Confucius: The Secular as Sacred* (New York: Harper & Row, 1972) has done a lot to bring out both the centrality and the uniqueness of ritual as it has functioned in the Confucian tradition.

2. *Analects* 13.23. See also 1.12, 2.14, and 15.22.

3. Ibid., 3.12.

4. Ibid., 3.3.

5. Ibid., 2.3.

6. Ibid., 15.5. See also 2.1.

7. David L. Hall, *The Uncertain Phoenix: Adventures toward a Post-Cultural Sensitivity* (New York: Fordham University Press, 1982), p. 249.

8. See D. C. Lau's Introduction to *Mencius* (Harmondsworth: Penguin, 1970); and for an analysis of its implications see Mark E. Lewis, "The Imperial Transformation of Violence," (Ph.D. diss., University of Chicago, 1985).

9. For this distinction between *jen* and *min* see David L. Hall and Roger T. Ames, *Thinking through Confucius* (Albany, N.Y.: SUNY Press, 1987), chap. 3.

10. *Li* is frequently used as shorthand for conceptual clusters. See Kenneth DeWoskin, *A Song for One or Two: Music and the Concept of Art in Early China* (Ann Arbor, Mich.: University of Michigan Press, 1982), esp. pp. 174ff.; and Hall, *Thinking through Confucius*, chap. 2.

11. See Bernhard Karlgren, *Grammata Serica Recensa*, Museum of Far Eastern Antiquities Bulletin no. 29 (Stockholm, 1987), p. 213.

12. See Brian E. McKnight, *The Quality of Mercy* (Honolulu: University of Hawaii Press, 1981). McKnight demonstrates that, amnesties being so frequent, China was in fact relying upon pressures within the community to restore all but the most egregious violations of social order.

13. *Analects* 12.13.

14. Ibid., 13.11–13.12.

15. *Hsün Tzu* brings these two terms together for the first time in the extant corpus with decidedly negative import: "For this reason, neither promise of power (*ch'üan*) nor personal advantage (*li**) can subvert the exemplary person." See *Hsün Tzu*, Harvard-Yenching Sinological Index Series, supp. 22 (Taipei: Chinese Materials Center, 1966 reprint): 3.1.49.

16. See A. C. Graham, *Studies in Chinese Philosophy and Philosophical Literature* (Singapore: Institute of East Asian Philosophers, 1986), p. 8. He is keen to correct his earlier understanding of *hsing** as "that which one starts with" to make it more representative of the whole process of one's existence.

17. Donald J. Munro, *Concept of Man in Contemporary China* (Ann Arbor, Mich.: University of Michigan Press, 1979), pp. 19–20, 57. Munro develops the notion of an innate and unchanging nature.

18. See T'ang Chün-i, "The T'ien Ming ("Heavenly Ordinance") in Pre-Ch'in China," *Philosophy East and West* 11, no. 4 (1961): 195–218; and 12, no. 1 (1962): 29–50.

19. See *Analects* 6.30; and the *Ta-hsüeh* ("Great Learning"), which is the classic statement for this coextensive relationship.

20. Donald J. Munro, "The Shape of Chinese Values in the Eye of an American Philosopher," in *The China Difference*, ed. Ross Terrill (New York: Harper & Row, 1979), p. 40.

21. See *Analects* 12.1: "Authoritative humanity proceeds from oneself — how could it come from others?"

22. Munro, "Shape of Chinese Values," p. 41.

23. Tu Wei-ming, "Confucianism: Symbol and Substance in Recent Times," in *Value Change in Chinese Society*, ed. R. W. Wilson, A. A. Wilson, and S. L. Greenblatt (New York: Praeger, 1979), p. 46.

24. See *Analects* 12.17. See also 13.6 and 13.13.

25. Ibid., 8.13 and 15.17.

26. Ibid., 1.2 and 2.21.

27. See Victor H. Li, *Law without Lawyers* (Boulder, Colo.: Westview Press, 1978), esp. chap. 4.

28. See Emily M. Ahern, *Chinese Ritual and Politics* (Cambridge: At the University Press, 1981), p. 1; and Sarah Allan, "Shang Foundations of Modern Chinese Folk Religion," in *Legend, Lore and Religion in China*, ed. Alvin P. Cohen and Sarah Allan (San Francisco: Chinese Materials Center, 1979), p. 3. They argue, basically, that gods are dead people.

29. Henry Rosemont, Jr., "Kierkegaard and Confucius: On Following the Way," *Philosophy East and West* 36, no. 3 (1986), and *Confucianism and Contemporary Ethics* (forthcoming); and Fingarette, *Confucius: The Secular as Sacred*. The insights of these two scholars

with respect to the nature of morality also apply to rationality; witness the relatively minor role of rational skepticism as a motive force in the tradition.

30. See Roger T. Ames, "Taoism and the Nature of Nature," *Environmental Ethics* 8, no. 4 (1986) for this argument.

31. Andrew J. Nathan, "Political Rights in the Chinese Constitutions," in *Human Rights in Contemporary China*, ed. R. Randle Edwards, Louis Henkin, and Andrew J. Nathan (New York: Columbia University Press, 1986), p. 79.

32. Ibid., pp. 82–83.

33. See, for example, Articles 14 and 19 of the 1982 People's Republic of China Constitution.

34. Cited in R. Randle Edwards, "Civil and Social Rights: Theory and Practice in Chinese Law Today," in *Human Rights in Contemporary China*, ed. Edwards.

35. Nathan, "Sources of Chinese Rights Thinking," in *Human Rights in Contemporary China*, ed. Edwards, p. 161.

36. David McMullen, "Bureaucrats and Cosmology: The Ritual Code of T'ang China," in *Rituals of Royalty*, ed. David Cannadine and Simon Price (Cambridge: Cambridge University Press, 1987).

Author Index

217

Subject Index